The Earliest Modern

Government Schools in China

The Earliest Modern
Government Schools
in China

By KNIGHT BIGGERSTAFF

Professor of Chinese History
Cornell University

Cornell University Press

ITHACA, NEW YORK

LIBRARY
UNIVERSITY OF MIAMI

LA
1131
.B55

© 1961 by Cornell University

CORNELL UNIVERSITY PRESS

First published 1961

This work has been brought to
publication with the assistance of
a grant from the Ford Foundation.

Library of Congress Catalog Card Number: 61-14951

PRINTED IN THE UNITED STATES OF AMERICA
BY VAIL-BALLOU PRESS, INC.

LIBRARY
UNIVERSITY OF MIAMI

To Camilla

EAF 3-8-63

Preface

THIS book consists of a general survey of the steps taken by the Chinese government prior to the first Sino-Japanese War (1894–1895) to introduce modern schools, followed by detailed studies of the first three important schools established by Chinese governmental agencies. My purpose, besides describing the character and achievements of the dozen or more schools surveyed, is to examine and, as far as possible, to account for the resistance to educational change during the second half of the nineteenth century. It is my hope that this analysis may fill one of the many blank spaces in our knowledge and understanding of the modernization of China.

The Wade-Giles system of romanizing Chinese characters is used throughout the book except for occasional exceptions sanctioned by general usage—as "Peking." The date given when a memorial was "submitted to the Throne" or "received in Peking" was the actual day on which it was formally acted upon by the Emperor, as indicated by the date under which it appears in the *Ch'ou-pan i-wu shih-mo* or the *Tung-hua hsü-lu.* The date given for a memorial found only in the collected writings of an official was the day on which it was dispatched to Peking. According to H. B. Morse, the tael—mentioned frequently in this study—was worth 80 English pence in 1864, 76 in 1874, 67 in 1884, and 38 in 1894. Translations from the Chinese not attributed to other sources are mine.

For help in the preparation of the manuscript I am especially grateful to Wu Hsin-min (Mrs. John F. Brohm) for assistance with translations from the Chinese; to my wife, Camilla, for editorial assistance; and to Mrs. Mary K. Menke and Mrs. Tazu A. Warner for typing and retyping.

Grants from the Rockefeller Foundation and the United States Educational Foundation in China (Fulbright agency) made possible my research in Nanking in 1949 and are gratefully acknowledged here. It gives me pleasure to be able to express my sincere gratitude to Professor Li Siao-yüen, Director of the Institute of Chinese Cultural Studies and Librarian of the University of Nanking, for hospitality and generous bibliographical assistance during my stay there in 1949, and to Mr. Wang Shou-i, a graduate student in the National Central University, who served as my research assistant in Nanking. I wish also to acknowledge a grant-in-aid from the Faculty Research Grants Committee of Cornell University. Finally, I wish to express my gratitude to the Hoover Institution on War, Revolution, and Peace at Stanford University and to the University of California Library at Berkeley for allowing me to use their splendid research resources.

To Dr. Richard Irwin of the University of California at Berkeley go my thanks for permission to use his unpublished manuscript on the writings of John Fryer.

KNIGHT BIGGERSTAFF

Ithaca, New York
February 28, 1961

Contents

Abbreviations

Calendar	*T'ung-wen Kuan t'i-ming lu* or *Calendar of the Tungwen College*
CCTI	*Ch'uan-cheng tsou-i hui-pien*
CSWP	*Huang-ch'ao ching-shih-wen hsü-pien*
IWSM	*Ch'ou-pan i-wu shih-mo*
KFYK	*Kuang fang-yen Kuan ch'üan-an*
KH	Kuang-hsü period, 1875–1908
NCH	*North-China Herald*
Shih-lu	*Ta-Ch'ing li-ch'ao shih-lu*
TC	T'ung-chih period, 1862–1874
THHL	*Tung-hua hsü-lu*
WHTK	*Ch'ing-ch'ao hsü wen-hsien t'ung-k'ao*

I

Background and History

of the Schools, 1861-1894

The Seedtime of Chinese Modernization
THE early decades of the nineteenth century found China
virtually untouched by Western influences. Legitimate trade
with Europeans was confined to Canton and Kiakhta, both
far from the center of the country. Christian missionary activity, which had flourished during the seventeenth century,
had been proscribed since 1724. The British Macartney embassy (1792–1793) had failed completely in its effort to persuade the Chinese government to open diplomatic relations
and to permit the expansion of Anglo-Chinese trade. The
Amherst mission of 1816, which had similar aims, was a fiasco.
By the end of the 1830's, however, Great Britain was prepared
to use force to improve the position of its merchants in China,

1

and the so-called Opium War (1840–1842) breached the hitherto solid Chinese wall against Europeans.

The period between 1840 and 1895—that is, between the first application of military force by Great Britain during the Opium War and China's overwhelming defeat in the first Sino-Japanese War—was the time when the seeds of modernization were sown in China. During this half century aggressive Western missionaries, merchants, and officials introduced ideas and methods developed by an alien civilization and scattered them widely. At the same time China was subjected to ever-growing pressure to accommodate itself to the modern world. The educated class which controlled China and whose members were smugly satisfied with Chinese civilization as they had inherited it from their ancestors stubbornly resisted all change. After 1860 a few innovations were introduced by the central government or by individual provincial officials, but these were all related to the defense of the country against foreign encroachments and were regarded by their proponents as superficial adjustments to Western pressures. Not until after China's humiliating defeat in 1895 by a modernized and hitherto despised Japan did the seeds of modernization begin to sprout and the Chinese people give serious consideration to the need for fundamental change.

As a result of the treaties that China signed with Great Britain, the United States, and France (between 1842 and 1844) following its first defeat at the hands of a Western power, the strategically located island of Hongkong was ceded to the British, five Chinese ports were opened to foreign residence and trade, and in other respects the way was prepared for Western penetration. Chinese efforts during the 1850's to restrict the activities of foreigners led to a series of Anglo-French military operations between 1856 and 1860 which resulted in the Treaties of Tientsin (signed with Great Britain, France, the United States, and Russia in 1858) and of Peking (signed with Great

Britain and France in 1860), and thus the doors of China were thrown wide open to foreign influence. Thereafter foreign legations were established in Peking, the number of foreign-controlled trading ports was increased, and Christian missionaries were permitted to preach their alien doctrines throughout the country.

The International Settlement in Shanghai became the principal base of foreign influence in China. Not only was Shanghai the center of Western trade and finance, but it also became the headquarters of many of the Christian missionary bodies, and much of the missionary publishing was done there. Secondary centers of foreign influence were the Western legations and the head office of the foreign-manned Imperial Maritime Customs Administration in Peking, the British colony of Hongkong, and the foreign residence concessions in Tientsin, Canton, and Hankow.

Most of the Westerners who lived in China and Hongkong regarded China as hopelessly backward and favored changes in the direction of Westernization. The merchants, seeking more favorable trading opportunities, urged, among other things, the opening of mines and construction of railways and telegraph lines. They taught their Chinese employees and agents Western business methods, and they operated steamship lines along China's coast and navigable rivers. The foreign settlements and concessions where they lived were governed in a Western rather than a Chinese fashion and tended to be more orderly and better administered than Chinese cities. The missionaries were even more enthusiastic advocates of change in China than the merchants. Their primary purpose, of course, was to convert the Chinese people to Christianity. But many of them, particularly among the Protestants, regarded their mission as broader than the mere preaching of the Christian religion. Western civilization was their message—its social and political ideals and its material culture, as well as the tenets of the

Christian faith. They operated schools and hospitals, translated both secular and religious writings into Chinese, and published periodicals and books in great numbers. Finally, many foreign diplomatic and consular officials and the numerous foreign employees of the Chinese government also worked for change in China. Their motives varied according to their individual predilections: some wished to strengthen the Chinese government in the interest of stability and order, others were interested in supporting the activities of foreign merchants and missionaries, and still others sought to "improve" the China they had come to admire and respect.

There were a few Chinese during the early 1840's and more after 1860 who also promoted the adoption by China of certain products of Western civilization. Lin Tse-hsü, the Imperial commissioner at Canton whose actions in 1839–1840 precipitated the Opium War, recognized the military superiority of the West and urged that China use modern weapons and warships. What is more, he collected information about the West and himself experimented with modern guns and ships prior to his dismissal from office in September 1840.[1] Later, in 1842–1843, a series of Imperial edicts ordered the governments of the coastal provinces to modernize their maritime defenses, using such phrases as "it is necessary to change" and "must not follow old methods"; but little action resulted, and the Imperial court itself soon reverted to ultraconservatism.[2] In the early 1840's there was published the *Hai-kuo t'u-chih* ("An Illustrated Gazetteer of Maritime Nations"), which had been compiled by Wei Yüan, a leading historian and geographer,

[1] Gideon Chen, *Lin Tse-hsü: Pioneer Promoter of the Adoption of Western Means of Maritime Defense in China* (1934), pp. 6–10; Ssu-yü Teng and John K. Fairbank, *China's Response to the West* (1954), pp. 28–29. See Lin's biography by Tu Lien-che in Arthur W. Hummel, ed., *Eminent Chinese of the Ch'ing Period* (1943–1944), pp. 511–514.

[2] Chen, *Lin Tse-hsü*, pp. 54–60; John K. Fairbank, *Trade and Diplomacy on the China Coast* (1953), pp. 184–185.

and which incorporated some data supplied by Lin Tse-hsü. This work contained a plan for Chinese defense that included construction of a navy yard and an arsenal near Canton where Western skilled workmen under French and American direction would teach Chinese how to build ships and manufacture arms and where Western pilots would give instruction in navigation and gunnery.[3] Although the *Hai-kuo t'u-chih,* which went through several editions, appears to have had no immediate effect on Chinese actions, it no doubt had some influence during the 1860's when Chinese minds were somewhat more open to new knowledge than during the late 1840's and the 1850's.

The series of setbacks suffered by the Imperial government during the 1850's at the hands of the T'aip'ing, Nien, and other rebels and the succession of foreign military encroachments between 1856 and 1860 culminating in the Anglo-French occupation of Peking finally moved a group of thoughtful Chinese and Manchus to give serious attention to reform. This group, embracing some of the highest metropolitan and provincial officials, instituted what later became known as the T'ung-chih Restoration (1861–1870). The program advanced by these men undertook to revitalize the increasingly ineffectual government by re-establishing traditional standards and practices that had fallen into decay and, at the same time, to put forward certain innovations which they hoped would meet the new conditions without conflicting with orthodox Confucianism.[4] These innovations, which were introduced during the first two decades after 1860, included a new system of diplomatic relations, several modern arsenals and shipyards, some up-to-date military and naval units, a fleet of merchant steamers, and four modern

[3] 1849 reprint ed. 1, p. 40 (Wei Yüan's preface is dated 1842); Chen, *Lin Tse-hsü,* pp. 5–6; Teng and Fairbank, p. 35. See Wei's biography by Tu Lien-che in Hummel, pp. 850–852.

[4] Mary C. Wright, *The Last Stand of Chinese Conservatism* (1957), pp. 7–8.

government schools that will be discussed in detail below: the Peking, the Shanghai, and the Canton T'ung-wen Kuan and the Foochow Navy Yard School.

The most effective promoters of such innovations in the 1860's were five of the leaders of the T'ung-chih Restoration: Prince Kung and Wen-hsiang in the national capital and Tseng Kuo-fan, Tso Tsung-t'ang, and Li Hung-chang in the provinces. Prince Kung and Wen-hsiang were the most influential officials in Peking, where they dominated both the Grand Council and the newly founded foreign office, the Tsungli Yamen. Prince Kung (1833–1898), a younger brother of the Hsien-feng Emperor, was one of the three ruling regents during the minority of his nephew the T'ung-chih Emperor. Wen-hsiang (1818–1876), a Manchu bannerman who had won the civil service degree of *chin-shih,* was considered by Westerners the outstanding statesman in the capital, and he was also highly regarded by the Chinese.[5]

Tseng Kuo-fan (1811–1872), a native of Hunan, was unquestionably the most influential and highly respected official in China during this period. He served as governor-general of Liang-chiang from 1860 to 1868—and concurrently as Imperial commissioner for the suppression of the T'aip'ing rebels from 1860 until the capture of the T'aip'ing capital in 1864—and as governor-general of Chihli, the metropolitan province, from 1868 to 1870.[6] Tso Tsung-t'ang (1812–1885), also a Hunanese, was a successful military commander against the T'aip'ings, and he served as governor-general of Chekiang and Fukien from 1863 to 1866 and of Shensi and Kansu from 1866 to 1880. An unusually honest and outspoken official, Tso exercised great influence in Peking, though his preoccupation with the suppression of revolt in the northwest and Sinkiang prevented his

[5] See biographies by Fang Chao-ying in Hummel, pp. 380–384, 853–855.
[6] See biography by Teng Ssu-yü in Hummel, pp. 751–756.

playing an active role in developments in the coastal provinces after the 1860's.[7] Li Hung-chang (1823–1901), a native of Anhwei, was a protégé of Tseng Kuo-fan. He gained his first fame between 1862 and 1865 when, as governor of Kiangsu, he took an important part in the suppression of the T'aip'ing rebellion. Already a major figure in the T'ung-chih Restoration movement, Li's power and influence continued to grow throughout the long period of his incumbency (1870–1895) as governor-general of Chihli, and he became the leading official promoting modernization in China.[8]

Although the central government rejected leadership in China's slow progress toward modernization after the death of Wen-hsiang and the political eclipse of Prince Kung in the 1870's, pressure for change—at least in the material realm—continued to come from officials in the provinces. The period from the late 1870's to 1894 witnessed the building of a nationwide telegraph system, further modernization of military and naval forces and facilities, the first railway construction, the beginnings of modern mining, and some industrial development.

Li Hung-chang's chief rival as a progressive statesman after 1885 was Chang Chih-tung (1837–1909), a native of Chihli. Chang launched a number of new enterprises while governor-general of Liang-kuang between 1884 and 1889, but his principal base of operations as an innovator was Wuchang, where he served as governor-general of Hu-kuang from 1889 to 1907, except for brief temporary appointments in Nanking and Peking. Although his interests were wide, Chang was most concerned with schools, railway developments, and the manufacture of steel.[9] Other provincial officials who actively promoted modernization during the twenty years before the Sino-Japanese War included Shen Pao-chen (1820–1879), Ting Jih-

[7] See biography by Tu Lien-che in Hummel, pp. 762–767.
[8] See biography by William J. Hail in Hummel, pp. 464–471.
[9] See biography by Meribeth Cameron in Hummel, pp. 27–32.

ch'ang (1823–1882), Liu K'un-i (1830–1902), and Liu Ming-ch'uan (1836–1896).[10] Three Chinese diplomats stationed abroad during this period who also pressed vigorously for changes in their homeland were Kuo Sung-tao (1818–1891), China's first minister to England; Tseng Chi-tse (1839–1890), the elder son of Tseng Kuo-fan and minister to England from 1879 to 1888; and Hsüeh Fu-ch'eng (1838–1894), minister to England from 1890 to 1894.[11]

As mentioned earlier, the primary motive of most Chinese advocates of change prior to 1895 was to strengthen the country against Western pressures. They were aware that what they all regarded as China's moral superiority could not compensate for inferiority in arms. Because of the widespread opposition within the educated ruling class to changes of any kind, those who suggested innovations during the period under review were compelled to justify their proposals in terms of military defense. It is not certain whether Prince Kung saw in Chinese participation in the Western system of diplomatic relations anything more than the opportunity it afforded China to anticipate Western aggression and thus be able to counter it, or whether Li Hung-chang advocated the construction of telegraph and railway lines in order to derive economic benefits for China or only to improve Chinese defenses against foreign invasion. Both clearly recognized that justification of such measures in terms of military necessity was required to secure the acquiescence of a large majority of Chinese officials. Suntzu's admonition, "Know the other side as one knows oneself in order to secure victory in all battles," was often cited to justify such steps as establishing diplomatic missions abroad, making

[10] See biographies in Hummel by Teng Ssu-yü (pp. 642–644), Fang Chao-ying (pp. 721–723), Teng Ssu-yü (pp. 523–524), and Hiromu Momose (pp. 526–528).

[11] See biographies by Tu Lien-che in Hummel, pp. 438–439, 746–747, 331–332.

provision for the study of foreign languages, and sending students abroad. And the scientific foundation of the manufacture of arms in the West was generally given as the reason for encouraging study by the Chinese of modern mathematics and sciences.

Traditional Education and Major Proposals
for Its Modification

Education has long been a major concern of the Chinese, for China has been administered since ancient times by an educated elite. For most of the thirteen-hundred-year period prior to its abolition in 1905, a system of civil service examinations supplied the principal key to public office. Preparation for the examinations involved acquisition of a thorough knowledge of the classics and of the orthodox interpretation of them and skill in the use of accepted forms of literary expression. Practical knowledge was considered of no use to the scholar-official and so was relegated to clerks and artisans. In the Chinese society of the nineteenth century public office yielded the greatest prestige and power, as well as the means of acquiring wealth; hence it was the object of the more promising sons of all ambitious families, whether of the scholar class or not. All Chinese who could afford to do so studied for the government examinations. Even those who passed only the first of these, and so remained ineligible for a coveted official post, entered a privileged class, the members of which were treated by the government and regarded by their fellows as superior men.

There was a regular hierarchy of civil service examinations. Candidates who had passed what may be called preliminary tests, given in succession by the district magistrate and the prefect, participated in the prefectural examination (*yüan-k'ao*) conducted twice every three years by the provincial director of studies. From 1 to 2 per cent of those who entered this series of tests were awarded what is called the first degree, the *sheng-*

yüan or *hsiu-ts'ai*. Another first degree, called the *chien-sheng*,
could be purchased or was occasionally awarded by the Emperor; although it had less prestige than the earned degree, it
gave the same privileges, including admission to the provincial
examination. The second degree, the *chü-jen*, was awarded to
from 1 to 2 per cent of the *sheng-yüan* and *chien-sheng* who
took the provincial examination (*hsiang-shih*) given triennially
in each provincial capital and in Shun-t'ien fu, the prefecture
of Peking. *Chü-jen* were eligible to take the triennial metropolitan examination in Peking (*hui-shih*), as a result of which
usually from 200 to 325 were awarded the highest degree, the
chin-shih. Corresponding hierarchies of examinations were also
administered for the military and for bannermen; the word
"military" was added to the degrees won by the former, and
"translation" to those won by the latter. Almost all government
officials were selected from the body of *chin-shih, chü-jen,* and
kung-sheng—the last being *sheng-yüan* who had failed to pass
the next higher examination but had nevertheless been recommended to the central government because of unusual scholastic competence.[12]

Throughout the Ch'ing dynasty the civil service examinations
consisted of three parts: (1) composition of essays on topics
selected from the *Four Books* (*Analects* of Confucius, *Mencius,
Great Learning,* and *Doctrine of the Mean*) and an original
poem; (2) essays on topics selected from the *Five Classics*
(*Changes, History, Songs, Rites,* and *Spring and Autumn An-
nals*); and (3) discussion questions. Although the third part
had at one time dealt with current political and economic
problems, by the end of the eighteenth century there was a

[12] Chung-li Chang, *The Chinese Gentry* (1955), pp. 5, 11–14, 21–
26; Etienne Zi, *Pratique des examens littéraires en Chine* (1894), pp.
35–64, 92–94, 103–104, 213–218. Western writers sometimes refer to
these three degrees as the bachelor's, master's, and doctor's degrees.
Chang, with some justification, objects to the use of the word "degree";
but since it is widely used, I retain it.

shift to noncontroversial philological questions. During the nineteenth century greatest stress was laid in the examinations on literary style and calligraphy, at the expense of knowledge and understanding. There had come to be, therefore, less study of the ancient books themselves than of the sterile literary form known to impress the examiners and of actual essays which had been successful in earlier examinations.[13]

The overwhelming majority of schools in China were private. They were generally taught by men who had won the first degree or who had tried but failed to win it, although holders of higher degrees and even some active officials were to be found conducting classes or tutoring the children of the well to do or candidates for the higher degrees. Private schools were ordinarily supported by the tuition fees of the students, by individual families or clans, or even by village subscription. Their curricula were, of course, determined by the content of the civil service examinations, for which all education was preparatory. Government schools, whose educational importance had been great in some of the earlier dynasties, provided comparatively little actual instruction during the Ch'ing period. They were to be found, particularly after their revival was pressed during the T'ung-chih Restoration, in virtually all district capitals and larger cities, but in most cases no regular classes were taught. Their primary function was to give monthly or semimonthly examinations to any who wished to take them. Monetary prizes were awarded for the best essays, but even more attractive to the participants appears to have been the practice in writing which such examinations afforded —that is, preparation for the civil service examinations. Some government schools, as those in Soochow during the 1890's, had sufficient endowment to support a teacher and from fifteen to twenty resident students. But even in such schools the principal activity was the conducting of periodical examinations

[13] Chung-li Chang, pp. 174–179.

for from several hundred up to a thousand students who were studying elsewhere.[14] In spite of the obvious defects of the Chinese educational system it produced some outstanding as well as many ordinary officials, all of them steeped in the ethical principles of the classical tradition and familiar with the precedents in accordance with which Chinese society and the Chinese government had operated for more than two thousand years.

Chinese education, as it had long been practiced, was regarded by virtually all Chinese as the best, in fact, the only possible system until near the end of the nineteenth century, but there were a few independent thinkers around the middle of the century who began to call for some knowledge of the West and of the studies basic to Western technology. As noted above, Wei Yüan had suggested as early as 1844 that China might profitably learn some things from the West. Although he doubtless would have rejected any change in the traditional classical education, he did propose the employment of Western experts to teach Chinese artisans and soldiers how to manufacture arms and to build and navigate modern ships. Also in the early 1840's Ch'i-kung, the governor-general at Canton, is reported to have suggested modifying the civil service examinations to the extent of introducing some new subjects, including mathematics and "manufacturing," and a censor is said to have made a similar proposal in 1851; but nothing came of either suggestion.[15]

At the beginning of the 1860's Feng Kuei-fen, a respected scholar and educator of Soochow who served for several years as an adviser to Li Hung-chang, made a vigorous plea that Chi-

[14] Ping Wen Kuo, *The Chinese System of Public Education* (1915), p. 61; A. P. Parker, "The government colleges of Suchow," *Chinese Recorder*, 24 (1893), 534–540, 579–584.

[15] *Tung-hua hsü-lu* (1909), Kuang-hsü (KH) 82, p. 10 (hereafter cited as THHL).

nese be encouraged to study Western subjects. In three essays entitled "On seeking Western knowledge," "On the manufacture of foreign weapons," and "On the establishment of a T'ung-wen Kuan in Shanghai," which presumably were written before the end of 1861, Feng deplored Chinese ignorance of the West and proposed measures to overcome it.[16] He recognized that continuing contact with the Western powers was unavoidable, and he blamed the humiliating military and diplomatic defeats China had suffered in the two preceding decades on backwardness in military technology and dependence upon incompetent Chinese "linguists" to interpret Western words and Western conditions.

Feng appears to have been particularly worried about the latter weakness. A number of foreigners had learned the Chinese language and familiarized themselves with Chinese affairs, he wrote, and some had even read the Chinese classics and histories, but no educated Chinese could speak a European language or knew anything about the West. In negotiating with Westerners, Chinese officials were entirely dependent upon "linguists," either unemployed merchants of Cantonese or Ningpoese origin who had picked up a smattering of a foreign language or graduates of missionary schools who had come from poor families of uncertain social status and who had been partially foreignized and in some cases actually converted to Christianity. These "linguists," lacking a real understanding of either China or the West and having only a superficial acquaintance with a foreign language, were a great handicap to China

[16] *Chiao-pin-lu k'ang-i* (preface dated 1861; 1892 ed.), pp. 67–74, 99–101. It is clear from his references to the Peking school that Feng Kuei-fen wrote his essay "On the establishment of a T'ung-wen Kuan in Shanghai" after the decision had been made to open a T'ung-wen Kuan in Peking. Yet it must have been written before the end of 1861 because of the date of the preface to the collection. Translations of the first two of these essays appear in Teng and Fairbank, pp. 51–54. See Hiromu Momose's biography of Feng in Hummel, pp. 241–243.

both in negotiations with foreigners and in the appraisal of Western strength and intentions. What was needed, Feng believed, was to teach foreign languages and cultures to educated and intelligent Chinese who could be depended upon to advance their country's interests.

Feng therefore urged the establishment in Shanghai and Canton of schools that could give such instruction. He suggested that boys of promise be recruited in districts near these ports and taught foreign languages and mathematics by Western teachers. They should at the same time continue their study of the traditional Chinese subjects under competent Chinese teachers so that their progress toward official careers would not be impeded. After completing a three-year course they should be sent to Peking to take the regular civil service examinations, and thus the government would be supplied with interpreters of high quality. In these same schools he proposed that books on Western countries and on modern science and technology be translated into Chinese in order that such information might be widely disseminated.

Feng Kuei-fen also recommended the establishment of an arsenal and a shipyard in each Chinese port to manufacture the modern arms and ships that were so badly needed for defense. He urged that foreign experts be employed to teach modern techniques to educated Chinese, who in turn would train many Chinese artisans. When the products of these arsenals and shipyards matched those manufactured by foreigners, he said, the Chinese responsible should be rewarded with the *chü-jen* degree and be permitted to enter the metropolitan examination in Peking on an equal basis with regular candidates. When the products surpassed those made by foreigners, the ones responsible should be awarded the *chin-shih* and allowed to enter the Palace examination. This last was Feng's most radical proposal, and that nothing ever came of it is not surprising. It is interesting that in spite of his orthodox training and his experience as an official and educator—or perhaps because of them—Feng Kuei-fen was critical of what he regarded as overemphasis in the civil service examinations on literary style and calligraphy. Moreover, he declared that China would benefit if half the candidates for office would apply themselves to the mastery of Western knowledge and modern technology. He was one of the first Chinese to point out that China's small neighbor, Japan, though only recently subjected to foreign pressures, was rapidly becoming strong by learning from the West. Chinese were in no way inferior intellectually to foreigners, he wrote, and could learn to do anything done by Europeans.

On January 13, 1861, Prince Kung, Kuei-liang,[17] and Wen-hsiang presented the epoch-making memorial to the Throne in which they proposed the establishment of a foreign office. In the same memorial they urged the opening of a school of foreign languages in Peking, pointing out the difficulty of carrying on diplomatic relations with the Western powers when no Chinese official could speak or understand a European language or had any knowledge about those countries. The languages of England, France, and the United States were to be taught by Chinese who were familiar with those languages and who would be recruited in Canton and Shanghai. At the same time an inactive Russian school that dated from the mid-eighteenth century was to be revived. The students were to be drawn from the Eight Banners.[18] Failing to locate com-

[17] He lived from 1785 to 1862 and was a grand councilor and the father-in-law of Prince Kung. See biography by Fang Chao-ying in Hummel, pp. 428–430.

[18] *Ch'ou-pan i-wu shih-mo* (1930), Hsien-feng 71, pp. 24–25. This important collection of documents on foreign matters is cited hereafter as IWSM; the reign periods Hsien-feng and T'ung-chih are indicated by HF and TC. For translations of relevant parts of this memorial see Chap. II, 95–96, or Teng and Fairbank, pp. 73–74. The Eight Banners constituted the regular national army under the Ch'ing dynasty and

petent Chinese teachers of foreign languages in the port cities, the Tsungli Yamen (the new foreign office) recommended that Westerners be employed to teach in the T'ung-wen Kuan, as the new school was called.[19]

Inspired by the opening of the new school in Peking and perhaps prodded by Feng Kuei-fen, Governor Li Hung-chang of Kiangsu dispatched a memorial (much of it straight out of Feng's essay mentioned above) that was received in the capital on March 11, 1863, and in it he advocated the opening of foreign-language schools in Shanghai and Canton. Li deplored China's ignorance of foreign languages and conditions, in contrast with the foreign powers some of whose officials had acquired a knowledge both of the Chinese language and of Chinese history and institutions. He favored admitting only traditionally educated youths to these schools and then continuing their classical education while they studied a foreign language. Upon completion of the course, he wrote, they should be admitted to the civil service examinations; this would make possible the assignment to provincial offices of some regular officials who were not completely ignorant of foreign languages and conditions. He also expressed the hope that instruction in foreign languages would lead to the teaching of Western mathematics, science, and technology and thus prepare the way ultimately for Chinese manufacture of armaments and steamships. Li's proposal was promptly authorized,[20] and mod-

------

included all living Manchus and all Chinese and Mongols whose forebears had been associated with the Manchu conquest of China in 1644. Members of the Eight Banners are referred to in English as bannermen, in Chinese as *ch'i-jen*.

[19] IWSM, TC 8, pp. 29–30. W. A. P. Martin's translation of T'ung-wen Kuan is "School of Combined Learning" (*A Cycle of Cathay* [1896], p. 301).

[20] IWSM, TC 14, pp. 2–6. A part of Li's memorial is translated by Teng and Fairbank, pp. 74–75.

ern schools were soon opened in Shanghai and Canton, each of them called T'ung-wen Kuan.

In this same spring of 1863, a memorial written by a district magistrate named Kuei Wen-ts'an, forwarded to the Throne by the Censorate, took up the matter of Chinese ignorance of the outside world. Kuei suggested that when officials were needed in the offices of the superintendents of trade (who dealt with foreign affairs in the treaty ports) they should be selected by a special examination on the geography, products, customs, and political concepts of the Western powers as set forth in such books as the *Hai-kuo t'u-chih* and the *K'un-yü t'u-shuo*.[21] He thought, moreover, that such tests should not be limited to board secretaries but should be open to all, from incumbent officials down to commoners. He also urged that China follow the example of Japan and send youths abroad to learn how to build ships and manufacture arms. If this proved to be impossible, "coast defense schools" should be established at various ports where both persons familiar with mathematics, astronomy, and the geography of foreign countries and persons knowing how to build ships and manufacture guns, gunpowder, barometers, and sextants should be employed to teach young Chinese recruited for such study. In commenting on these proposals, the ministers of the Tsungli Yamen evidently approved the intention, but they deprecated the suggestion that officials be selected to deal with foreign affairs solely on the basis of their familiarity with the limited material about the West so far printed in China. The new language schools in Peking, Shanghai, and Canton, they said, would ultimately supply trained personnel of assured quality for these positions. Although the sending of young men abroad for tech-

---

[21] The second book is a small work on world geography written in Chinese late in the seventeenth century by Ferdinand Verbiest, a Jesuit missionary (A. Wylie, *Notes on Chinese Literature* [1922], p. 58).

nical training appeared desirable, it would be difficult, they said, to find men to send at the present time. With regard to the proposal that "coast defense schools" be set up to teach modern technology, they quoted Li Hung-chang to the effect that once Western languages had been mastered in the new language schools the techniques of manufacturing steamships and modern weapons would gradually be understood in China.[22]

The Tsungli Yamen did not respond at this time to the suggestion of Kuei Wen-ts'an that centers be established in the ports to teach modern science and technology. However, Tso Tsung-t'ang, the newly appointed governor-general of Fukien and Chekiang, who was conducting military operations against the T'aip'ing rebels, seems to have been thinking along the same line. In the course of a discussion of means of strengthening China carried on in 1866 between the foreign office and a number of high provincial officials, Tso strongly urged that China build and operate its own steamships, saying that he had had in mind for three years a project for the training of Chinese in both shipbuilding and ship operation.[23] In a memorial dated June 25, 1866, Tso proceeded to outline his ideas. A modern navy yard should be built at the port of Foochow in Fukien province with a school attached where European specialists would train Chinese recruited from all levels of society to serve as ship construction engineers and technicians and as ships' officers. He criticized two ideas prevalent among the literati, namely, that Chinese should limit themselves to the finer things, leaving mechanical competence to foreigners, and that building ships in imitation of the West would be demeaning to China. Prince Kung and the two Empresses Dowager, who constituted the regency during the minority of the T'ung-chih Emperor, evidently accepted Tso's argument, for an Imperial edict was issued on July 14 authorizing construction of

[22] IWSM, TC 15, pp. 31–34.   [23] IWSM, TC 42, p. 48.

the Foochow Navy Yard and including the proposed technical training school.[24] Before the end of the year preparation for the new school at Foochow was well advanced, and Chinese education moved forward another small step in the direction of modernization.

Even more extreme than the proposals out of which came the new language schools in Peking, Shanghai, and Canton and the new Navy Yard School at Foochow was the suggestion submitted to the Throne by the Tsungli Yamen in December 1866 and January 1867 that a new department of mathematics and astronomy be added to the Peking T'ung-wen Kuan and that admission to it be limited to holders of advanced civil service degrees. The Tsungli Yamen declared that a knowledge of mathematics and astronomy was basic to the manufacture of armaments and machinery and to the movement of ships and armies and thus their mastery was essential to Chinese security. Since the bannermen studying in the foreign-language departments of the T'ung-wen Kuan could not be expected to master both these subjects and a foreign language, the ministers indicated that a higher quality of student would have to be recruited for the new department. Such students, they urged, should be sought among young men holding *chü-jen, kung-sheng,* and *chin-shih* degrees and even among junior members of the Hanlin Academy, who were the most highly respected officials of the empire. Large stipends and rapid promotion would have to be assured to induce these persons to take up such unconventional study; and Westerners possessing expert knowledge of these subjects would have to be employed as teachers.[25]

[24] *Ch'uan-cheng tsou-i hui-pien* (1902?), 1, pp. 1–9 (hereafter cited as CCTI). Most of Tso's memorial is translated by Teng and Fairbank, pp. 81–83.

[25] IWSM, TC 46, pp. 3–4, 43–46. For fuller discussion of this proposal and the controversy it induced, see Chap. II, pp. 108–119. The terms "mathematics" and "astronomy" appear to have been used in the name

This proposal was at once attacked by conservative officials, led by the influential grand secretary Wo-jen,[26] who condemned astronomy and mathematics as mere skills unworthy of officials educated in the classics and who deplored the use of foreign teachers and of monetary awards and promises of rapid promotion to attract members of the elite as students. The way to strengthen China, these opponents said, was to cultivate the Confucian virtues and to build morale by appointing wise officials and protecting the welfare of the people. The purpose of the examination system was to ensure that officials would know the doctrines of Confucius and Mencius and would follow the way of the sage kings of antiquity. Learning the principles required in manufacturing modern guns and building steamships could contribute nothing. It would be better, they said, to overcome the foreigners than to copy them, to think of means to destroy their steamships instead of building steamships in imitation. China should strengthen its morale and character rather than be frightened by foreign ships and machines. Finally, if instruction should be given in mathematics and astronomy, Westerners—"our enemies," because of their arrogance and unreliability and the danger that they would lead their Chinese students astray—should not be used as teachers.

The ministers of the Tsungli Yamen fought back vigorously, declaring that the foreign threat and the need to develop mod-

---

of the new department because they were old Chinese terms and so presumably more acceptable to traditionalists than a word such as "science," which was new. The intention was from the beginning to offer instruction in chemistry, physics, and mechanics as well as in mathematics and astronomy.

[26] A Mongol bannerman (*chin-shih* in 1829) who in 1861 became president of the Censorate and in 1862 chancellor of the Hanlin Academy, president of the Board of Works, tutor to the child Emperor, and a grand secretary. He died in 1871. See biography by Fang Chao-ying in Hummel, pp. 861–863. For a translation of one of Wo-jen's memorials on this subject (March 20, 1867) see Teng and Fairbank, pp. 76–77.

ern naval and military strength to counter it were obvious. Such development, they asserted, was impossible without mastery of modern mathematics and astronomy. Because they recognized the danger that simple Chinese might be led astray by Western teachers, the ministers had recommended that those assigned to study these new subjects should be drawn from the indoctrinated official class in the belief that they would be least vulnerable. Tseng Kuo-fan, Tso Tsung-t'ang, Li Hung-chang, and other high provincial officials were cited as supporters of this means of overcoming China's military weakness. It was completely unrealistic, the Tsungli Yamen declared, to argue that the foreign threat could be counteracted by relying solely upon the Confucian virtues of propriety and righteousness.

An Imperial edict authorized the proposed new department and declared that mathematics and astronomy were not mere crafts, that they should be understood by all scholars; moreover, studying them would in no wise conflict with study of the classics and the way of the ancient sage kings. In the end, however, even though the proposed new department was actually set up in the T'ung-wen Kuan, the conservative opposition succeeded in preventing the enrollment of members of the educated class as students. In the face of both public criticism and organized secret pressure, no young official, in spite of the Imperial endorsement, would risk jeopardizing his career by pursuing a course that departed from tradition. Hence this attempt on the part of the progressive statesmen of the T'ung-chih period to broaden and modernize the knowledge of at least a few of the younger officials of the empire came to naught.[27]

The next significant educational innovation was the so-called Chinese Educational Mission to the United States. This con-

[27] IWSM, TC 47, pp. 15–16, 24–25; TC 48, pp. 1–4, 12–14, 18–19; TC 49, pp. 13–24.

sisted of 120 boys who between 1872 and 1875 were sent in groups of 30 to secure a complete American education from elementary school through college. The experiment lies beyond the scope of the present study because it was unrelated to the schools under discussion except at one point: when the students were abruptly recalled to China in 1881, they were assigned to the telegraph and other schools in Tientsin or to the Navy Yard School at Foochow for further study. The mission is therefore briefly touched upon here since it was another step, albeit an abortive one, in the direction of modernizing Chinese education.

The Chinese Educational Mission to the United States was proposed in 1871 by Tseng Kuo-fan and Li Hung-chang at the instigation of an American-educated Chinese named Yung Wing. Its purpose was to train young Chinese in the scientific and mechanical arts that Tseng and Li regarded as essential to the strengthening of China's defenses. Nearly all the students were recruited in the port cities of the south where boys from ten to fourteen years of age could be found who had already begun Western studies in missionary and other modern schools. After brief preliminary instruction in Shanghai they were taken to Connecticut; there they boarded in groups of two or three in private homes in Hartford and nearby towns and enrolled in local schools. Living in this way they quickly adjusted themselves to American life, with the result that some of the Chinese teachers who had accompanied the mission in order to teach Chinese subjects and manners became alarmed and notified Li Hung-chang and other high officials in China that the boys were becoming denationalized. As a consequence the whole mission was recalled to China before most of the students had entered colleges.[28]

[28] For fuller discussion see Thomas E. La Fargue, "Chinese Educational Commission to the United States," *Far Eastern Quarterly*, 1 (1941), 59–70, and *China's First Hundred* (1942); Teng and Fairbank, pp. 91–93

More directly related to the subject under study were the proposals to send graduates of the Foochow Navy Yard School and, later, graduates of the Tientsin Naval Academy to Europe for advanced study. Three T'ung-wen Kuan students were members of the Pin-ch'un mission that visited Europe in 1866 to observe Western manners, customs, and conditions; six accompanied the Burlingame mission that toured the United States and Europe between 1868 and 1870; and two accompanied the Ch'ung-hou mission of apology to France in 1870–1871.[29] In none of these cases, however, did the students carry on formal study while abroad.

On May 26, 1872, Shen Pao-chen, director-general of the Foochow Navy Yard, submitted a memorial to the Throne urging that graduates of the Foochow school in shipbuilding and seamanship and skilled young artisans from the navy yard be sent abroad for further training.[30] Provoking no response in Peking, Shen renewed the suggestion the next year in more specific terms in a memorial presented on December 26. Graduates of the shipbuilding division, he said, should be sent to

(including a translation of the Tseng-Li memorial proposing the mission); Yung Wing, *My Life in China and America* (1909). Ninety-four of the original 120 students returned to China from the United States. Of these one group of 21 was assigned to the telegraph school in Tientsin, another of 23 was divided between the Foochow school and the Shanghai arsenal, and the remaining 50 were scattered among Li Hung-chang's other schools and modern agencies in Tientsin (Li Hung-chang, *Li Wen-chung kung ch'üan-chi* [1908], 53, p. 16).

[29] See Biggerstaff, "The first Chinese mission of investigation sent to Europe," *Pacific Historical Review*, 6 (1937), 310; "The official Chinese attitude toward the Burlingame mission," *American Historical Review*, 41 (1936), 687; "The Ch'ung Hou mission to France, 1870–1871," *Nankai Social and Economic Quarterly*, 8 (1935), 637, 639.

[30] IWSM, TC 86, p. 21. Shen says in this memorial that Tseng Kuo-fan had some years earlier proposed that Chinese youths be sent to England to learn Western skills and that the province of Fukien had considered a similar project but had been prevented from carrying it out by lack of funds. I have found no other reference to either of these suggestions.

France for from three to five years of advanced study, and graduates of the navigation department to England for a similar period; upon returning to China, both groups should be replaced by later graduates. Such a procedure, he said, would assure the country an ample supply of highly trained shipbuilding engineers, ships' officers, and Chinese teachers of Western subjects. This time the Tsungli Yamen and the Throne approved Shen's proposal, although it was not put into effect until 1877, when the first group of Foochow graduates left for three years of advanced training in Europe.[31]

Neither Feng Kuei-fen's belief, expressed in 1861, that persons possessing a knowledge of foreign languages should be admitted to the higher civil service examinations nor his criticism of the content of those examinations was generally acceptable in official circles, and subsequent efforts to obtain places in the official hierarchy for men trained in modern subjects met with little success. The first regulations of the Canton T'ung-wen Kuan, approved in August of 1864, provided that students who could demonstrate knowledge of a foreign language after completing the three-year course would be given the official title of interpreter (*fan-i kuan*) and permitted to take the provincial examination for the (presumably *fan-i*) *chü-jen* degree.[32] Actually, in addition to the title, they were awarded a somewhat inferior first degree: either a *fan-i-sheng* or a *chien-sheng* (presumably an *en-chien-sheng*).[33] In contrast to this privileged status accorded graduates of the Canton school, who except for two or three in the first graduat-

---

[31] IWSM, TC 92, pp. 16, 23–24; CCTI, 15, p. 24.

[32] IWSM, TC 27, p. 8. "Translation M.A."

[33] *Kuang fang-yen Kuan ch'üan-an*, p. 69 (hereafter cited as KFYK). The *fan-i-sheng* had been invented for bannermen, and the *en-chien-sheng* was also sometimes bestowed on bannermen (Chung-li Chang, p. 13). These degrees had less prestige than the regular *sheng-yüan* degree, but they nevertheless admitted the holders to the provincial military and civil service examinations.

ing class were all bannermen, the graduates of the Peking T'ung-wen Kuan, though given official rank, were neither given degrees nor admitted automatically to the provincial examinations, though most of them, at least in the beginning, were also bannermen. The 1863 regulations governing the Shanghai T'ung-wen Kuan (later called the Kuang fang-yen Kuan) stipulated that graduates of that school whose competence both in a foreign language and in Chinese was demonstrated in an examination conducted by the superintendent of trade would be awarded the *sheng-yüan* degree and that the best of them would be recommended by the superintendent for admission to the special *chü-jen* examination given in Peking.[34] However, this regulation was never applied, and civil service degrees were not awarded to Kuang fang-yen Kuan graduates until after 1893, when the granting of *fan-i-sheng* and *chien-sheng* degrees was authorized following the precedent of the Canton T'ung-wen Kuan.[35]

In the early 1870's there were two or three proposals made by high officials to modernize both the civil and military examinations and to open additional modern schools. Shen Pao-chen, director-general of the Foochow Navy Yard, and Ying-kuei, governor-general of Min-che, proposed in 1870 that a special examination be given in mathematics; but the step was opposed by ministers of the responsible boards in Peking on the grounds that there was no one competent to grade such an examination. In May 1872 Shen renewed this proposal, pointing out that Li Shan-lan, a professor in the Peking T'ung-wen Kuan, was thoroughly familiar with Western mathematics and declaring one Yang Pao-ch'en, a former prefect, to be a master of Chinese mathematics—between them capable of grading any possible examination questions in mathematics. Should China abolish the useless military examinations, Shen said, and introduce an urgently needed examination in mathematics, within

[34] KFYK, pp. 8–9.   [35] KFYK, p. 73.

a few decades Chinese talent would be plentiful, and further dependence upon foreign experts would be unnecessary.[36] Again the proposal was ignored in the capital.

The Japanese invasion of Formosa during the summer of 1874,[37] though ultimately settled without resort to war, inspired among responsible Chinese officials renewed discussion of China's military weakness. The difficulty of organizing and co-ordinating Chinese defense operations because of the shortage of Chinese personnel familiar with modern military equipment and methods and the slowness of the primitive communication system worried leading statesmen.

In a memorial submitted to the Throne on December 12, 1874, Li Hung-chang attributed the greater rapidity of communication and mobility of troops in Western countries to the existence of telegraph and railway lines, and he deplored the persistence of Chinese ignorance of modern military science even though the country had been under almost constant foreign military threat for more than thirty years. He expressed regret that preparedness for civil office was still measured by ability to turn phrases and for military rank by skill in horsemanship and use of the bow and arrow. Although he recognized that sweeping changes in the examination system were not feasible, he urged modification at least to the extent of permitting candidates to offer foreign learning as one of the subjects in which they might be examined. The way to acquiring Western knowledge already appeared to be open, he said, because of the presence of the T'ung-wen Kuan in Peking and the recent dispatch of boys to study in the United States, but appearances were deceiving because the official class continued to oppose Western studies. If the Imperial court failed to force a change in this attitude by breaking the restraints of ancient

[36] IWSM, TC 86, p. 21; THHL, KH 82, p. 10.

[37] See H. B. Morse, *The International Relations of the Chinese Empire,* II (1918), 270–275.

usage and encouraging mastery of what was of real use, Li feared that the dangerous condition of China could not be alleviated.

In the same memorial Li Hung-chang went on to propose that "schools of foreign learning" be established in every coastal province. The subject matter to be taught in them should include physics, chemistry, mensuration, mapping, machinery, steamships, electricity, and military science and fortifications. High officials with some knowledge of the modern world should be placed in charge of these schools, he wrote, and an effort made to recruit as students Chinese who already had some interest in or some knowledge of these subjects. Skilled foreigners should be employed as teachers, as well as graduates in mathematics of the T'ung-wen Kuan and the Kuang fang-yen Kuan and Chinese who had studied abroad. The graduates of these proposed schools should be sent to navy yards, arsenals, or military units for practical experience, after which they should be given civil or military rank and assigned to posts along the coast where their knowledge would be of greatest use to the government.[38]

Li's proposals that more modern schools be established and that a modern subject be admitted to the civil service examinations were regarded by the Tsungli Yamen as both compatible with the traditional system and necessary if China was to develop men capable of dealing with the problems created by relations with the West, but there was strong opposition elsewhere in the government. Action was therefore postponed until some future time when these projects might receive "universal support." [39] Four years later, under a mounting demand on the

[38] IWSM, TC 99, p. 30.

[39] THHL, KH 3, p. 15. L. W. Pilcher, in "The new education in China," writes without citing any authority that, even though Li's proposal was not acceptable to the government, questions bearing on mathematics and the physical sciences were gradually introduced into many of the provincial examinations (*Chinese Recorder*, 20 [1889], 309).

part of a few high officials to strengthen the naval defense, the Imperial court acknowledged the need for additional naval training facilities and ordered discussion of steps that might be taken to develop them.[40] As will be brought out, Li Hung-chang opened several new modern schools in Tientsin within the next few years: a telegraph school in 1880, a naval academy in 1881, and a military academy in 1885. And in 1880 the School of Western Studies was inaugurated at Canton.

"Foreign learning" was not formally admitted to the civil service examinations as an optional subject until 1887, and even then the concession was severely limited. In April of that year the Empress Dowager submitted for discussion to the Tsungli Yamen and the Boards of Ceremonies and Civil Office a memorial from a censor named Ch'en Hsiu-ying, who urged that scholars thoroughly competent in mathematics be given some advantage in the examinations. Ch'en proposed that, while two-thirds of both the provincial and metropolitan examinations continue to be devoted to the *Four Books* and the *Five Classics,* candidates be permitted to devote the other third to mathematics; that mathematics papers be sent to the Tsungli Yamen to be graded; that the traditional portions of the examinations of candidates offering mathematics be judged with some leniency; and that mathematics candidates who passed the examination be rewarded with rank equal to that awarded those passing a wholly traditional examination.

On May 18 the Tsungli Yamen, presumably after discussing the censor's proposal with the two boards, recommended that *sheng-yüan* and *chien-sheng* admitted to provincial examinations for the *chü-jen* degree be allowed to write on a question in mathematics in addition to those on the traditional examination subjects. The papers of those demonstrating a command of mathematics should be sent to the Tsungli Yamen for grading, and the candidates themselves summoned to Peking by the same agency for a special examination in theoretical science,

[40] THHL, KH 31, p. 6.

mathematics, mechanical engineering, military and naval tactics, naval gunnery and torpedoes, or international law and Western history. Those passing this special test would be admitted to the next regular examination for the *chü-jen* conducted in the national capital, where one out of each twenty "mathematicians" entering the examination but not more than a total of three for each examination would be awarded the regular *chü-jen* degree, provided they demonstrated in the examination a reasonable command of the traditional subject matter. Although eligible for the *chin-shih* examination, as other *chü-jen* were, these "mathematicians" were to be given no special advantage there but must compete on equal terms with the thousands of *chü-jen* who had won that degree by demonstrating superiority in the traditional curriculum. The Throne ordered this recommendation put into effect.[41]

Although a real modification in favor of modernization was thus made in the civil service examination system, its practical effect was negligible. At three-year intervals a maximum of three persons with a command of modern subjects including mathematics who had already secured the first degree by examination or by purchase but who were unable to earn the second degree by the traditional process might secure that degree because of their modern knowledge. The quota of *chü-jen* for the entire country in the triennial examination of 1891, according to figures compiled by Chung-li Chang, was 1529.[42] This provision for no more than three out of a total of more

[41] THHL, KH 82, pp. 10–11. For a translation of this document see R. S. Gundry, *China Present and Past* (1895), pp. 387–393, or *Foreign Relations of the United States, 1887*, pp. 228–230.

[42] P. 129. In 1889 over sixty eligible candidates submitted essays to the Tsungli Yamen under this special provision. Of these, thirty-two were admitted to the regular provincial examination conducted in Peking, and of the thirty-two admitted only one secured the *chü-jen* degree. Of the thirty-two admitted to the examination thirteen were from the Peking T'ung-wen Kuan, seven from Kiangsu, four from Chihli, two each from Kiangsi, Chekiang, and Fukien, and one each from Anhwei and Kwangsi (*Chinese Recorder*, 20 [1889], 89–90).

than 1500 promised no significant infiltration of modern-trained persons into the upper level of Chinese officialdom.

On November 10, 1889, Governor-general Chang Chih-tung of Liang-kuang proposed expansion of the naval and military academy that had evolved from the Canton School of Western Studies, mentioned above, by adding instruction in mining, chemistry, electricity, plant science, and international law. All these subjects, he declared, were needed to strengthen China, and he had already requested the Chinese minister to England to recruit teachers, one for each subject. He envisioned a student body of 250 and suggested that they be recruited from the Foochow Navy Yard School, the Kuang fang-yen Kuan in Shanghai, and the Canton T'ung-wen Kuan; thus all would possess a basic knowledge of mathematics and a foreign language before admission.[43] Nothing came of this proposal, presumably because of its author's transfer to the governor-generalship of Hu-kuang.

Chang Chih-tung carried the idea with him, however, for on November 29, 1893, he forwarded a memorial to Peking in which he set forth his plans for a Tzu-ch'iang Hsüeh-t'ang (Self-strengthening School) to be established in Wuchang. Four general subjects were to be taught: European languages, science, mathematics, and commerce; and each department would commence with twenty students, all drawn from the provinces of Hupeh and Hunan. The languages, he wrote, are necessary for the conduct of foreign relations; the sciences— and he listed chemistry, mechanics, electricity, and optics— are fundamental to many studies; mathematics is the foundation of manufacturing; and commerce is related to wealth and power.[44] There was some delay in the opening of this school, as will be seen later.

[43] Chang Chih-tung, *Chang Wen-hsiang kung ch'üan-chi* (1928), 28, pp. 7–9.
[44] *Ibid.*, 34, pp. 5–6.

The Schools Themselves

The modern schools established by the central government and by various provincial governments between 1861 and 1894 fall into seven categories: (1) schools to train interpreters and foreign affairs specialists; (2) schools to train engineers and skilled workmen for the new shipyards and arsenals; (3) schools to train deck and engine-room officers for the modern navy—these will be called naval academies; (4) schools to train army officers, that is, military academies; (5) schools to train personnel for the telegraph administration; (6) a naval and military medical school; and (7) a school of mining engineering. It should be noted that all these schools were related by their sponsors to national defense and that they were generally regarded by the Chinese as completely outside the regular concept and system of education.

The three schools to train interpreters and experts in foreign affairs—the Peking, the Shanghai, and the Canton T'ung-wen Kuan (within a few years the name of the Shanghai school was changed to Kuang fang-yen Kuan)—were the first modern government schools opened in China. Instruction began in the English department of the Peking T'ung-wen Kuan during the summer of 1862, with an English Protestant missionary employed as teacher. In the same year a long-established but ineffective Russian school was transferred to and became a department of the T'ung-wen Kuan. Classes in French and Russian began in April 1863, the former taught by a French ex-priest and the latter by the interpreter at the Russian legation. The students in the three classes, totaling thirty, were drawn from the Eight Banners. They were supposed to be about fifteen years of age, to be familiar with both the Manchu and Chinese languages, and to possess "natural ability and cleverness." Besides a foreign language, they studied regular Chinese subjects under teachers who held at least the second civil service degree. Those who stood high in the triennial examinations of the school conducted by the Tsungli Yamen were rewarded with the eighth or ninth official rank, and their Chinese teachers were rewarded with promotions in the official hierarchy. The school was controlled directly by the Tsungli Yamen and was located in adjoining buildings. It was financed from a fund consisting of 30 per cent of the tonnage dues collected on foreign ships at the treaty ports.[45]

The Peking T'ung-wen Kuan succeeded in training few competent interpreters during its early years, probably because of frequent changes in teachers and the low quality of most of the students. The effort of the Tsungli Yamen in 1867 to attract *chü-jen, chin-shih,* and even young members of the Hanlin Academy to a new department of mathematics and astronomy failed, as already noted; the initial class in this department turned out so badly that only five members were still in the school in 1869. But an important gain from this attempt to strengthen the T'ung-wen Kuan was a considerable broadening of the curriculum of the school, hitherto confined to foreign languages and Chinese. A Frenchman, Anatole Billequin, brought out from Europe in 1867, taught chemistry to all students; and W. A. P. Martin, an American ex-missionary who had taught English in the school since 1864, began to teach political economy and international law. After his return in 1869 from a period of advanced study in the United States, Martin also taught physics. Li Shan-lan, one of the most eminent Chinese mathematicians of his day, who had been one of the Chinese pioneers in modern science and mathematics associated with Tseng Kuo-fan and Li Hung-chang in Kiangsu, was appointed professor of mathematics in 1869. The failure of the Peking T'ung-wen Kuan to attract good students locally, even though all students received substantial stipends, led the Tsungli Yamen to secure authority

[45] For fuller treatment of this school and for documentation, see Chap. II.

late in 1867 to bring the best graduates of the Shanghai and Canton schools to the capital for advanced study. It is interesting to note that in later years some of the outstanding alumni of the Peking school were men who had come to it from these two schools, particularly from the first.

With the assumption of the presidency of the T'ung-wen Kuan by W. A. P. Martin in the fall of 1869 and the promise of continuous financial backing and moral support by Robert Hart, head of the Chinese Imperial Maritime Customs and an influential adviser to the Tsungli Yamen,[46] the school took on new life. The enrollment was increased at once to one hundred, and for more than thirty years thereafter a broad education was given to the youths who were to serve as China's interpreters and experts in foreign affairs in the foreign office, in some provincial governments, and in the diplomatic and consular offices opened in foreign lands from 1876 onward.

Two curricula were offered throughout this thirty-year period. (1) An eight-year curriculum included a foreign language —English, French, Russian, German (from 1871), or Japanese (from 1895); traditional Chinese subjects; Western mathematics, including calculus, mechanics, and theoretical navigation; physics, chemistry, astronomy, geology and mineralogy; and international law and political economy. (2) A five-year curriculum that omitted instruction in a foreign language and in

[46] Robert Hart (1835–1911) was inspector-general of the Chinese governmental agency called the Inspectorate of Customs (more often referred to as the Chinese Imperial Maritime Customs or the Chinese Customs) from 1863 until 1911, though he spent the last four years in virtual retirement in England. An Irishman and a graduate of Queen's College, Belfast, he went to China in 1854 as a student interpreter in the British consular service. He joined the new Inspectorate of Customs in 1859 as deputy commissioner. He was without question the most influential foreigner in China during more than forty years, and he had a major part in the modernization of that country. For a full biography see Stanley F. Wright, *Hart and the Chinese Customs* (1950). For a biographical note on Martin, see Chap. II, note 51.

Chinese and added Chinese mathematics otherwise roughly
duplicated the eight-year curriculum. The five-year curriculum
made possible concentration in mathematics and science, in
contrast to the concentration on a foreign language that char-
acterized the longer curriculum, but over the years few students took advantage of it. The quality of the students drafted
from the Eight Banners remained low, but as the years passed
and as increasing numbers of nonbannermen were attracted,
the general level in the school rose slowly. In addition to Martin
(who taught in the T'ung-wen Kuan for more than thirty years),
Billequin (twenty-nine years), and Li Shan-lan (thirteen
years), other long-time teachers were Charles Vapereau (who
taught French for twenty-five years), J. Dudgeon (a Scotch
doctor of medicine who taught a course in physiology for
twenty-three years), two graduates of Queen's College, Belfast,
S. M. Russell (who taught astronomy for twenty-one years) and
C. H. Oliver (who began teaching English in 1879, taught
physics from 1888, and succeeded Martin as president in 1895),
and Hsi Kan (a graduate of the T'ung-wen Kuan who had come
to it from the Shanghai T'ung-wen Kuan and who became professor of mathematics in 1886). The school was reasonably well
equipped with classrooms, a library, and other facilities; a chemistry laboratory was built in 1876, and an astronomical observatory and a physics laboratory were erected in 1888.

Besides classroom instruction, two related educational activities were carried on at the Peking T'ung-wen Kuan. Resident graduates were called next door to the Tsungli Yamen
from time to time to serve as interpreters or translators. And
members of the faculty, assisted by advanced students and
resident graduates, translated more than a score of Western
books into Chinese. These included books on international law,
foreign laws, mathematics, and the sciences. The translations
were printed by the school's own press and distributed to various governmental offices by the Tsungli Yamen.

Construction of the Shanghai T'ung-wen Kuan, proposed in Li Hung-chang's memorial of March 11, 1863, mentioned earlier, was begun in the summer of that year. The first set of regulations fixed the maximum enrollment at forty local youths "of superior intelligence and character" and not more than thirteen years of age who had been recommended by reputable officials or members of the gentry. Provision was also made for the admission of ten special students to be selected either from minor officials awaiting posts or from adult members of the gentry. English and mathematics were to have the leading places in the curriculum, but considerable attention was also to be given to the Confucian classics, Chinese history, and Chinese composition—the subject matter of the regular civil service examinations.[47]

Instruction in English was begun on March 28, 1864, by Young J. Allen, an American Protestant missionary. The other subjects were taught by Chinese, and even Allen was replaced by a Chinese after six months, although he was re-employed in February 1867 when the Chinese had proved to be incompetent. The first class of nine students completed the course in the spring of 1867, and the six best were recommended for transfer to the Peking T'ung-wen Kuan for advanced study. The Shanghai T'ung-wen Kuan was controlled by the Shanghai customs intendant and was financed from the local tonnage dues on shipping.

At the end of the 1860's some modifications were made in this school, including its name, which was changed to Kuang fang-yen Kuan. When the Kiangnan Arsenal was moved to a new site on the outskirts of the city early in 1870, it was decided to move the language school there too and to place it under the administration of the arsenal, together with a recently established department for the translation of foreign books into

[47] For a fuller account of this school and for documentation, see Chap. III.

Chinese. An attempt was made at this time to expand the school by adding a number of technological departments, but in the end the technical training was left separate, and the Kuang fang-yen Kuan continued for thirty-five years to concentrate on foreign languages and mathematics, with all of its students also regularly studying traditional Chinese subjects.

The instruction in English was given by Young J. Allen until 1881, when he was succeeded by Shu Kao-ti (also referred to as Dr. V. P. Suvoong), a Chinese with an American education, who continued to teach English until 1905, at which time the Kuang fang-yen Kuan evidently ceased to exist. French was taught from 1870 to 1881 by John Fryer, an English ex-missionary who was the head of the arsenal's translation department. After Fryer's withdrawal, French was taught until 1903 by a succession of Chinese and Frenchmen. The most effective of these appears to have been Alphonse Bottu, who taught during the late 1880's. German was taught for a few years during the preceding decade by Carl T. Kreyer, an American missionary, but this language was dropped after his departure. All mathematics courses appear to have been taught by Chinese scholars, as were the traditional Chinese subjects. The curriculum was supposed to take three years to complete.

Some of the best graduates of the Shanghai school were sent from time to time to the Peking T'ung-wen Kuan for more advanced study, although this was not done with any regularity. Their quality was evidently comparatively high for they generally stood out among the graduates of the Peking institution.

The Canton T'ung-wen Kuan opened on June 23, 1864, under regulations based in part on those of the Shanghai school. It was stipulated that there should be twenty regular students between thirteen and nineteen years of age, all to be intelligent representatives of old and honorable families. Of these, sixteen were to be Manchu and Chinese bannermen from the Canton garrison who knew both the Manchu and Chinese languages, and four were to be local Chinese. It was also stipulated that up to ten Manchu and Chinese expectant officials over the age of twenty might study a foreign language as special students. The regular curriculum, consisting of English, mathematics, and Chinese, was to require three years to complete, and there were to be two professors, a Westerner and a Chinese. Graduates were to be assigned as interpreters to provincial or garrison offices and to be admitted to the provincial examinations. The costs of operating the school were to be met from the tonnage dues on foreign shipping at Canton; and the customs intendant at Canton was assigned administrative control, including responsibility for the employment of teachers, under the joint supervision of the Canton Tartar general and the governor-general of Liang-kuang. An American whom it has been difficult to identify from the Chinese transcription of his name (T'an-shun) began the instruction in English and possibly in mathematics; and Wu Chia-shan, a second-class compiler of the Hanlin Academy, was the first teacher of Chinese.[48] Sometime prior to 1874 Theos. Sampson was appointed the foreign professor and "headmaster" of the school, a position he continued to hold at least until 1889. There were generally from three to five Chinese teachers.[49]

[48] IWSM, TC 27, pp. 6–10. "T'an-shun" was succeeded in the summer of 1865 by "Ha-pa-an-te," probably Rev. A. P. Happer of the American Presbyterian Mission, who in turn was succeeded two years later by W. L. G. Badham (IWSM, TC 62, p. 21; *Chronicle and Directory for China, Japan, and the Philippines for the Year 1868*, p. 181). American Consul F. D. Cheshire wrote to George F. Seward, the American minister to China, on March 29, 1880, that the course of study consisted "chiefly of the English language, together with but subordinate to which there are geography, arithmetic, history, algebra, mathematics and astronomy." Since the students were liable to dismissal only if they failed in English, they made less effort in other subjects. Cheshire also reported that control of the school was left almost entirely to the Tartar general, who made all appointments of students and staff on a patronage basis (*Foreign Relations of the United States, 1880*, pp. 281–282).

[49] *Chronicle and Directory for China . . . 1877*, p. 258; *1889*, p. 375.

In the beginning the Tsungli Yamen protested the provision for only one foreign teacher, saying that both English and French, and if possible Russian, should be taught. It also called for fuller elaboration of the provisions for the rewarding and use of graduates; it demanded that bannermen be awarded the *fan-i sheng-yüan* degree and admitted to either the provincial translation examination or the regular provincial civil service examination, that other graduates be awarded the *chien-sheng* and admitted to the provincial civil service examination, and that all graduates be given the title of interpreter. Finally, the Tsungli Yamen insisted that all graduates who had secured a thorough knowledge of a European language should be sent to Peking to be examined and assigned to official positions according to their ability. An edict issued on August 19, 1864, ordered these amendments added to the Canton regulations, although I have found no evidence that any foreign language other than English was taught in the Canton school before 1897.[50]

Late in 1867 six members of the first graduating class—one local Chinese and five bannermen—were sent to the Peking T'ung-wen Kuan, where they took examinations that demonstrated their competence in English and mathematics. The one Chinese was thereupon given the *chien-sheng* degree and the five bannermen the *fan-i sheng-yüan* (under the regulations these awards should have been made before they left Canton), and all took and presumably failed to pass the 1868 examination for the *chü-jen*. They were then sent back to Canton and

[50] IWSM, TC 27, pp. 18–19. An item in the *Ta Ch'ing li-ch'ao shih-lu* (hereafter cited as *Shih-lu*) dated Nov. 7, 1879, refers to a memorial from the incumbent Tartar general in Canton which mentioned that further funds were needed in order to add facilities for the study of French and German at the Canton T'ung-wen Kuan (*Shih-lu*, KH 99, p. 19). But John Fryer, in the *Educational Directory for China*, published in 1895, indicates that only English was being taught there in the early 1890's (p. 82).

assigned as salaried interpreters to the Tartar general's office
or the customs house, continuing their studies at the local T'ung-
wen Kuan.[51] Five graduates of the next class were granted the
first degree in 1871 in Canton,[52] and thereafter outstanding
members of succeeding classes were similarly rewarded triennially. The number sent to Peking is not known.[53]

More detailed regulations for the treatment of graduates of
the Canton T'ung-wen Kuan were authorized by the Throne
on April 6, 1869; they were based upon a recommendation submitted on December 1, 1868, by Governor-general Jui-lin and
drawn up by the ministers of the Tsungli Yamen after discussion with the Board of Civil Office. (1) Only the most intelligent graduates should be sent to Peking for examination by the
Tsungli Yamen, and then only when recommended by the
provincial governor. Those who demonstrated in Peking that
they were outstanding should either receive appointments as
board secretaries or be assigned as expectant officials to provincial offices. This group was to include graduates who had

[51] IWSM, TC 56, pp. 22–23; TC 62, p. 20. At least three of these men
(Ts'ai Hsi-yung, Na-san, and Tso Ping-lung) ultimately returned to the
Peking T'ung-wen Kuan, for they are found listed in 1879 as alumni
either stationed overseas or actually teaching in the Peking school. See
Calendar of the Tungwen College (cited hereafter as *Calendar*), first issue
(1879), pp. 9, 15. Unless otherwise indicated, pages cited from the
1879 and 1888 *Calendars* are to the English text. The 1893 and 1898
Calendars are entirely in Chinese.

[52] IWSM, TC 84, p. 29.

[53] KFYK, p. 71. These same graduates were also admitted to the
provincial examinations in Canton, although I have not been able to
discover whether any actually passed. In 1880 a memorial to the Throne
from Liang-kuang Governor-general Chang Shu-sheng and others stated
that graduates had been sent to Peking after 1867 (THHL, KH 36, p. 3).
In the same year Consul Cheshire wrote that fourteen Cantonese students had been sent to Peking "about ten years ago," of which six were
still attached to the Peking T'ung-wen Kuan and three held appointments
abroad (*Foreign Relations of the United States, 1880*, p. 282). If a total
of fourteen Canton T'ung-wen Kuan graduates went to Peking before
1880, all but six must have gone later than 1870.

passed a provincial examination and had subsequently been awarded the *chü-jen* degree. *Chü-jen* might be recommended for the title of magistrate. (2) Other graduates who had served capably as interpreters for three years, had demonstrated a mastery of the Manchu language in a provincial translation examination, and had also completed the three stages of the regular provincial civil service examination but failed to pass it though possessing a clear smooth Chinese literary style should be awarded the title of prefectural secretary, assistant district magistrate, or banner garrison captain. (3) Persons in both the first and second groups should be assigned to posts in provinces where there was foreign trade or, when asked for, in provinces where there were foreign missionaries. (4) Interpreters who proved to be incompetent should be returned to the school for three additional years of study. If still incompetent they should be dismissed, though allowed to continue to wear the official gown and button of a *chien-sheng*.[54] These provisions were expected to attract good students and to stimulate both students and graduates to greater effort.

The original plan to admit both bannermen and local Chinese to the Canton T'ung-wen Kuan was not followed very long. Governor-general Jui-lin reported to the Throne in 1872 that the Chinese students who had been admitted had proved to be quite useless.[55] Those who had matriculated, he said, presumably had done so only to secure the monthly stipend of three taels, for they had been irregular in attendance and lacking in interest, and nearly all had dropped out after a year or two. Consequently, he requested that thereafter admission of both regular and special students be restricted to bannermen,

[54] IWSM, TC 62, pp. 19–21; TC 65, pp. 12–15.

[55] Although Jui-lin did not mention an exception, the one Chinese in the first class sent to Peking, Tso Ping-lung, clearly was not "useless" for he became one of the leading graduates of the Peking T'ung-wen Kuan.

and this evidently was authorized.[56] American Consul F. D. Cheshire expressed the view in 1880 that the local Tartar general was more interested in having the school supply stipends for bannermen than interpreters for the government.[57]

In the same year Jui-lin also declared that the appointment of graduates of the Canton T'ung-wen Kuan as interpreters in provincial and garrison offices had not worked out as anticipated. These positions had proved to be only nominal, he said, for when foreigners came to negotiate, they ordinarily brought along their own interpreters. Whatever the reason, he complained that the official Chinese interpreters had little to do, with the result that they either hung about the offices to which they had been assigned in complete idleness or stayed at the T'ung-wen Kuan studying Chinese subjects in preparation for the provincial civil service examinations—meanwhile forgetting the foreign language the school had been established to teach. Jui-lin proposed that the position of interpreter be abolished and that all graduates who were not good enough to be sent to Peking or to pass the provincial civil service examinations continue foreign-language study in the school on a fixed salary that would subject them to call by one government office or another for interpreting duties as needed. In the end, he said, all the promising ones would either be called to Peking or earn the title of prefectural secretary or assistant district magistrate according to the formula provided in the school regulations,

[56] IWSM, TC 84, p. 29. Chinese bannermen, of course, continued to be accepted. Consul Cheshire, in reporting that only bannermen were admitted to the Canton T'ung-wen Kuan, favorably contrasted them with Chinese officials. He felt that bannermen were more bound to the government than Chinese and more loyal both by training and because of self-interest. Cheshire is the authority on the monthly stipend of three taels (*Foreign Relations of the United States, 1880*, p. 282).

[57] *Loc. cit.* Jui-lin's proposal regarding interpreters, discussed in the next paragraph, seems to support this view. Jui-lin was a bannerman himself.

and the rest would be dropped. This proposal was authorized on February 29, 1872.[58]

The Canton T'ung-wen Kuan apparently continued to operate on this basis until the first years of the twentieth century. The primary emphasis remained on foreign-language instruction, with departments of Russian and Japanese added to the original English department in 1897 and a French department added in 1900. In 1901 there were seventy students enrolled in English, and forty each in Russian and Japanese and, presumably, in French; and there were more ready to enter the school who were excluded by the inadequacy of its funds.[59] Elementary mathematics and smatterings of modern science were also taught, as well as Chinese. The teaching staff was said to be untrained and poorly supervised. In 1903 the school was amalgamated with another banner school under the name

[58] IWSM, TC 84, pp. 29–31; TC 85, pp. 12–13. According to Cheshire, not one graduate of the Canton T'ung-wen Kuan had been called upon to serve his government between 1870 and 1880. Most received a first degree, and three or four held nominal appointments as interpreters, receiving additional pay. "But," he wrote, "year after year passes and boys of 17 grow up to be 27, marry and become fathers and go on with their foreign studies without so much as a word of encouragement from their own authorities. Under such discouraging circumstances it must be that studying is often done in a perfunctory way, and yet while some of the students have, as I understand, a very good knowledge of English, wanting only practise outside the school walls to render it equal to that of any Chinaman who has not had the advantage of living abroad, they constantly witness men of less technical knowledge than themselves, men of lower stamp altogether, men picked up here and there without any proper steps being taken to ascertain their fitness, called upon to perform the very duties for the performance of which the students of the Tung wen Kuan are in theory specially educated" (*loc. cit.*).

[59] Imperial Maritime Customs, *Decennial Reports, 1892–1901*, II, 191. In 1904 there were said to be 60 students in the English department, 40 in the Russian, 37 in the Japanese, and 42 in the French. A total of approximately 250 had studied in the school during the previous eleven years (O. F. Wisner, "Western education in south China," *East of Asia Magazine*, June 1904, pp. 81–82).

I-hsüeh Kuan; in 1906 the name was again changed, this time to Fang-yen Hsüeh-t'ang. Under the latter name the school continued to emphasize foreign-language instruction, but its graduates might become either language teachers in the new public schools or official interpreters. At this time nonbannermen were once more admitted as students.[60]

The second and third types of schools opened by Chinese government agencies after 1860 had their prototypes in the two divisions of a school established in 1867 as a part of the Foochow Navy Yard.[61] One division, known as the French School (because French was the foreign language taught and used there and because its foreign teaching staff consisted of Frenchmen), trained young men of some education to design and build ships' hulls and machinery and young workmen to serve as foremen in the various construction departments of the navy yard. The other division, known as the English School, trained deck and engine officers for the ships built in the navy yard.

As noted earlier, the Foochow Navy Yard was the creation of Tso Tsung-t'ang, governor-general of Fukien and Chekiang in the mid-1860's and one of the more progressive high-ranking Chinese officials during the period covered by this study. A vigorous advocate of self-strengthening, Tso believed that China could not control its own destiny unless it was able to build and man its own warships. To this end he had proposed the employment of French engineers to build a modern navy yard near Foochow on the coast of Fukien, of French scholars as well as French engineers and skilled workmen to teach ship-

[60] Wisner, *loc. cit.;* THHL, KH 36, pp. 3–4; KFYK, p. 71; Fryer, *Educational Directory,* p. 82; *Ch'ing-ch'ao hsü wen-hsien t'ung-k'ao,* p. 8665 (cited hereafter as WHTK).

[61] This school was called the Ch'iu-shih T'ang in the beginning, but the name disappears almost at once from the documents. It will here be called the Foochow Navy Yard School, approximating the Chinese name Ch'uan-cheng Hsüeh-t'ang by which it was ordinarily called.

building, and of English naval officers to teach the command
and operation of modern ships. He was persuaded that within
five years of the completion of the plant Chinese could be
trained to operate both the navy yard and the attached school,
and thus China would be freed from continuing dependence
upon foreigners in this important sphere. The new navy yard
was authorized on July 14, and the school on December 30,
1866.

Prosper Giquel, a French naval officer who had been employed by the Chinese Maritime Customs, and Paul d'Aiguebelle, a French naval officer who had commanded French
troops that co-operated with Tso Tsung-t'ang in the suppression
of the T'aip'ing rebellion, were appointed joint foreign directors
of the navy yard, including the school; and Shen Pao-chen, a
former governor of Kiangsi province, who later became an
influential and progressive governor-general of Liang-chiang,
was appointed director-general of the whole enterprise under
the supervision of the governor-general of Min-che, the governor of Fukien, and the Tartar general at Foochow.[62] The
construction and operation of the navy yard and school were
financed from maritime customs collections in the province
of Fukien. It was the intention to recruit the students locally
from among intelligent youths of respectable families who had
had a traditional classical education, but there was also some
recruiting in Hongkong where young Chinese who had studied
English could always be found.

The French division of the Foochow school, which became
the prototype of government schools to train engineers and
skilled workmen for the new shipyards and arsenals built during and after the 1860's, consisted of three departments: naval
construction, naval design, and apprentice. The naval con-

[62] For a fuller discussion of the Foochow Navy Yard School and for
documentation, see Chap. IV. In 1869 d'Aiguebelle resigned leaving
Giquel sole foreign director.

struction department trained its students to design and build ships and marine engines. The curriculum, which took five years to complete, consisted of French, mathematics through calculus, physics, mechanics, and practical instruction in the construction of hulls and the construction and operation of machinery. In their final year the students of this department spent a part of each day actually working in one or another subdivision of the navy yard, learning to apply their theoretical knowledge and to direct workmen. Instruction was given by from three to six men holding appointments as professors of French, mathematics, and physics and chemistry, as well as by engineers from the operating divisions of the navy yard. All the teachers in the French division were Frenchmen during the initial period. Between 1874 and 1897 the instruction was given by one or two Frenchmen, by Chinese graduates of the school, and for a time by an Englishman. Then for several years commencing in 1897 a new group of French teachers was associated with L. Médard, who taught in the school during all three periods.

The department of design seems to have taught at a more elementary level than the department of naval construction, its aim having been to train youths to prepare drawings and specifications for the construction of engines. Besides French and elementary mathematics, the students were taught drawing and a thorough knowledge of engines of all kinds. The course appears to have required three years to complete, including eight months of practical application in the various navy yard shops. Prior to 1874 most of the instruction was given by a navy yard foreman and a professional draftsman, both French. Many of the students who completed this course were then admitted to the more advanced department of naval construction.

The apprentice department gave technical training to promising young workmen who might look forward to careers as foremen. Classes of one and a half hours' duration were held each morning and evening before and after the apprentices put in a regular day's work in the navy yard. The curriculum was similar to that of the design department: French, elementary mathematics, drawing, and engines, and the instruction was presumably given by the same teachers. The apprentices clearly were of a class different from the students in the other two departments and could not have had the same career expectations.

The best graduates of the French division, including a few of the apprentices, were sent to France for from three to six years of advanced training. They went in four different groups, which left China in 1877, 1882, 1886, and 1897.

Besides the formal instruction given in the French division, the navy yard itself served as a kind of training school for the many Chinese workmen employed there who had had no previous experience with machinery or modern tools. The teaching role in this case was played by the more than thirty French foremen and skilled workmen employed by the Foochow Navy Yard prior to 1874 and by their Chinese successors thereafter.

The second government-operated technological training center was located at the Kiangnan Arsenal (and shipyard) in Shanghai.[63] Formal training never had as important a place there as at Foochow, perhaps because it was not set up as a basic part of the enterprise, as had been done in the beginning by Giquel and his colleagues at the Foochow Navy Yard. Or perhaps it was never expected that foreign supervision of the Kiangnan Arsenal could be dispensed with, as was anticipated at Foochow. In any event, the proposed expansion of the Kuang fang-yen Kuan in 1870, mentioned above, which contemplated adding instruction in mineralogy and metallurgy, metalworking, machine design and operation, and naval and military

[63] See Chap. III for fuller discussion and documentation.

sciences and tactics, was never carried out. In 1881 the teaching departments at the arsenal, outside the Kuang fang-yen Kuan, were listed as naval architecture, marine engineering, and military science (ordnance?). It is not clear when these began, though an ordnance department was said to have been established in 1874. Little is known about these departments, even in 1881, except that instruction was being given in mathematics, drawing, military science, gunnery, and a foreign language—presumably English—and that they were being financed by the Maritime Customs. In 1879 three foreigners were listed as teachers, specializing in engineering science, shipbuilding, and military science respectively. Sometime during the 1880's these three departments were reduced to two: (1) the drafting division, consisting of ten or more students and twenty apprentices from the various shops of the arsenal, all of whom studied mathematics and drawing, a foreign language, and Chinese, and (2) an artillery training battalion. Finally, about 1898, these surviving technical training departments were combined and expanded to form a school of technology.

I have not ascertained whether the evening classes for arsenal workmen contemplated in 1870 were ever begun. On-the-job training for workmen certainly was provided—otherwise the arsenal could not have carried on—but it was probably quite informal. Although the arsenal continued to be supervised by foreign engineers, these were always few in number. The Chinese engineers and skilled workmen who actually operated the arsenal were trained there, formally in the technical training departments and informally in the shops.

Training somewhat comparable to that given at the Kiangnan Arsenal was also provided at the Tientsin Arsenal. Authorized in 1866 and equipped in 1869, this northern ordnance-manufacturing and ship-repair plant took on importance with the appointment of Li Hung-chang as governor-general of

Chihli in 1870. To operate the plant, Li brought experts from abroad and Chinese technicians from the Kiangnan Arsenal and from foreign-owned shipyards and factories in Hongkong and elsewhere. An arsenal school (Ch'iang-p'ao Hsüeh-t'ang) was set up,[64] and on-the-job training was given not only to Chinese technicians and workmen but also to Korean artisans who were sent by their government to Tientsin for this purpose in the 1880's.[65]

More closely patterned upon the Foochow Navy Yard School was the Hsi-hsüeh Kuan (School of Western Studies), established by Governor-general Chang Shu-sheng and Governor Yü-k'uan at Whampoa, near Canton, in 1880. Three years earlier, when Liu K'un-i was governor-general of Liang-kuang, he had set aside a fund of 150,000 taels for the teaching of foreign subjects; a part of that money was now drawn upon to build this school, and the interest on the balance was used for operating expenses.[66]

According to regulations dated June 9, 1881, under which this school was to operate,[67] all the students were to learn English and to study mathematics and Chinese. The Hsi-hsüeh Kuan was to consist of two divisions: one to train deck officers for the navy, the other to train engineers for ship construction, mining, and ordnance and also engine-room officers for the navy. The sturdiest of the best students were to be assigned to the deck officer training division, the best educated and most intelligent to the technical training division. The best students in the latter division were to be trained as engineers and the

[64] At least by 1893, for naval cadets were ordered in that year to devote six months to study in that school (THHL, KH 115, p. 5).

[65] IWSM, TC 25, pp. 1–4; TC 44, pp. 16–18; Li Hung-chang, 17, p. 35; 46, pp. 44–46; WHTK, p. 9831; THHL, KH 36, p. 18; KH 37, p. 3.

[66] Chang Chih-tung, 21, p. 25; Huang-ch'ao ching-shih-wen hsü-pien (1888), 120, p. 14 (cited hereafter as CSWP).

[67] KFYK, pp. 54–59. I have not been able to ascertain just how far this plan was carried out.

second best as engine-room officers. The least able students in both divisions were to concentrate on the English language, and it was thought they might ultimately serve as diplomatic officials and interpreters. The curriculum for engineers was to include such subjects as calculus, mechanics, chemistry, natural science, steam engines, ship construction, and ordnance. After completing a five-year program of study, the graduates were to be sent to various industrial plants for a period of practical experience. Thereafter the best of the graduates were to be sent abroad for three years of advanced training. The curriculum for prospective ships' engineers was to include the study of mechanics and of steam engines and to be followed by a period of actual metalworking in a factory.

Following the practice at the Foochow school, the students were to be selected from reputable local families on the basis of general intelligence and competence in Chinese scholarship or to be recruited in Hongkong from the growing number of young Chinese who were studying English there. It was hoped that the better students might include some who had previously passed the first civil service examination. A foreigner was to be employed to teach engineering and the most advanced English classes; elementary English and mathematics were to be taught by Chinese, preferably by graduates of the Foochow school. When Chang Chih-tung was appointed governor-general of Liang-kuang in 1884, he tells us, he found the students in this school "promising" and changed its name to Po-hsüeh Kuan (School of Wide Learning); but he gives no information about its operations. Three years later, however, Chang and the incumbent governor of Kwangtung, Wu Ta-ch'eng, converted the institution into a combined naval and military academy, presumably abandoning instruction in engineering.[68]

[68] Chang Chih-tung, 21, pp. 25–26. The navy yard built in 1885 at Whampoa, presumably adjacent to the school, had constructed seven

The third type of modern school sponsored by the Chinese government between the early 1860's and the early 1890's trained ships' officers for the Chinese navy and may properly be called a naval academy. The prototype is to be found in the English division of the Foochow Navy Yard School. China's unfortunate experience with the British-officered and British-controlled Lay-Osborn flotilla in 1863 [69] convinced the Tsungli Yamen and high provincial officials such as Tso Tsung-t'ang that China must not only build its own warships but also provide officers to command them; thus it was only natural that such training should be provided at China's first navy yard at Foochow.[70]

The naval division of the Foochow school consisted of three departments: theoretical navigation, practical navigation, and engine room. All three were taught by Englishmen not only during the initial period but also during the two decades after 1874, although Chinese professors appear also to have been used occasionally. The curriculum of the department of theoretical navigation included English, mathematics through plane and spherical trigonometry, nautical astronomy, navigation, geography, and some Chinese and required three and one-half years to complete. Graduates, unless physically unprepared for the rigors of life aboard ship, went immediately into the department of practical navigation. Those under par physically were used as tutors in this or other schools or as translator-interpreters.

---

small warships and assembled nine torpedo boats purchased in Germany, without the help of any foreigners, before 1893. Presumably some of the engineers operating this navy yard had been trained in the engineering division of the Hsi-hsüeh Kuan/Po-hsüeh Kuan (Imperial Maritime Customs, *Decennial Reports, 1882–1891*, p. 574).

[69] Morse, *International Relations*, II, 35–45; John W. Rawlinson, "The Lay-Osborn flotilla: Its development and significance," *Harvard Papers on China*, 4 (1950), 58–93.

[70] For fuller discussion of this division of the Foochow school and for documentation, see Chap. IV.

The department of practical navigation operated in a school ship attached to the navy yard. The teaching staff during the early years consisted of a captain, a master gunner, and a boat- swain—all on leave from the British navy. The curriculum in- cluded seamanship, gunnery, and ship command and required two years to complete. Part of the time the training ship re- mained at Foochow, but there were also long cruises which gave the cadets practical experience at sea. All graduates were given rank in the Chinese navy, and the best were qualified to serve as captains or mates.

The third department was established to train engine-room officers for the ships built in the navy yard. Whereas the stu- dents in the other two departments were educated young men recruited in Fukien or in Hongkong, these were skilled work- men who had been sought out in Hongkong and Shanghai. The curriculum included English, elementary mathematics, drawing, description and operation of engines, and the use of various gauges. The students were taught how to asemble en- gines, and for practical experience they installed the engines in some of the ships built at the yard. Graduates were assigned to new ships as they were commissioned.

Three groups of graduates of the English division of the Foo- chow Navy Yard School were sent to England for three years of advanced training—in 1877, 1882, and 1886. They spent a part of the time in the Royal Naval College at Greenwich and a part serving as cadets on British warships. Although the naval division at Foochow became moribund after the Sino- Japanese War, it was temporarily revived under Chinese pro- fessors before 1905 and again shortly after the 1911 Revolution.

The second Chinese naval academy, the Tientsin Shui-shih Hsüeh-t'ang, authorized in 1880, was established in 1881 by Li Hung-chang within the grounds of the Tientsin Arsenal to train officers for his new Peiyang naval squadron. Li hoped to attract able boys from the better families, as he said the Foo- chow school had succeeded in doing, but he was evidently unsuccessful in the beginning for he himself wrote that too many of the early applicants were either stupid or too old. However, he increased student stipends in 1882 from one to four taels per month, fixed the age of entering students at below seventeen, and tightened the entrance requirements with respect to the family background and the formal Chinese education of applicants—presumably with better results. The first two directors of the school had served previously as officials at the Foochow Navy Yard, one as director of the yard and the second as a proctor in the school, and the Foochow pattern appears to have been followed closely in Tientsin.[71] The first regular class of thirty students studying navigation had graduated by 1884, although Pao reports that eight students of the Educational Mission to the United States who had been assigned to this department after their recall to China graduated in 1882.[72]

The Tientsin Naval Academy consisted of two departments. One to train deck officers was opened in 1881, and the other for engine-room officers was opened in 1882.[73] The curriculum of the navigation department included English, geography, algebra, geometry, trigonometry, calculus, mechanics, astronomy, navigation, sailing, surveying, and torpedo firing. That of the engine-room department included English, arithmetic, algebra, geometry, trigonometry, mechanics, physics, ships' engines,

[71] Li Hung-chang, 40, p. 47; THHL, KH 82, p. 21; *North-China Herald* (cited hereafter as NCH), Nov. 29, 1882.

[72] WHTK, p. 8677; Pao Tsun-p'eng, *Chung-kuo hai-chün shih* (1951), p. 231.

[73] THHL, KH 79, pp. 29–30. The second department had been converted from a torpedo and telegraph school that had been established in the arsenal about 1877 in which an English telegrapher named Betts for three years had taught simple English, arithmetic, geography, and presumably telegraphy. After graduation—and more than twenty were reported to have graduated in 1879—the students were assigned to forts and telegraph stations (Consul Denny in *Foreign Relations of the United States, 1880*, p. 286; Pao, pp. 230–231).

mechanical drawing, applied engineering, and torpedo repair.[74] The Chinese classics and Chinese composition were also
taught—"to steady the students' character." Finally, all students were subject to military drill; and the prospective deck
officers were taught how to fire weapons and were exercised
on dummy ships' masts.[75] An English naval captain who helped
conduct the annual examination in 1890 suggested to Li Hung-
chang that the cadets be taught boxing, gymnastics, and fenc-
ing "to develop their pluck, nerve and self-confidence," [76] but
this may have been asking too much physical activity of a
Chinese officer. Yen Tsung-kuang (Yen Fu), a graduate of the
Foochow naval division who had received advanced training
in Europe, was dean (*tsung-chiao-hsi*) and professor of navigation and mathematics for a number of years. There were also
three Englishmen on the faculty: William McLeish, who taught
English and mathemathics, and H. W. Walker and G. H. Hearson, both engineers of the British navy who taught the engine-
room officers.[77]

Although the first class apparently graduated within three
years, regulations dating from sometime during the 1880's
stipulated that cadets being trained as deck officers should
spend four years at the academy, followed by a year on a training ship, then three more months at the academy, and finally
three months on a regular warship before taking their final examinations. In 1893 Admiral Ting Ju-ch'ang, the commander
of the Peiyang squadron, expressed the view that an even longer
period of training was desirable. He proposed that the four
years of study in the academy be followed by six months in an
ordnance school, another six months on a torpedo training ves-

[74] THHL, KH 82, p. 21. [75] WHTK, p. 8677.
[76] NCH, July 18, 1890.
[77] Ch'ih Chung-hu, "Hai-chün ta-shih-chi," in Tso Shun-sheng, *Chung-kuo chin-pai-nien shih-tzu-liao hsü-pien* (1933), p. 329; *Chronicle and Directory for China . . . 1889*, p. 480; NCH, July 18, 1890; *Foreign Relations of the United States, 1888*, p. 301.

sel, and then finally two years at sea on a general training ship, seven years thus elapsing from admission to the academy to completion of training.[78] No evidence has been found that this proposal was carried out.

Pao Tsun-p'eng says that the Tientsin Naval Academy came to an end in 1900 during the Boxer troubles, when its students were scattered. Prior to that time, he reports, eight classes graduated from the navigation department, including the group of returned students from the United States and a class that had been transferred from the short-lived Peking naval school, with a total of 164 graduates. The engine-room officer department graduated 85 students in five classes.[79] One group of 9 Tientsin graduates was sent to England in 1886 for three years of advanced training.[80]

The deck officer division of the Hsi-hsüeh Kuan/Po-hsüeh Kuan at Whampoa, near Canton (briefly described above), and the naval division of the Shui-lu-shih Hsüeh-t'ang (Naval and Military Academy) that succeeded it in 1887 followed the model of the English division of the Foochow school, with some adjustment to local conditions. In the beginning there was a five-year curriculum, but after the 1887 reorganization six years were required to complete the course: three to be spent in the school and three on a training ship.[81] The original

[78] THHL, KH 115, pp. 5–6. In 1891 Li Hung-chang wrote that a minimum of ten years of training was desirable for naval officers (72, p. 22). Besides training naval officers, the Tientsin Naval Academy is said to have had a translation department. Liang Ch'i-ch'ao lists it with the T'ung-wen Kuan and the Kiangnan Arsenal as centers where foreign books had been translated into Chinese (Joseph R. Levenson, *Liang Ch'i-ch'ao and the Mind of Modern China* [1953], p. 27, n. 63).

[79] Pp. 231–232. Pao's figures are not very reliable: those he gives for each class add up to 154 in the case of the navigation department and 73 for the engine-room department.

[80] Li Hung-chang, 55, pp. 14–15; CCTI, 41, pp. 8–11. For their names, see Chap. IV, notes 94–98.

[81] Chang Chih-tung, 28, pp. 2–7; Imperial Maritime Customs, *Decennial Reports, 1882–1891*, p. 575.

curriculum included English, mathematics, naval astronomy, navigation regulations, and seamanship, besides training in the use of small arms and some military drill, with only six months on the training ship.[82]

After 1887 the naval division consisted of two departments, one for the training of deck officers, the other for engine-room officers. It had been intended that the initial class in each department should have seventy students, thirty to be drawn from students already enrolled in the Po-hsüeh Kuan who had achieved proficiency in English and mathematics, twenty junior military officers "of experience and demonstrated courage," and twenty holders of the first degree who were less than thirty years of age. On November 10, 1889, however, Chang Chih-tung wrote that the naval division had started in 1887 with upwards of seventy students transferred from the Po-hsüeh Kuan, divided between the two departments. Of these only thirty-eight remained in 1889 after the elimination of those who had failed to measure up to the standard set. Chang went on to say that the senior class in the deck officer's department at the time he wrote had only fourteen students. It may be that some of their original classmates were still studying in the department but had been demoted to a lower class. This senior class was expected to be ready for assignment to a training ship within the year.

In September 1889, thirty-seven students were transferred to the deck and engine-room officer departments of the Canton academy from the English division of the Foochow school where they had already completed from three to four years of study. And in October 1889 twenty youths with some Chinese education were brought to the school from Tientsin. These students were to concentrate at first on English and mathematics and only later to be assigned to either the naval or the military division of the school for more specialized training.[83]

[82] KFYK, pp. 54–59.   [83] Chang Chih-tung, 28, pp. 3–6.

Why students were recruited in distant Tientsin rather than in Canton is not easy to explain.

Wu Chung-hsiang, who had served ten years as a proctor at the Foochow school and had then set up the Tientsin Naval Academy for Li Hung-chang, was brought to Whampoa by Chang Chih-tung as a consultant during the planning of the naval and military academy, and he later became the first director of the naval division. An Englishman named F. T. Richards, who had previously taught at Foochow, was appointed professor in the deck officer department, teaching theoretical navigation, nautical astronomy, and English. Another Englishman named Edmonds taught the engine-room officers. And there were four Chinese teachers who gave instruction in navigation and seamanship, engineering, English, and Chinese. New buildings were erected, and the engine-room officer department was said to have been unusually well equipped with modern mechanical appliances. A training ship, the S.S. *Huang-chin,* was ordered to be readied for use by the time the first class had completed its three years of study ashore. It was to be commanded by Chinese officers, but instructions were sent to the Chinese minister in England to employ a foreign professor for the school ship and two other foreigners to teach gunnery and the handling of sails and tackle. The interest from the endowment originally set up by Liu K'un-i was insufficient to operate the school even on the modest scale contemplated, and it was necessary to secure additional money from the coast-defense funds of Kwangtung province.[84]

I have been unable to discover what became of the seventy-five naval students mentioned in Chang Chih-tung's memorial of November 10, 1889. The 1893 edition of *Decennial Reports* of the Maritime Customs gives a total of only twenty-five cadets in the naval division at that time. Probably some of those miss-

[84] *Ibid.,* 21, pp. 25–28; 28, pp. 2–4.

ing had meanwhile been assigned to naval posts and the rest dismissed for one reason or another. During the governorship of Kang-i (1892–1894), one of the most notorious reactionaries of the period, the Whampoa Naval and Military Academy was closed, the foreign staff was dismissed, and the modern vessels of the Kwangtung flotilla were tied up. According to a contemporary Maritime Customs report the school remained closed for the remainder of the 1890's,[85] although Pao Tsunp'eng states that it reopened between 1895 and 1899.[86] Whichever is right, the combined naval and military academy evidently was in operation once more by 1901. F. T. Richards was again teaching naval subjects, a German named G. L. Hummel taught in a new torpedo department, and the English and German languages were taught by Chinese instructors. Pao reports that the school was divided into separate naval and military academies in 1902. By 1904 all the teachers were Chinese.[87] There were 150 cadets enrolled in the Whampoa Naval Academy in 1911, at which time Brunnert and Hagelstrom listed it as one of the three naval academies of the Imperial Chinese government.[88]

Three other naval academies were established before the Sino-Japanese War: one at the Imperial summer palace outside Peking during the winter of 1887–1888, one at the operating base of the Peiyang squadron at Weihaiwei in 1889, and the

[85] Wen Ching, *The Chinese Crisis from Within* (1900), p. 161; Imperial Maritime Customs, *Decennial Reports, 1882–1891*, p. 576; *1892–1901*, II, 195.

[86] P. 228. He says that the original joint academy was reorganized as a naval academy during the governor-generalship of T'an Chung-lin and that the two academies which were created in 1902 represented a second reorganization.

[87] Pao, p. 228; *Chronicle and Directory for China . . . 1901*, p. 293; *Directory and Chronicle for China . . . 1904*, pp. 355–356.

[88] Imperial Maritime Customs, *Decennial Reports, 1902–1911*, II, 153; H. S. Brunnert and V. V. Hagelstrom, *Present Day Political Organization of China* (1912), p. 345.

third at Nanking in 1890. The first of these, called the K'un-ming Lake Naval Academy, was created to provide naval training for bannermen. It was modeled on the Tientsin academy, and its first graduating class was sent there in April 1892 for additional training. The Peking academy was closed three or four years later. The school building at Weihaiwei was destroyed in 1894 and that academy was closed, too.[89] Wang Wen-chieh lists torpedo and submarine-mine training schools that were opened during this period in Tientsin (1879), Taku (1881), Dairen (1887), Weihaiwei (1894), and Port Arthur (1894).[90] All of these, like the Tientsin, Weihaiwei, and Peking naval academies, were adjuncts of the Peiyang squadron and the North China coastal defense command built up by Li Hung-chang.

Comparable in importance to the English division of the Foochow school and the Tientsin Naval Academy was the Kiangnan or Nanyang shui-shih Hsüeh-t'ang, established at Nanking in 1890 to train officers for a new Nanyang naval squadron based in Kiangsu. Tseng Kuo-ch'üan,[91] a younger brother of Tseng Kuo-fan, who was governor-general of Liang-chiang for six years prior to his death in November 1890, was responsible for the setting up of this academy, and it continued to receive the warm support of his succesor Liu K'un-i. At first the port of Shanghai, with its shipyard at the Kiangnan Arsenal, seemed the appropriate place for this academy, but Nanking's isolation from the distractions of the metropolis and its status as the seat of the governor-general of Liang-chiang finally led to its selection. Shen Tun-ho, who after studying in England had served as special adviser on foreign affairs to the governor-general, drew up the plans for the academy and was

[89] Li Hung-chang, 72, p. 22; Pao, pp. 232–236.
[90] "Shih-chiu shih-chi Chung-kuo chih tzu-ch'iang yün-tung," *Fukien Culture*, 3 (Dec. 1947), 16–18.
[91] See biography by Teng Ssu-yü in Hummel, pp. 749–751.

named its first director. The administration building and student living and dining quarters were in Chinese style, the classroom building, the laboratories, and the faculty residences in Western style. A dummy ship's mast, an athletic and drill field, and a target-practice area were provided. The regulations under which the Nanking school operated were based on those of the Tientsin academy.[92]

Two experienced British naval officers, John Penniall and Hugh R. Hearson, were the first professors of navigation and engineering respectively. The Chinese teaching staff, which numbered sixteen in 1905, included several graduates or former instructors of the Tientsin school some of whom had had advanced training in Europe. As at Tientsin and Whampoa, the academy was divided into two departments, one to train deck officers, the other engine-room officers. And for a time, commencing in 1893, instruction was given to a succession of three small classes studying submarine mines and torpedoes. The curriculum of the navigation department required five years to complete, with two of those years to be spent aboard a training ship. The engine-room course took six years, including six months working in the shops of the Kiangnan Arsenal and six months aboard a training ship. The subjects taught, besides English and Chinese, were mathematics, mechanics, hydrostatics, navigation and nautical astronomy, marine engineering, applied mechanics, engineering, drawing and design, physics, chemistry, physical geography, mechanical work, rifle practice, and gymnastics. A Lieutenant H. V. Simpson of the British navy was employed in 1894 to teach the cadets their duties as naval officers. Drill and gymnastics were taught by German officers, and the submarine-mine and torpedo instruction was given by Chinese who had been trained in France.

When the Nanking Naval Academy opened in December 1890, it proved to be difficult to recruit promising students, for

[92] NCH, Oct. 26, 1894.

the prerequisites included a knowledge of English and of the Chinese classics, as well as good character, intelligence, and alertness. Of the first group of several hundred who applied for admission, only one hundred were admitted, and some of these were later dropped. Some had studied previously in the Foochow Navy Yard School, and others at English schools in Shanghai. Outside examiners, John Fryer of the Kiangnan Arsenal translation department in 1892 and two British naval officers in 1894, were very favorably impressed with the knowledge and ability demonstrated by the cadets.[93] At the end of the Ch'ing dynasty the naval academy at Nanking was one of the three still training officers for the Chinese navy. According to Pao Tsun-p'eng, seven classes, with a total of 107 cadets, graduated from the navigation department between 1896 and the 1911 Revolution, and six classes, totaling 91 cadets, from the engine-room department.[94]

Military academies, that is, schools to train army officers along modern lines, appeared comparatively late in nineteenth-century China. In 1862 the top commanders of the government's armies engaged in the suppression of the T'aip'ing rebellion were ordered by the Emperor to select junior officers to be sent to Shanghai and Ningpo for several months to learn modern military methods from British and French officers; after this training they were to be reassigned to combat forces, where they would be expected to pass along their knowledge.[95] Later a few high provincial officials, notably Li Hung-chang,

[93] WHTK, p. 8679; "Nan-yang shui-shih Hsüeh-t'ang k'ao-shih chi-lüeh" (presumably by John Fryer), *Ko-chih hui-pien,* 7 (Winter 1892), 47–48; NCH, Nov. 18, 1892, Oct. 26, 1894; Fryer, *Educational Directory,* p. 84; Nathaniel Gist Gee, *The Educational Directory for China* (1905), p. 133; *The Engineer* (London), June 8, 1900, p. 600; Pao, pp. 235–236.

[94] Brunnert and Hagelstrom, p. 345; Pao, pp. 235–236.

[95] IWSM, TC 10, pp. 15–16. For a translation of excerpts from this edict see Teng and Fairbank, p. 68.

employed French or, after the Franco-Prussian War, German army officers to train their troops; and Li sent seven of his own officers to Germany in 1876 to learn "the art of war." [96]

The first actual school for the training of army officers was the Wu-pei Hsüeh-t'ang (Military Preparation Academy) established in Tientsin in 1885 by Li Hung-chang. On June 17 of that year Li wrote to the Emperor that his new school was to be patterned on the military academies found in Western countries. As teachers he planned to use some German army officers, specialists in various branches of military science, whom he had brought to Tientsin the previous year to train his army. Western countries, Li wrote, had learned the necessity for trained professional leadership of their armies. They therefore selected boys with intelligence and ability from respectable families for thorough schooling in military science and tactics. This training was followed by actual experience with troops, after which they were commissioned as officers. Mere bravery and crude talent, without proficiency in military science, would not save China from foreign encroachment, he said; the training of professional army officers in modern military academies was essential.

Ostensibly because of financial stringency it was decided at first to train only selected petty officers and soldiers and to make the course a short one. Provincial military commanders as far away as Kwangsi and Szechwen, in addition to the commanders of units under the control of Li himself, were ordered to send promising candidates to Tientsin, where early in 1885 a first class of over a hundred was selected, including a few civil officials who had expressed a desire to study military science. The curriculum consisted of astronomy, geography, science, surveying, drafting, mathematics, construction of fortifications, and infantry, cavalry, and artillery drill and opera-

[96] Li Hung-chang, 41, p. 23; Helmuth Stoecker, *Deutschland und China im 19. Jahrhundert* (1958), p. 127.

tions. Once each month the students were taken by their instructors to nearby military posts for several days of target practice and participation in military maneuvers. Li had anticipated that the course would be completed in one year, but it turned out that classes were graduated every two years. Since the students knew no foreign language and most of them presumably had had little Chinese education, instruction had to be by word of mouth and demonstration, the foreign staff teaching through interpreters. Upon completing the course the graduates were returned to the military units from which they had come so that their new knowledge might be widely employed.[97] It seems obvious that these men of limited education could not have acquired more than a superficial acquaintance with modern military science within the two-year period. Yet the program must have been regarded as successful, for each graduating class was succeeded by a new one, at least until 1892.[98] However, even in his memorial of June 1885 Li Hung-chang was aware that this short course would not solve China's military leadership problems. The astronomy, mathematics, and natural sciences from which Western military studies were derived could not be mastered without a command of Western languages, he wrote. When more funds were available, another division (or school) would be established to which select youths from respectable families would be admitted for professional military training. After completing their studies they would be assigned as officers to various military units, where they would secure practical experience and thus ensure a continuous supply of competent army officers. Li recognized that inducements would be required not only to attract students to the military academy but also to persuade them to study con-

[97] Li Hung-chang, 53, pp. 42–44; 60, p. 48. For a translation of Li's June 1885 memorial see Cyrus H. Peake, *Nationalism and Education in Modern China* (1932), pp. 10–12.

[98] Li Hung-chang, 74, p. 23. In the same 1885 memorial Li mentions a similar training school for selected petty officers and soldiers that had been established at Shanhaikuan.

scientiously; he therefore proposed that superior students as well as their instructors be recommended to the Throne for commendation every two years.[99]

In the spring of 1887 a long-term officers' training program was added to the military academy at Tientsin. Forty youths between thirteen and sixteen years of age, sons of military officials or other reputable families and possessed of at least the essentials of an orthodox Chinese education, were selected by examination. If they showed promise after a three-month trial period and committed themselves to five years of schooling, during which they would not ask for leave to take the regular civil or military examinations or to get married, they were allowed to proceed. During the first three years the cadets were to study a foreign language (presumably German), arithmetic, algebra, geometry, mechanics, astronomy, natural science, geography, and mapping, as well as Chinese history and the Chinese classics. In the fourth and fifth years the curriculum was to include gunnery, military drill, construction of fortifications, and other technical military subjects. The students were to be tested regularly and rewarded if deserving. At the end of five years they were to be encouraged to take the government civil or military examinations with a view to permanent military service. In the beginning only one foreigner and two Chinese were employed as teachers, but three German professors, Captains Richter, von Briwen, and von Auer, were there in 1889.[100] An engineering department must have been added by 1890 because in the 1925 *Who's Who in China* there are listed three prominent railway engineers who say they graduated from such a department during the early 1890's.[101]

The military academy was destroyed in the fighting at Tien-

[99] *Ibid.*, 53, pp. 42–44.

[100] *Ibid.*, 60, p. 49; NCH, April 13, 1887; *Chronicle and Directory for China . . . 1889*, p. 479.

[101] Pp. 5–6, 651–652, 944–945.

tsin during the Boxer uprising in 1900 and was never rebuilt. Within two or three years it was replaced by several levels of military schools set up in Paotingfu by Yüan Shih-k'ai after he became governor-general of Chihli.[102]

The other Chinese military school that came into existence during this period was a division of the Shui-lu-shih Hsüeh-t'ang, the combined naval and military academy near Canton mentioned earlier, which was converted from the Po-hsüeh Kuan in 1887 by Chang Chih-tung. The military division of this school was expected to accommodate seventy students, who in the beginning were to be drawn partly from the student body of the Po-hsüeh Kuan, partly from experienced junior army officers, and partly from holders of the first civil or military degree who were between twenty and thirty years of age. The course was to be three years in length and to include instruction in German and traditional Chinese studies as well as in technical military subjects. There were three departments, cavalry and infantry, artillery, and military engineering; three months of each year were to be spent in camp. Graduates were to be eligible for both military and civil service examinations. The faculty consisted at first of two German army officers and several Chinese.[103]

How many students entered the first class, whence they came, or how long it took them to complete their training I have not been able to ascertain. In his November 10, 1889, report Chang Chih-tung wrote that twenty (presumably young) army officers

[102] Ralph L. Powell, *The Rise of Chinese Military Power, 1895–1912* (1955), pp. 114, 145.

[103] Chang Chih-tung, 21, pp. 25–26; CSWP, 120, pp. 13–14. A Maritime Customs officer writing in 1892 says that there were about seventy-two students at that time, and he mentions a Captain Tenckhoff and Lieutenants Appelius and Lange, all German army officers, as having taught in the school. He also mentions a foreign professor of botany, who, however, had been dropped because little interest was shown in his subject (Imperial Maritime Customs, *Decennial Reports, 1882–1891,* p. 576).

had been brought from Tientsin in June 1888 to study in the Canton school; and he also said that the first class of nineteen students had completed its training and was ready to return to active military service.[104] If these are references to the same class, the course took only a year; if the graduating class had commenced its training at the time the school was reorganized in 1887, the course required two years. In any event the original plan for a three-year military curriculum appears not to have been carried out. As mentioned earlier, this combined naval and military academy was closed during the early 1890's, but reopened later; and in 1902 it was divided to form separate naval and military academies.

Among the earliest modern innovations in communications introduced by the Chinese was the telegraph. When the Tsungli Yamen in 1867 solicited the opinions of a number of high provincial officials regarding the desirability of permitting foreigners to build and operate telegraph lines in China, the response was unanimous opposition; but Li Hung-chang and Shen Pao-chen said that the telegraph might be beneficial to China if installed and operated by the Chinese themselves.[105] It was Li who actually took the initiative when construction of a telegraph system was begun more than a decade later. After experimenting for a year with a telegraph line connecting army headquarters in Tientsin with a fort at Taku, on September 18, 1880, he requested Imperial authorization to build a telegraph line from Tientsin to Shanghai as a measure of national defense. Permission was promptly granted, and construction was begun with military funds. After completion the enterprise was taken over by the Imperial Telegraph Administration, an official-supervised and merchant-managed company admin-

[104] Chang Chih-tung, 28, pp. 3, 6.
[105] See Biggerstaff, "The secret correspondence of 1867–1868: Views of leading Chinese statesmen regarding the further opening of China to Western influence," *Journal of Modern History*, 22 (June 1950), 129–130.

istered by Sheng Hsüan-huai under Li's aegis and capitalized by the sale of shares to merchants and other individuals.[106]

In his September 1880 memorial Li Hung-chang stated that he intended to establish a school in Tientsin with foreign teachers to train telegraph operators; and in a set of regulations attached to that memorial he stipulated that the school should be a part of the new telegraph administration and that all of its graduates should be assigned to the telegraph service. The Tien-pao Hsüeh-t'ang (Telegraph School) opened on October 6, 1880, with a faculty of Danes employed on a one-year basis to teach "the science of electricity and the technique of sending telegrams." Graduates who failed to make good on the job were to return to the school for additional training.[107]

Declaring in a memorial submitted to the Throne on December 23, 1882, that the Tientsin-Shanghai telegraph line, which had been completed before the end of 1881, had already proved its usefulness, Li proposed that a second line be built to Canton, connecting with the first line at Soochow. This additional construction was also authorized. One of the ten regulations attached to this memorial provided that the Tientsin Telegraph School continue for another year in order to supply telegraphers for the new line. Li proposed that from forty to fifty new students, recruited among Chinese who knew English, be added to the thirty-two students remaining in the school. He

[106] THHL, KH 36, pp. 12–13; Albert Feuerwerker, *China's Early Industrialization* (1958), pp. 191–192. For a biography of Sheng see *ibid.*, pp. 58–95; for a brief study of the Imperial Telegraph Administration see *ibid.*, pp. 190–207.

[107] THHL, KH 51, pp. 2–4; Fryer, *Educational Directory*, p. 85. The telegraph system was installed on contract for the Chinese by the Danish Great Northern Telegraph Co. The first class in the school included at least twenty-three members of the Chinese Educational Mission to the United States that had been recalled to China in 1880 (Li Hung-chang, 53, p. 16). Li's office was to assume the major expense of opening and operating this school and a similar school to be opened in Shanghai (Feuerwerker, p. 203).

expected that their training would be finished in time for them to take over the positions created by the completion of the new line the following year.[108]

Although it had been intended to close the telegraph school after 1883, this decision was reversed, for there are later reports of its continuing operation. In 1889 the professorial staff consisted of C. H. O. Poulsen and V. Culmsee, both Danes, and Na-san, a graduate of the Peking T'ung-wen Kuan.[109] The two aims of the school, as set forth in 1895 by Poulsen, who was the assistant director, were, in general, "to introduce into China the science of electricity and magnetism and the application of those kindred forces in various forms of apparatuses for different purposes" and, more specifically, "to educate Chinese students in the theory of electricity and magnetism and the art of telegraphy for service in the stations of the Imperial Chinese Telegraph System."

In 1895 there were fifty students in the school, divided among four classes. They ranged from sixteen to twenty-two years of age, they received monthly stipends of from three to ten taels according to their class, and those who had entered with a good foundation of English and mathematics could expect to graduate in four or five years—clearly a much more thorough training than was given during the early years of the school. The curriculum in 1895 consisted of the following subjects: "telegraph practice, preliminary traffic questions, rules and regulations of instruments, rules of international telegraph convention, electricity and magnetism, electrical testing, various kinds of telegraph systems and instruments, railway telegraph apparatuses, construction of land and submarine lines, surveying of telegraph routes, science of materials, telegraphic geography, mathematics, drawing, electric lighting, English

[108] THHL, KH 51, pp. 2–4; *Huang-ch'ao cheng-tien lei-tsuan* (1903), 461, p. 4.
[109] *Chronicle and Directory for China . . . 1889*, p. 480.

and Chinese." The textbooks used were "C. H. O. Poulsen's Electro-Telegraphy and other books written by him for the students." Since its beginning 300 students had graduated from the school. Chin-t'ang, a graduate of the Peking T'ung-wen Kuan, was director of the Tientsin Telegraph School in 1895 and also professor of English. Poulsen taught the technical subjects, possibly assisted by Chang Chin-fen and T'an Chi-hsiang, who also presumably taught Chinese.[110]

The Tientsin Telegraph School was still functioning in 1900, evidently with an all-Chinese faculty. But it was no longer listed in the 1902 *Chronicle and Directory for China,* so presumably it had been closed.[111] While the telegraph system was being extended during the 1880's, other telegraph schools were opened in Shanghai, Foochow, Canton, and perhaps elsewhere, but these appear to have been intended to train an initial crew of operators for the region in which they were located and to have been closed when this task was completed.

The sixth type of government-sponsored modern school was a medical school for army and navy surgeons. By successfully treating the wife of Li Hung-chang after old-fashioned Chinese practitioners had failed, Dr. John K. Mackenzie of the London Missionary Society won Li's support for a small modern hospital that was opened in Tientsin in 1880 and was called, in English, the Viceroy's Hospital. A year later Dr. Mackenzie offered to give modern medical training to some of the students recalled from the Educational Mission to the United States, preparing them to be medical officers in the armed forces, with the result that the I-yao Kuan, or Viceroy's Hospital Medical School as it was called in English, opened on December 15, 1881, with eight students. Instruction was given by Dr. Mackenzie and such British and American naval surgeons as happened to be stationed in Tientsin; clinical teaching was done

[110] Fryer, *Educational Directory,* pp. 85–86.
[111] *Chronicle and Directory for China . . . 1900,* p. 133; *1901,* p. 145.

in the hospital. Li paid all the expenses of the school from provincial defense funds. The first class, reduced to six, graduated in 1885; all were awarded the ninth civil rank and an honorary fifth or sixth rank. Its two ablest members remained in the school as teachers, and the rest were assigned to army posts or naval vessels. A second class of four, all of whom were graduates of the Hongkong Normal School, entered in 1883 and graduated in 1887. A third class of twelve, all graduates of the Hongkong Central School, took longer to complete their work because of deficiencies in their English—in fact, two were transferred to the telegraph school.[112]

After the death of Dr. Mackenzie in 1888 the Viceroy's Hospital was purchased by the London Missionary Society, and Li, with funds contributed by local merchants, built a new government hospital in Tientsin to which the medical school was attached. In 1893 a new building was erected for the school, now called the Pei-yang I-hsüeh T'ang (Peiyang Medical College). Dr. Lin Lien-hui, the outstanding member of the first graduating class, was the director, and general medical supervision was exercised by Dr. Andrew Irwin, Maritime Customs medical officer for Tientsin. The teaching staff included both Chinese and foreign doctors, and all expenses were met from the coast-defense funds following the precedent of the Tientsin naval and military academies. The curriculum followed the standard practice of medical schools in the West.[113] In 1900 this school had a teaching staff of three Chinese and two foreign doctors, and in 1906 the staff was even larger.[114]

The last type of government-sponsored modern school opened prior to the Sino-Japanese War was the Mining and Engineering College of the Hupeh province Board of Mines. In

[112] K. C. Wong and Wu Lien-teh, *History of Chinese Medicine* (1936 ed.), pp. 440–442.

[113] *Ibid.*, p. 479; Li Hung-chang, 78, pp. 31–32.

[114] *Chronicle and Directory for China . . . 1900*, p. 127; *Directory and Chronicle for China . . . 1906*, p. 631.

April 1890 a laboratory was opened in Wuchang to analyze coal and ores from the two provinces of Hupeh and Hunan, and in July 1891 a class was organized to study the methods of analyzing coal and iron ore. In June 1892 this class was expanded to form a "college," and courses were added in chemistry and physics. By 1895 there were twenty students in the college, receiving instruction from Henry H. Robinson, M.A. (Oxon.), Low Kuo-jui (who had been educated at Rensselaer Polytechnic Institute in the United States), and other Chinese teachers.[115]

Obstacles and Accomplishments

It can be stated categorically that none of the officials who were responsible for the modern schools described in this survey wanted to replace Chinese civilization with Western civilization or the Chinese system of education with an alien system. All of them appeared to have accepted the concept stated at the beginning of the 1860's by Feng Kuei-fen in his essay "On seeking Western knowledge," namely, that China's established principles and the teachings of the sages were basic; what was needed was that these be supplemented by the techniques that had enabled the Western powers to achieve wealth and national strength. This idea is better known in the more succinct formulation made at the end of the 1890's by Chang Chih-tung: "Chinese learning for fundamentals, Western learning for practical use" (*Chung-hsüeh wei t'i, hsi-hsüeh wei yung*). Even Li Hung-chang, the most vigorous Chinese advocate of adaptations from the West during this period, appears, as Ssu-yü Teng and John K. Fairbank have said, "to have thought

[115] Imperial Maritime Customs, *Decennial Reports, 1882–1891*, p. 190; Fryer, *Educational Directory*, p. 86. A class in practical chemistry and mineralogy had been organized at Kaiping (near Tientsin) many years earlier for seven members of the Educational Mission to the United States recalled to China in 1881. It was taught by an American named E. K. Buttles (*Foreign Relations of the United States, 1883*, p. 201).

that the Chinese political and educational systems and Chinese culture and customs were all superior to those of foreign countries—except for cannon, railways and machinery." [116]

Although these modern schools were strongly supported by such powerful statesmen as Prince Kung, Tseng Kuo-fan, Tso Tsung-t'ang, Li Hung-chang, and Chang Chih-tung, who believed that Chinese spiritual values would be strengthened by such practical borrowings, the overwhelming majority of the ruling class, the Confucian literati, disapproved of the deviation from the traditional pattern of education which these schools represented, regarding them as incompatible with, and therefore a threat to, the Chinese way of life.[117] Much of the opposition was relatively inert, but some was vehement. Not unnaturally, perhaps, large numbers of Chinese distrusted foreigners and everything foreign. Cultural pride and ignorance of the outside world could explain this attitude, particularly among the ruling class, but experience with Western arrogance and aggression inevitably added resentment to this natural feeling. In general, Chinese who worked closely with foreigners were suspected by their countrymen. Those who went as far as to learn a foreign language were, at times, even regarded as traitors.[118] Yen Ching-ming, a minister of the Tsungli Yamen from 1884 to 1886, is said to have told a friend that "no gentleman with a sense of honor cared to learn about foreign affairs." [119]

[116] *Chiao-pin-lu k'ang-i*, p. 69; Teng and Fairbank, pp. 86, 164, 169; Hellmut Wilhelm, "The problem of within and without," *Journal of the History of Ideas*, 12 (1951), 59–60.

[117] See Joseph R. Levenson, *Confucian China and Its Modern Fate* (1958), pp. 59–78, for an interesting philosophical discussion of this conflict.

[118] M. J. O'Brien letter, NCH, Jan. 25, 1870; Ch'i Ju-shan, "Ch'i Ju-shan tzu-chuan," *Chung-kuo i-chou*, no. 237 (Nov. 8, 1954). A copy of these reminiscences of a T'ung-wen Kuan graduate was sent to me from Taiwan by the late Ts'ui Shu-ch'in.

[119] Ssu-ming Meng, "The Organization and Functions of the Tsungli Yamen" (Harvard Ph.D. dissertation, 1949), p. 141.

There was mistrust of the use of foreigners as teachers, particularly when the foreign teachers were Christian missionaries. It was almost impossible for Chinese to believe that a Westerner would honestly share with Chinese students knowledge in the various fields that gave European powers military superiority over China. Surely the foreign teacher would supply misinformation harmful to China or use his position to subvert his students—to undermine their loyalty to their cultural heritage and to their government.[120] In the beginning even Prince Kung and Wen-hsiang tried to recruit the teachers of foreign languages required by the Peking T'ung-wen Kuan among Chinese in Shanghai and Canton; only when it became clear that no suitable Chinese teachers could be found did they employ foreigners. And it should be remembered that one of the complaints made by the uncompromising traditionalist Wo-jen against the plan to reorganize that same school in 1867 was directed against the provision to employ foreigners to teach mathematics and astronomy. "Why must we learn from foreigners?" he wrote; ". . . the foreigners are our enemies. . . . It cannot but end after a few years by driving the Chinese people fully to yield to the foreigner."[121] Yet because not enough competent Chinese were developed to meet the need, particularly the need for advanced instruction, modern schools continued to employ some foreign teachers until the middle of the twentieth century.

Opponents also charged that these modern government schools were intended to serve as alternate routes to regular

[120] Although most of the foreign teachers in these schools appear to have served China faithfully, the fears of conservative critics were not entirely baseless. Some missionaries, as Young J. Allen, and even ex-missionaries such as W. A. P. Martin, considered it their moral duty to introduce their students to Christian ideals—even though it was done subtly. Moreover, no one can doubt that the Western knowledge spread through these schools contributed ultimately to the subversion of traditional Chinese civilization.

[121] IWSM, TC 47, pp. 24–25.

civil and military office, as substitutes for the traditional government examinations, and for this reason there was particularly strong opposition to them among those who held official degrees. The original plan to reward all graduates of the Shanghai T'ung-wen Kuan with the first civil service degree was never put into effect—presumably having been blocked by the Board of Civil Office or by the educational commissioner for Kiangsu province. Although graduates of the Canton T'ung-wen Kuan were given a first degree, it was a special degree that the ruling Manchus had earlier created for the purpose of slipping into the official system bannermen who could not pass the regular examinations, and as such, it had long been depreciated by the Chinese literati. Shen Pao-chen and Li Hung-chang tried unsuccessfully during the 1870's to secure modification of the regular civil service examinations in order to give some advantage to candidates who had mastered mathematics and other Western subjects at the expense of a complete command of the traditional curriculum. So strong was the resistance that when a concession to modern knowledge was finally made in the regular examinations in 1887 it was, as noted, so limited as to be practically meaningless. Virtually all of the few graduates of modern schools who held regular civil service degrees prior to the twentieth century won them by passing the examinations in the regular way, having mastered the traditional curriculum in addition to Western subjects. Entrenched officialdom effectively blocked the replacement of traditional Confucianism by modern knowledge as a key to official position and prestige until after the abolition of the old examination system in 1905. Opposition to compromise with modernism was most often expressed in terms of principle; but one cannot doubt that many educated Chinese feared what they regarded as a threat to the privileged position conferred upon them by their mastery of the subject matter of the traditional examination.

The conservative literati also disapproved of attempts to recruit members of their own class as students in the modern schools. Most of these schools offered admission to a certain number of officials, at least as special students, but the prevailing attitude within the educated elite appears to have discouraged the interest of all but a few who were attracted by the large stipends and the promises of rapid promotion. The spectacular debate on this issue which was evoked in 1867 by the creation of a new department of mathematics and astronomy in the Peking T'ung-wen Kuan has already been examined. This department was to have been open only to young scholars holding at least the second civil service degree. The scientific and mathematical knowledge which Prince Kung and Wen-hsiang regarded as essential for national defense and as demanding the attention of the best Chinese minds was dismissed by Wo-jen and other spokesmen for the traditionalists as mere craftsmanship to be eschewed by the educated and left to ordinary men. Properly educated officials did not require such information to conduct the affairs of state, they said. Exposed to it they might become confused, possibly even lose their sense of values, to the lasting misfortune of China. It is of considerable significance that, in spite of the support given the creation of this new department of study by leading statesmen in the central and provincial governments and in spite of the rejection in several Imperial edicts of the contrary arguments of Wo-jen and like-minded censors, the influence of these uncompromising anti-Westerners was so great that the plan failed completely because none of the desired type of young scholars applied for admission.

It is important to keep in mind that the modern government schools opened between 1861 and 1895 were regarded as *training* schools and that the training given was specifically related in each case to national defense, either military or diplomatic. It was only this justification that made it possible for the promoters of the schools to secure authorization for such innovations in the first place. It also explains why the greatest advance was made in the 1860's, when China was still badly shaken by the military and diplomatic defeats that had culminated in 1860 in the Anglo-French occupation of the Imperial capital. As the memory of this humiliation faded, the need for radical defensive measures—including schools such as these—appeared to be less urgent. New crises, such as the Russian occupation of Ili in the 1870's, the Japanese expedition to Formosa in 1874, the war with France (1883–1885), and Japan's machinations in Korea, stimulated fresh bursts of concern about national defense. These later threats to China's security gave the necessary justification for Li Hung-chang's schools in Tientsin, for example, and to Chang Chih-tung's promotion of a modern school in Kwangtung. However, it was not until China's shattering defeat by its despised neighbor Japan in 1894–1895 that a serious self-examination comparable to that of the early T'ung-chih period again took place.

Although the curricula of all the schools examined in this study included enough instruction in mathematics and a foreign language to supply the basic tools necessary for the specialized training that was their *raison d'être,* only the Peking T'ung-wen Kuan (after its reorganization in 1867, but more especially after Martin had put some vitality into the school in 1870) can be said to have provided the equivalent of a Western liberal arts education. Even in this exceptional case the breadth of the curriculum was justified on the grounds that T'ung-wen Kuan graduates had to be familiar with all aspects of Western knowledge in order to perform their diplomatic duties—in other words, that this, too, was specialized training. Several of the graduates of the Foochow Navy Yard School who went to England or France for advanced study managed to take courses that were much broader than the training in naval science or engineering for which they had been sent, but they were exceptional.[122] Thus, general education remained the monopoly of the traditional schools until after 1895.

Modern general education, with liberal arts subject matter corresponding to that offered in American and British schools and colleges during the same period, was first introduced into China, other than at the Peking T'ung-wen Kuan, by Protestant Christian missionary schools. St. John's College (in Shanghai), Tengchow College (in Shantung province), Canton Christian College, Peking (Methodist) University, North China College (at Tungchow, near Peking), and the University of Nanking, all were opened during the 1880's (St. John's in 1879). Although these institutions began at the preparatory school level and provided comparatively little instruction on the collegiate level prior to the twentieth century, their curricula approximated those of contemporary American secondary schools (for example, mathematics, science, history, geography, political economy, English, and Bible) plus the Chinese classics.[123]

Growing dissatisfaction with the backwardness of their country among the newly developing business class and other Chinese residents of the treaty ports, but particularly among young literati who felt humiliated because of the defeat of China by a modernized Japan in 1895, led to demands for governmental reform, including educational reform. One consequence was the appearance under official auspices of new and broader modern educational institutions. The Chung-hsi Hsüeh-t'ang (Sino-Western School) and Nan-yang Kung-hsüeh (Southern Public School) were opened in Tientsin and Shanghai respectively in 1896 and 1897 by Sheng Hsüan-huai, director-general of the Imperial Railway Administration. Each

[122] Wang Hsin-chung "Foochow ch'uan-ch'ang chih yen-ke," *Tsing Hua hsüeh-pao,* 8 (Dec. 1932), 46–48. Two of these men, Yen Tsung-kuang (Yen Fu) and Ma Chien-chung, ultimately became leading scholars and educators.

[123] Jessie Gregory Lutz, "The Role of the Christian Colleges in Modern China before 1928" (Cornell Ph.D. dissertation, 1955), pp. 33–84.

was sponsored by the governor-general of the province in which it was located, and both were financed with funds supplied by the China Merchants Steam Navigation Company and the Imperial Telegraph Administration. Although Sheng intended that these schools should be technological colleges—which they did ultimately become—they opened as general preparatory schools.[124] The Tzu-ch'iang Hsüeh-t'ang, which, as noted earlier, Chang Chih-tung in 1893 proposed to establish in Wuchang, was finally opened in 1896. Its original purpose was to provide a broad education for youths from Hupeh and Hunan, but the school actually began by concentrating on the teaching of foreign languages and later, according to Lund, came increasingly to emphasize military science.[125]

Even more important to the introduction of liberal arts education of the Western pattern than these three schools was the Imperial University of Peking (Ching-shih Ta-hsüeh-t'ang), established by the central government in August 1898, during the so-called Hundred Days of Reform. Modeled in part on the Peking T'ung-wen Kuan and drawing some of its faculty, including its first dean of Western studies (*hsi-hsüeh tsung-chiao-hsi*), W. A. P. Martin, from that school, the new university survived the abolition of the Kuang-hsü Emperor's reforms in September 1898 and went on to become the leading educational institution of modern China.[126] These developments between 1895 and 1898 mark the beginning of a new stage in the his-

[124] Peake, *Nationalism*, pp. 31–34; Feuerwerker, pp. 69–70; THHL, KH 136 p. 13; Ting Chih-p'in, *Chung-kuo chin ch'i-shih nien lai chiao-yü chi-shih* (1935), pp. 5–6. Both foreign and Chinese teachers were employed, and the curricula of the two schools included geography, astronomy, mathematics, general science, chemistry, mineralogy, and gas engines (Sheng Hsüan-huai in THHL, KH 136, pp. 12–13).

[125] Renville C. Lund, "The Imperial University of Peking" (University of Washington Ph.D. dissertation, 1956), p. 49, n. 88; Hsü T'ung-hsin, *Chang Wen-hsiang kung nien-p'u* (1946), p. 103.

[126] For the founding and early history of this university, which was later called Peking National University, see Lund, *passim*.

tory of Chinese education and are beyond the scope of this survey.

When their achievements are measured against the expectations of their founders, the schools examined appear to have been only partially successful. They produced a small body of reasonably competent diplomatic officials, the personnel for a nationwide telegraph service, and a number of naval and army officers and dockyard and arsenal technicians. But the training of most graduates was far from thorough. Moreover, besides serious students the schools harbored a large number of incompetents who learned little, if anything, yet remained on the rolls drawing their stipends.

A look at the obstacles that confronted these modern schools will be of assistance in seeking an explanation of their shortcomings. Probably the most serious impediment was the difficulty of recruiting promising students. A partial explanation of this is to be found in the prevailing opposition to modern schools among the Confucian literati who dominated Chinese society. Since the recognized road to prestige and position in China was through the civil service examination system, no person with any hope of passing those examinations would choose any other course. Given this fact and the prevailing attitude toward foreign subjects and foreign teachers, it was virtually impossible to persuade any but those without a traditional education or the hopelessly unpromising to enter these unorthodox schools. Even when large stipends and attractive living conditions were provided and promise of some kind of governmental position was held out, comparatively few able students presented themselves.

Both the Peking and the Canton T'ung-wen Kuan could and did draft their students from the Eight Banner schools. Perhaps because the Canton graduates were awarded an official degree, even though a lesser one, that school seems not to have encountered as much resistance as the Peking T'ung-wen Kuan.

It was said that the families of bannermen called to the Peking school regarded studying there such a disgrace that they resisted it with every available means and that only boys who were so stupid or so lazy that they could make no progress in the banner schools or whose families were without political influence of any kind actually enrolled. The best students in the Peking T'ung-wen Kuan were those who had previously graduated from the Kuang fang-yen Kuan in Shanghai or the Canton T'ung-wen Kuan. Of the few degree holders who actually entered the new department of astronomy and mathematics in spite of the Wo-jen tirades in 1867, nearly all proved to be middle-aged or elderly incompetents who were attracted by the large stipends; they took no interest in their studies, and some even tried to hide their connection with the school. Not until the 1890's, according to Ch'i Ju-shan, had this attitude changed sufficiently so that respectable Chinese families began to seek admission for their sons. Even in the late 1890's Sun Chia-nai wrote of the poor quality of students attracted to the T'ung-wen Kuan.[127] The Kuang fang-yen Kuan evidently had less difficulty than the Peking T'ung-wen Kuan attracting good students, perhaps because Shanghai was a more foreignized city with correspondingly less prejudice against foreign studies, although even the students in this school were regarded by many as potential traitors.[128] Among Kuang fang-yen Kuan students were the sons of mercantile families and of Christian converts who no doubt found it more difficult than the sons of officials to enter the bureaucracy by the regular route.[129]

Although Li Hung-chang reported that the Foochow Navy Yard School had succeeded in attracting the sons of local gen-

---

[127] *Chung-kuo i-chou,* no. 237; M. J. O'Brien letter, NCH, Jan. 25, 1870; *Huang-ch'ao cheng-tien lei-tsuan,* 230, p. 27.

[128] Lou Tseng-tsiang, *Souvenirs et pensées* (1945), p. 20.

[129] *Ibid.,* p. 21; John Fryer letter of July 5, 1867, Letter Journals, Fryer Papers, University of California (Berkeley) Library.

try, it is known from other sources that many of its students were recruited in Hongkong and Shanghai, where they had studied English or had had some experience with modern technology. For unexplained reasons the naval and military academy at Canton failed to recruit enough students locally and found it necessary to seek them among partially trained students at the Foochow school and from military units as far away as Tientsin. Li Hung-chang evidently succeeded in finding students for his Tientsin schools within his jurisdiction, though he was helped in the beginning by being able to assign to the naval academy, the telegraph school, and the medical school many of the nearly one hundred returned students of the Educational Mission to the United States, who had much better basic preparation than prospective students available in China. The short-course students in Li's military academy were already in the army and needed only to be ordered to the school. A number of the early classes in his medical school were recruited from the colonial government schools in Hongkong. The Nanking Naval Academy secured some of its students from the Foochow Navy Yard School and others from private schools in Shanghai that taught English.

The quality of instruction differed among these schools and even within the same school at various times. The foreign teachers who continued to serve over a period of years—there were a number of these in the Peking T'ung-wen Kuan, several in the Kuang fang-yen Kuan and the Foochow school, and at least one each in the Tientsin Naval Academy and the Tientsin Telegraph School—appear to have taken their teaching seriously, perfecting their techniques, developing textbooks and other instructional aids, and even, in some cases, securing additional training abroad. Most of the naval, military, and engineering teachers were trained and experienced in the subjects they taught, though they were not always skillful teachers. Some of the schools, including the naval and military academy at Canton, evidently employed foreign members of the Maritime Customs or missionaries who happened to be nearby. Generally these were engaged for a short term, sometimes on a part-time basis. Even the schools that maintained permanent faculties had to pick up temporary teachers when their regular instructors resigned or died unexpectedly or were absent on leave. Such substitutes were seldom adequately prepared to teach the subjects they offered, and they frequently did not take their teaching responsibilities seriously. Ch'i Ju-shan is very critical of his foreign teachers at the Peking T'ung-wen Kuan during the early 1890's, charging that none had a college degree and that they made no effort to give serious instruction. The facts would not seem to sustain these charges in the case of the permanent members of the faculty, but such charges might have applied to employees of the Maritime Customs who, Ch'i says, were assigned to teach in the school while learning the Chinese language. Ch'i writes disparagingly of most of his fellow students, too, and describes their indifference to their studies and their devotion to nonacademic pleasures, causing one to wonder how they could have learned anything.[130] The teaching of classes most of whose members had no interest in learning but went through only those motions required to receive their stipends must have been discouraging to even the most dedicated teacher. Writing more than fifty years later, Ch'i probably exaggerates the situation; but there is little doubt that lack of interest and low morale were widespread among the student bodies of all the modern schools, and whether the quality of the teaching was the cause or the result of the low morale is difficult to say.

The Chinese teachers of foreign subjects were undoubtedly of uneven quality, but there is comparatively little information about them. All but a few, such as Li Shan-lan and Shu Kao-ti, were graduates of the modern government schools. In

[130] *Chung-kuo i-chou,* no. 240.

most cases they were selected because of outstanding ability, though sometimes they were appointed because weak physiques kept them from the more vigorous life of naval officers and engineers or because no other suitable position could be found for them.

The foreign-language problem was a major one in all the modern schools. Much of the instruction, particularly in scientific or technical subjects, was given by foreigners who knew little or no Chinese. Exceptions were Martin and the other permanent teachers in the Peking T'ung-wen Kuan, Fryer and Allen in Shanghai, and Médard and perhaps others at Foochow. The mastery of English, French, or German sufficient to follow technical lectures was a slow process, and many students found it difficult even after years of study of a foreign language to keep up with classes taught in that language. It was almost impossible to teach through an interpreter, particularly technical subjects, because few Chinese had either the requisite vocabulary or the experience to serve as such.[131] Throughout this period there was a continuing debate among foreign teachers, including missionaries, as to whether it was more efficient to teach in Chinese, which required mastery of the Chinese language by the foreign teacher and the translation of many European-language books into Chinese, or in a foreign language which the students must first take years to learn.[132] In most of these government schools the second alternative was followed. The great length of time required to gain genuine language competence was a primary reason why some of the schools sought as students youths who had already begun the

[131] Chester Holcombe, *The Real Chinese Question* (1909), pp. 138–139.

[132] A. P. Parker, a missionary educator, favored the first alternative. He quotes an article from the *Hu pao*, a Shanghai newspaper, which declared that by the time a student had mastered a foreign language he was advanced in age and his ardor had abated, with the result that he never did learn Western science (p. 584).

study of a foreign language in a Hongkong or Shanghai private school, in one of the colonial schools in Hongkong, or even in another Chinese government school such as that at Foochow. It was their competence in English which led to the assignment to some of these schools of most of the members of the Educational Mission to the United States after their recall in 1881.

Principal causes of low morale among the serious students in these modern schools were the comparatively low value placed upon their knowledge and usefulness by the government and by most officials after the completion of their studies and the difficulty many graduates encountered in trying to secure appropriate and respected permanent posts. That there was a continuing demand for the men trained in the Tientsin Telegraph School may be deduced from the fact that it continued to operate year after year even though it had originally been expected to close within a short time. This was exceptional, however, for most of the other schools found it difficult much of the time to place their graduates; moreover, even when graduates received prompt appointments, their special knowledge often was not used or appreciated. When the T'ung-wen Kuan type schools were opened in the 1860's, it was anticipated that their graduates would be snapped up by the various provincial governments which had dealings with foreigners. But this did not occur; very few actually secured provincial posts, presumably because the regular provincial officials did not want them about. The principal reason for this rejection, perhaps, was that the graduates did not wear the "old school tie" of the regular examination system; but it is also possible that many of the graduates proved to be not altogether competent to handle foreign relations or even to act as interpreters. One would think that interpreters would have been useful in the various governmental offices along the coast of China, but relatively few such appointments were made from these "interpreters' schools." There were always unemployed "resident graduates" in the schools, many of them devoting their time to traditional Chinese subjects in what was for almost all of them the vain hope of securing official positions by way of the regular examinations. Even the fairly rapid expansion of Chinese diplomatic and consular activities after the opening of the first Chinese legation abroad in 1877 failed to absorb all graduates of even the most advanced of these schools—the Peking T'ung-wen Kuan. Some Kuang fang-yen Kuan graduates secured appointments with the Maritime Customs, but others had to accept positions as interpreters or clerks with private business firms or remain unemployed.

The Foochow Navy Yard School trained more engineers than could be used. Some who could not be placed in the local navy yard found employment in other government shipyards and arsenals or as teachers in the modern schools in Tientsin, Shanghai, and Canton. But others found it necessary to accept engineering positions with foreign firms, and still others were reduced to working as translators or interpreters for foreign companies or even for foreign consulates. The naval academies also soon found themselves graduating more naval officers than there were posts available. It has already been noted that both the Whampoa Naval and Military Academy and the Nanyang Naval Academy admitted students who had already studied several years in the Foochow school, presumably youths who were regarded as surplus at Foochow. Meanwhile Foochow graduates, because they were older and more experienced than the earliest graduates of the Tientsin academy, held all the senior posts in the Peiyang squadron. So situated, it was claimed, they gave junior posts to later graduates of the Foochow school, to the disadvantage of young naval officers turned out by the academy at Tientsin.[133] In his discussion of the fail-

[133] Alexander Michie, *The Englishman in China* (1900), II, 400. A report in the *North-China Herald* of May 13, 1892, stated that engine-room officers graduating from the Tientsin Naval Academy could not se-

ure of the self-strengthening movement during the latter part of the nineteenth century, Wang Wen-chieh quotes Liang Ch'i-ch'ao's and Chang Chih-tung's criticisms of the failure of the Chinese government to make appropriate use of modern-trained personnel. Both Liang and Chang contrasted China unfavorably with Japan, pointing out that Japan placed its modern-trained young men in positions of influence and authority, whereas China, after investing heavily in modern education, failed to use and reward those who had been trained and allowed them to be scattered and their talents wasted.[134] In the face of such uncertainty regarding opportunities for attractive, permanent appointments, it was no wonder that not many able and ambitious youths applied for admission to these schools and that most of those who entered were not inclined to work hard at their studies.

Probably China's most urgent defensive need during the latter half of the nineteenth century was for a modern army. Such an army, to be effective, required modern-trained officers. Yet only two military academies, those at Tientsin and Canton, were established prior to the Sino-Japanese War, in contrast to six naval academies; and even these two were late in starting and concentrated for a time on short-course training. No satisfactory contemporary explanation has been found of this neglect of thorough training of up-to-date army officers, but perhaps it was not unrelated to the resistance to modification of the civil service examinations that was noted earlier. The regular officers of the military forces were probably fearful of the competition of modern-trained officers. There had previously been no navy, as such; therefore the naval officers trained to operate modern warships threatened no vested interests, and there was no organized resistance to the naval

---

cure appointments on ships of the Peiyang squadron because most of them had already been filled by graduates of the Foochow school.

[134] *Fukien Culture,* 3 (Dec. 1947), 34.

academies or even to the giving of regular military rank to their graduates.[135] It has been noted that the military academy at Tientsin began by giving a limited training of two years to men who were already enlisted men or petty officers in the army. Only in 1887 was a five-year curriculum introduced that was comparable to those offered in the Chinese naval academies and in European military academies. Not until after the defeat by Japan did modern-trained officers begin to exercise influence in the Chinese army; and still another decade passed before a hierarchy of modern military training schools appeared.[136] Characteristic of the conservative attitude of regular army officers in the early 1890's was the complete lack of support and understanding encountered by two members of the first class of the Tientsin medical school who were assigned to the army.[137]

Considerable criticism of these earliest modern schools by Chinese who knew them at first hand or who at least wrote about them while they were still in existence has been preserved. Already considered has been the early attack made on the Peking T'ung-wen Kuan on grounds of principle by Wojen and other conservative officials. Their views, it is worth repeating, were widely held and unquestionably provided the most serious obstacle to the spread of modern education prior to the Sino-Japanese War. Reference has also been made to some of the harsh criticisms of Ch'i Ju-shan. He declared that not a single distinguished diplomat was produced by the T'ung-wen Kuan in its forty years, that the few graduates, such as Lu Cheng-hsiang and Chou Tzu-ch'i, who became famous, acquired their knowledge after they had left the school and entered the foreign service.[138]

---

[135] Michie agrees with this interpretation: "The explanation of the great difference between the organisation of the sea and land forces seems to be that the former, being a new creation, was beyond the range of criticism and was unhampered by any traditions, while the reform of the army was merely patching a worn-out garment" (II, 398).

[136] Powell, pp. 180–184.   [137] Wong and Wu, p. 442.

[138] *Chung-kuo i-chou*, no. 240.

In 1881 the *North-China Herald* expressed disappointment at the extremely meager achievements of the Peking T'ung-wen Kuan, when it was considered how long it had been in existence and how much care and thought had been spent upon it.[139] A censor charged in 1889 that the teachers in this school had become lax and their students undisciplined. In 1896 another censor, reflecting the surge of reform sentiment after the Sino-Japanese War, criticized what he regarded as the low standards and limited curriculum of the T'ung-wen Kuan, declaring that it was a name without substance. In replying to this attack the Tsungli Yamen stressed the difficulty of giving adequate scientific training when mastery of a foreign language had to be acquired first. But it also admitted that discipline had been lax and examinations too easy to maintain a high level of achievement.[140]

The Foochow school shared in the criticism directed at the navy yard in 1880 when members of the foreign staff were declared by the Tsungli Yamen to be incompetent and lazy. Actually the Foochow Navy Yard suffered from poor management and insufficient funds through most of the first twenty years of the Kuang-hsü period, an exception being the period from 1885 to 1890 when P'ei Yin-sen was the director and strove, with limited success, to revitalize the various divisions including the school.[141] In 1896 Governor-general Pien Pao-ch'üan reported, after a thorough investigation of the Foochow Navy Yard brought on by the criticism of a censor, that graduates had been receiving inadequate training both in the school and abroad, with the result that operation of the yard was inefficient and outmoded.[142] Foochow students had even earlier been criticized by Wang T'ao, a prominent publicist, for not having kept up with Western technological ad-

[139] Nov. 15, 1881.
[140] WHTK, p. 10801; 1898 *Calendar*, pp. 6–11.
[141] THHL, KH 35, p. 13; KH 82, pp. 2, 5; KH 84, p. 15.
[142] CCTI, 46, pp. 9–10.

vances; he said they acquired terminology but not substance.[143]

In an epochal memorial presented to the Throne on June 12, 1896, in which he proposed the creation of a modern educational system culminating in a university in Peking, Vice-President Li Tuan-fen of the Board of Punishments was highly critical of what he regarded as serious shortcomings in all the modern schools established prior to the 1890's. Although their students studied Western languages and other Western subjects, he wrote, they did not master the knowledge that was basic to national strength and prosperity. Their studies were not sufficiently thorough for a mastery of science and manufacturing, and there was too little equipment in the schools for practical experiments, which resulted in overdependence upon book learning. Too few students were attracted to these schools, he went on, because the traditional examinations continued to offer greater promise of position and wealth. Finally, the students in these schools were too young to secure maximum benefit from the available instruction. In spite of these faults, however, Li felt that there still were too few modern schools and too few students in each school.[144] Later in the same year Sheng Hsüan-huai criticized the T'ung-wen Kuan and the Kuang fang-yen Kuan for not having produced broader and more talented graduates.[145]

There was both Chinese and foreign criticism not only of the training given by the Foochow naval division but also of its graduates who commanded the ships of the Fukien squadron when a superior French fleet destroyed almost the entire squadron off the navy yard in 1884. The poor showing made by the Peiyang squadron against the Japanese fleet in 1894 also

[143] Teng and Fairbank, p. 138.

[144] THHL, KH 134, p. 1. For a brief résumé of this memorial see Peake, *Nationalism*, pp. 25–28. A. P. Parker several years earlier quoted a statement from the *Hu pao* saying that "so far the results of these modern schools are not satisfactory"(p. 584).

[145] THHL, KH 136, pp. 12, 13.

prompted widespread criticism of the Foochow and Tientsin graduates who were the officers of the Chinese squadron and some of whom acquitted themselves badly.

These first modern government schools had numerous defenders, however, both Chinese and foreigners. The Tsungli Yamen gave strong support as long as it was dominated by Prince Kung and Wen-hsiang, but its position became somewhat ambivalent after 1884, when Prince Kung was succeeded as head by I-k'uang. The leading provincial officials, who among themselves had created all of these schools except the Peking T'ung-wen Kuan, also could be counted upon to defend them against attack. Prince Ch'un, who was made the head of the new Naval Office created in 1885 and who in that capacity inspected Li Hung-chang's naval and military academies the following year, praised them to the Empress Dowager and urged that such training be expanded.[146] Influential foreign employees of the Chinese government such as Robert Hart, W. A. P. Martin, and Prosper Giquel were, of course, strong supporters of the modern schools. But there was praise from other foreigners as well. For example, the *North-China Herald*, which tended to be highly critical of the Chinese government, at least once wrote favorably of the T'ung-wen Kuan (August 31, 1872), commended the skill with which naval officers who had graduated from the Foochow school handled their ships (September 27, 1881), and reported the impression of efficiency made by the Tientsin Naval Academy upon two foreign naval officers who had served there as examiners (May 13, 1894). A. P. Parker, an outstanding missionary educator, praised the modern government schools in 1893, saying that the education they gave was "solid and useful," that "the pupils educated there were of immediate use to the country." [147]

It is my own opinion that if one takes into account the magnitude of the obstacles confronting them the modern

[146] THHL, KH 76, pp. 10–11.   [147] P. 581.

schools opened by the Chinese government between 1861 and 1894 carried out with surprising success the functions for which they were created and made a substantial contribution to the modernization of China. In spite of the numerous difficulties with which they had to contend, the schools persisted, and they turned out graduates most of whom proved capable of performing the tasks for which they had been trained.

The three schools for interpreters manned the new Chinese legations and consulates established during and after the 1870's and supplied numerous foreign relations advisers and interpreters for the Tsungli Yamen, for those provincial and prefectural governments that asked for them, and for the Maritime Customs. The Peking T'ung-wen Kuan also supplied a number of teachers not only for its own staff but for the telegraph school and the military academy in Tientsin and the Kuang fang-yen Kuan. A number of T'ung-wen Kuan graduates, including several who had come to it from the Kuang fang-yen Kuan, rose ultimately to the post of minister plenipotentiary, and one, Lu Tseng-hsiang—later known as Lu Cheng-hsiang— became foreign minister and even served as premier under the republic. The translations of Western books prepared in and published by the translation department of the Kiangnan Arsenal and by the Peking T'ung-wen Kuan made a major contribution to the introduction of Western ideas and techniques into China. Finally, the Peking T'ung-wen Kuan opened the way and served as a model for the Peking University— China's first and greatest national university.

The French division of the Navy Yard School at Foochow trained the men who operated that important navy yard with a minimum of foreign assistance after 1874; and other graduates helped run government shipyards and arsenals in Shanghai, Tientsin, Canton, and other cities. Although the Foochow yard never afterward operated as efficiently as during the period of French tutelage from 1867 to 1874, it nevertheless carried on steadily, and its shortcomings were unquestionably attributable at least as much to poor administration and insufficient funds as to the training of its staff. Some Foochow engineering graduates taught French or engineering in other modern schools, and one, Kao Lu, became China's outstanding astronomer and, in 1930, minister of education in the Central Government at Nanking.[148]

The English division at Foochow and the Tientsin Naval Academy supplied the officers for both the Fukien and the Peiyang squadrons of the Chinese navy; Foochow graduates taught in their own school, in the Naval and Military Academy at Whampoa, and in the Tientsin Naval Academy; and Tientsin graduates taught in the Nanyang Naval Academy at Nanking.[149] The most successful graduates of the Foochow naval division were Yen Tsung-kuang—later known as Yen Fu—and Admirals Liu Kuan-hsiung, Sah Chen-ping, and Li Ting-hsin. The three admirals served successively as minister of navy under the republican government during the 1910's and 1920's, besides holding other naval and governmental posts.[150] Yen Fu became one of China's most prolific translators of Western writings and an influential educator.[151]

Outstanding among graduates of the Tientsin Naval Academy were Li Yüan-hung, Vice-President of China from 1912 to 1916 and President in 1916–1917 and again in 1922–1923; Admiral Y. L. Woo (Wu Yü-lin), who played a leading role in river conservancy and railway affairs in north China during the first decade of the republic; Chang Po-ling, eminent educational leader and founder and long-time president of Nankai University; and Wang Shao-lien, who after some years of teaching and educational administration, served as the Chi-

[148] 1931 *Who's Who in China*, p. 204.
[149] *Ko-chih hui-pien*, 7 (Winter 1892), 47.
[150] 1925 *Who's Who in China*, pp. 543–544, 640–641, 487–488.
[151] See biography by Chow Tse-tsung in Howard L. Boorman, ed., *Men and Politics in Modern China* (1960), I, 161–166.

nese assistant general manager of the Kailan Mining Administration from 1916 to 1927.[152] Admiral Tu Hsi-kuei, an early graduate of the naval academy at Nanking, became commander in chief of the Chinese navy in 1923 and minister of navy in 1926.[153]

Although the two military academies described above were established late, Chang Chih-tung wrote in March 1896 of the important place their graduates already held in the modernized units of China's armies.[154] Tientsin Military Academy graduates not only dominated the northern armies during the 1910's and 1920's but also were active in Chinese politics during that period, many of them as members of the Chihli Party. The more famous alumni of the Tientsin school included Feng Yü-hsiang and Wu P'ei-fu, "war lords" who played major political roles during the 1920's; Ts'ao K'un, President of the republic in 1923–1924; and Tuan Ch'i-jui, a leader of the Anfu Party who served as minister of war or premier of the Peking government much of the time between 1913 and 1919 and again in 1924. Several graduates of the engineering division held key positions in China's railways during these decades.[155] And graduates of the Peiyang Medical College were influential in the introduction of modern medical practices into the Chinese army and navy.

One cannot easily define the contribution of these early government schools to the general modernization of China because of the difficulty of isolating their influence and activities from those of foreigners—missionaries, merchants, teachers, and so on—and of Chinese who went abroad or who learned about Western or modern Japanese developments without going abroad or attending modern schools. The schools

[152] 1925 *Who's Who in China*, pp. 494–496, 889–890, 55–56; 1931, pp. 422–423.

[153] *Ibid.*, 1931, p. 394.   [154] THHL, KH 132, pp. 16–17.

[155] 1931 *Who's Who in China*, pp. 126, 446; 1925, pp. 736–738, 761–762, 5–6, 651–652, 944–945.

just surveyed trained young men for new activities—modern diplomacy, modern warfare, modern engineering, modern communications and transportation, as well as a few for modern medicine—and all of these became components of the Chinese civilization of the twentieth century. Moreover, the schools trained many teachers of modern subjects and in other ways helped prepare the way for the new system of education inaugurated by the Chinese government after 1900. But even in these respects their contributions were not unique.

In the end it took the catastrophic events between 1894 and 1901—the defeat by Japan, the scramble of foreign powers for concessions, and the Boxer upheaval together with the foreign armed invasion it prompted—to convince significant numbers of the Chinese ruling class that traditional ideas, institutions, and methods were no longer capable of protecting China. Once Chinese confidence in the tradition was lost, the resistance to change that had been so strong during the latter half of the nineteenth century began to crumble and demands for governmental organization and education modeled after those of Japan and Western nations could be acted upon. Although not the principal cause, the modern schools that have been described at least helped to prepare the way for the revolutionary changes of the twentieth century.

II

The T'ung-wen Kuan

Establishment

THE first modern school established by the Chinese government, and one of the more successful and influential of the
modern government schools opened prior to the Sino-Japanese
War, was the T'ung-wen Kuan.[1] It began as a school for the
teaching of foreign languages, and its primary function during the forty years of its existence was the training of interpreters and diplomatic officers for the Chinese government.[2]

[1] Literally, School of Combined Learning; called by W. A. P. Martin
the Tungwen College (Martin, *A Cycle of Cathay* [1896], p. 301). It
was sometimes referred to by other foreigners as the Imperial College.

[2] The material in this chapter is a revised and expanded version of my
article "The T'ung Wen Kuan" that appeared in the *Chinese Social and
Political Science Review*, 18 (Oct. 1934), 307–340. Two Chinese translations of that article were published, both entitled "T'ung-wen Kuan
k'ao," one by Hsü Shao-ch'ang, in *Wai-chiao yüeh-pao*, vol. 6, no. 3

The T'ung-wen Kuan had its origin in a memorial outlining a drastic reorganization of the machinery for conducting foreign relations which was submitted to the Throne on January 13, 1861, by Prince Kung, Kuei-liang, and Wen-hsiang. Of greatest importance in the memorial was the proposal to establish the Tsungli Yamen, China's first real foreign office; [3] but of particular relevance to this study was the section proposing a school of foreign languages. That portion of the memorial reads as follows:

In dealing with foreign countries, it appears necessary first of all to know their nature and temperament. Since we do not know their languages, there is complete misunderstanding. How can one hope for satisfaction?

At an earlier time a school was established for the study of the Russian language. That was a thoroughly sound idea, but it has now long been regarded as a mere formality, and no one is able to understand [Russian]. It would perhaps be well to consider encouraging effort by using monetary stimulants.

One hears that there are merchants in Kwangtung and Shanghai who have made a special study of the written and spoken languages of Great Britain, France, and the United States. Your Majesty is requested to order the governors-general and governors of those provinces to select two honest and reliable persons to be sent from each province to the capital and to bring with them foreign books. In addition, four or five intelligent youths less than thirteen or fourteen years of age should be selected from each of the Eight Banners to study. The salaries of the men sent [to teach] should be liberal, following the precedent for teachers in the Russian School; and after two years have distinguished the diligent from the lazy, the successful ones should be rewarded. When the banner students

---

(1935), the other by Fu Jen-kan, in *Chung-hua chiao-yü chieh,* vol. 23, no. 2 (1935). The latter translation was reprinted in *Chung-kuo chin-tai ch'u-pan shih-liao erh-pien* (1954), pp. 35–47.

[3] See Ssu-ming Meng, "The Organization and Functions of the Tsungli Yamen" (Harvard Ph.D. dissertation, 1949).

thoroughly understand the written and spoken languages [the teachers'] services should be discontinued.

It is also requested that Your Majesty order the [Russian] Language School to decide upon satisfactory regulations and to supervise study strictly.

All who master the foreign languages they study will be recommended for liberal rewards; all who do not attain mastery will at length be dropped.[4]

It was no doubt helpful to the promoters of the new language school to have the precedent of the Russian Language School; in fact, the original intention was to locate the new school in the Russian Language School. Actually the idea of teaching foreign languages was an old one in China. There was an official bureau of interpreters at least as early as the T'ang dynasty,[5] and a School of Interpreters had existed in the capital since the first reign of the Ming dynasty.[6] The Russian Language School (E-lo-ssu-wen Kuan) was said to have been established in 1757 under the aegis of the Grand Secretariat to train interpreters and translators of Russian. The students, limited to twenty-four in number, were drawn exclusively from the Eight Banners. Examinations were held every five years, and those who passed with distinction were

[4] IWSM, HF 71, pp. 24–25. For another translation see Teng and Fairbank, p. 74.

[5] Paul Pelliot, *Journal asiatique*, 11th ser., 4 (1914), 179.

[6] G. Devéria, "Histoire du Collège des Interprètes de Péking," *Mélanges Charles de Harlez* (1896), pp. 94–102. The theory upon which this school had been founded—as in the case of the T'ung-wen Kuan—was that ignorance of foreign peoples is a handicap in dealing with them; consequently the students were also required to secure a thorough knowledge of the geography, customs, and commercial resources of the country whose language they studied. For continuation of this school during the Ch'ing period see Pelliot, pp. 180–182, and *Ta-Ch'ing hui-tien* (1899), 39, p. 14. See also Norman Wild, "Materials for the study of the Ssu I Kuan," *Bulletin of the School of Oriental and African Studies,* 11 (1945), 617–640.

given official rank and assigned either to the Li-fan Yüan [7] or
to offices on the frontier where a knowledge of Russian was
needed. The students received a stipend of three taels each
month, and the teachers were chosen from among former students.[8] An Imperial edict was issued on January 20 ordering
the proposals of Prince Kung and his associates put into effect.[9]

On February 3, at the end of a long memorial devoted to
the organization of the Tsungli Yamen, Prince Kung, Kuei-
liang, and Wen-hsiang declared that the students in the new
language school, as well as their instructors, should be encouraged by being given the same stipends as those in the
old Russian School. Although the proposed instruction in
English, French, and "American" should properly be given at
the old Russian School, the ministers reported that the limited
space there made it necessary to provide separate quarters for
the new departments in the old Iron Money Bureau that had
been assigned to the Tsungli Yamen, a part of which could
easily be converted for use as a school. Moreover, being located
close to the foreign office, these new departments could be
kept under surveillance by the ministers.[10]

The promoters of the new school of Western languages gave
as their reason for such instruction the difficulty of maintaining
harmonious relations with foreign countries without a knowledge of those countries and of their languages, but another
reason was provided by certain provisions in the British and
French Treaties of Tientsin.[11] These treaties, signed in 1858,
had stipulated that in correspondence with the Chinese government thereafter British and French officials should write

[7] This office in the Peking government had charge of Russian relations.
[8] *Ta-Ch'ing hui-tien* (1818), 2, p. 19; J. Dudgeon, "Sketch of Russian
ecclesiastical intercourse with, and the Greek Church in, China," *Chinese
Recorder*, 4 (1871), 37; George Timkowski, *Travels of the Russian Mission through Mongolia to China* (1827), I, 369.
[9] IWSM, HF 72, p. 2.   [10] IWSM, HF 72, p. 32.
[11] Martin, *Cycle*, p. 295.

in their own languages—following European diplomatic procedure—and that such communications were to be accompanied by a Chinese translation only until the Chinese
government had trained its own translators.[12] Heretofore official communications from Western governments to the Chinese government had been written in Chinese or, often in the
case of Russia, in Manchu.

In a memorial presented to the Throne on August 20, 1862,
Prince Kung and the other ministers of the Tsungli Yamen reported on the progress that had been made with foreign-
language instruction since the first authorization and also submitted a set of regulations for the T'ung-wen Kuan, as the
new school was called. The search in Canton and Shanghai
for competent Chinese teachers had ended in failure. The
governor-general of Liang-kuang had written that he had no
one there to send; and the governor of Kiangsu had reported
that although such men were to be found in Shanghai their
ability was not great and the compensation they demanded
was high, so that it had not seemed worth while to send them
to the capital. Consequently some delay was experienced in
the launching of the enterprise.[13]

Reiterating their belief that it was necessary thoroughly to
understand conditions in foreign countries and to study foreign languages if China were not to be taken advantage of,
the ministers of the foreign office reported that the representatives of foreign governments had found it desirable to

[12] W. F. Mayers, *Treaties between the Empire of China and Foreign
Powers* (1906), pp. 60, 19. American notes addressed to the Chinese
government were still being accompanied by Chinese translations as late
as 1945–1946 when I served as Chinese secretary of the United States
embassy in Chungking. The explanation given for supplying a translation
in the middle of the twentieth century was that it produced a reply sooner
than a note sent without a translation.

[13] IWSM, TC 8, pp. 29–30.

employ Chinese to teach them the Chinese language. They wrote:

Since there are no Chinese possessing a thorough knowledge of foreign languages, Kwangtung and Kiangsu lacking any who could be sent to Peking, we could not avoid seeking suitable persons among foreigners. The English [secretary of legation] Thomas Wade informed us that his countryman J. S. Burdon, who understands Chinese, might temporarily fill the chair [of English], so we ordered him to visit this office for an interview. Although we do not know this man well, still he appears to be sincere and if employed only to teach students there would seem to be no grounds for him to make demands. Because the ten students earlier ordered selected entered the school on July 11, he is being tried out as their teacher. As clearly stated to Wade in advance, religious teaching will not be tolerated after the language lessons.

The memorial also reported that a Chinese named Hsü Shulin had been appointed to teach the students Chinese subjects.[14]

The ministers of the foreign office proceeded then to discuss the financing of the school. The foreign diplomatic representatives who had been consulted expressed the view that foreign teachers would demand what might appear to the Chinese to be large salaries. Burdon, already receiving a salary as a missionary, had consented to work for only 300 taels during the first year, but if he continued another year, he would certainly expect an annual salary of about 1000 taels.[15] By contrast, the salaries of the Chinese teachers, in accordance with the Chinese system, would begin at only eight taels per month, although they would receive their official stipends, board, and other allowances in addition. The ministers estimated that

[14] *Loc. cit.*

[15] A tael was worth about U.S. $1.60 in the early 1860's (H. B. Morse, *The Trade and Administration of China* [1908], p. xiii).

teachers' salaries and allowances, student stipends, wages and food for employees, and the other costs of the T'ung-wen Kuan would total several thousand taels each year. They reported that the Board of Revenue had no funds available for this purpose and that they had decided to request the setting aside of 30 per cent of the tonnage dues collected by the Maritime Customs on foreign ships at the various treaty ports for the support of the T'ung-wen Kuan.[16] Previously these dues had all been allocated for the construction and maintenance of light-houses and other aids to navigation, but from this time 30 per cent of the amount collected was remitted regularly to Peking for the support of the T'ung-wen Kuan and other governmental educational activities.[17]

The six regulations submitted and authorized at this time dealt with the selection and payment of students, teachers, and proctors and with the examination and rewarding of students. The precedent of the old Russian Language School was cited throughout, but many changes were introduced to meet the special needs of the new departments.[18]

The first regulation provided that all students in the T'ung-wen Kuan should be drawn from the Eight Banners. A total of thirty had already been selected, ten in the first instance and twenty more later, although a minimum of twenty-four was permissible. It was stipulated in the regulation that when re-placements were required each division of each of the Eight Banners should send two or three youths of about fifteen years who knew the Manchu language and possessed "natural ability and cleverness," from among whom the Tsungli Yamen would select the new students.

[16] IWSM, TC 8, pp. 30–31.   [17] Wright, *Hart*, p. 295.

[18] IWSM, TC 8, pp. 31–35. See also the *Calendar of the Tung-wen College*, first issue (1879), pp. 14, 20. Where there is disagreement, as there occasionally is, between a T'ung-wen Kuan *Calendar* and the Chinese documents in the *Ch'ou-pan i-wu shih-mo*, I am inclined to fol-low the latter as the more reliable source.

The second regulation dealt with teachers. Burdon, the recently invited professor of English, desired only a salary and had not requested official rank. If Chinese teachers of foreign languages were recruited in Canton or Shanghai, they should be rewarded periodically, presumably with official rank, and paid annual salaries also, though not on the same scale as foreign teachers. The teachers of Chinese should be selected from among the natives of Chihli, Shantung, Shansi, or Honan (because of their pronunciation) who were awaiting appointment as teachers of Chinese in the official schools for bannermen.[19] They should be tested and appointed by the Tsungli Yamen and paid salaries of eight taels per month. After two years of satisfactory service they should be promoted in rank and recommended for district magistracies; if they continued to teach two additional years, at the end of that time they should be sent to the provinces as district magistrates awaiting appointment. "When the number of students has increased later on and teachers of French and Russian are sought, Chinese and foreign teachers will be added according to the situation and assigned to teach in the different departments of the school." The third regulation provided for the appointment by the Tsungli Yamen from among its own functionaries of two proctors (*t'i-tiao*), one Chinese and one Manchu, to oversee all the affairs of the T'ung-wen Kuan.

The fourth and fifth regulations dealt with examinations. Monthly tests and quarterly and annual examinations were to be conducted by the staff of the T'ung-wen Kuan, with rewards, in order to stimulate diligent study, for those students showing the greatest achievement. At the end of each three-

[19] It proved difficult to recruit the required number of teachers of Chinese from this group. Accordingly on June 26, 1868, the Tsungli Yamen was authorized to examine for these positions *chü-jen* and *kung-sheng* of any province who had come up through the examination system and who could secure the permission of their provincial officials in the capital (IWSM, TC 59, p. 34).

year period a Great Examination (*ta-k'ao*) would be conducted by senior officials of the Tsungli Yamen. The better students would be rewarded with tutorships or the seventh, eighth, or ninth official rank according to their standing in these examinations, the poorer ones to be demoted but to continue their studies in the school. There was also provision for appointing the tutors and the outstanding students who received the seventh rank as secretaries awaiting assignment to boards or to other offices in the capital. The sixth regulation provided that all students should receive their regular subsistence allowances as bannermen and that those who were promoted should receive the following annual salaries: tutors, 80 taels; seventh and eighth rank, 40 taels; ninth rank, 32.5 taels. The subsistence allowances would continue to be paid by the banners to which the students belonged. The other payments were to be met from the tonnage dues appropriated for the use of the T'ung-wen Kuan.

On the same day, August 20, 1862, a memorial was presented to the Throne by the Grand Secretary Chia Chen and other ministers of the Grand Secretariat, urging that direction of the old Russian Language School be transferred from the Grand Secretariat to the Tsungli Yamen and that the school itself be incorporated into the T'ung-wen Kuan. The memorial reported that the Tsungli Yamen had called together the teaching staff and students of the Russian School a month or two earlier and upon examining them had discovered that none of the students was conversant with the Russian language and that of the five teachers only one had any understanding of Russian. Authorization was requested to dismiss all the students and the four incompetent teachers, who had been drawing stipends because of their supposed studies, and to transfer the Russian School and the one worthy teacher to the T'ung-wen Kuan. The proposals were approved by the Throne.[20]

[20] IWSM, TC 8, pp. 35–36.

On May 6, 1863, the Tsungli Yamen presented a memorial announcing to the Throne that French and Russian classes had been started on April 23 with ten students each.[21] The French and Russian ministers to China had been asked to recommend teachers. The former had proposed a French priest named Smorrenberg, whom the foreign office had at first rejected but finally appointed when assured that he was no longer engaged in missionary work and that he was a simple and honest man. Nevertheless it was stipulated that he must resign if discovered preaching his religion. The Russian minister had recommended one A. Popoff, interpreter at the Russian legation. He was already well known at the Tsungli Yamen and although not altogether trusted was regarded highly enough to be appointed a teacher in the T'ung-wen Kuan. Although not entirely clear, the Chinese documents give the impression that the agreements regarding the appointment of Smorrenberg and Popoff, and of Burdon the year before, were made by the Tsungli Yamen with the respective legations rather than with the men themselves.

The French minister had declared that a salary of 300 taels for a "trial year," as provided the year before for Burdon, would not be acceptable; therefore it had been agreed to pay both Smorrenberg and Popoff 1000 taels from the beginning of their service. Burdon was given the same amount, presumably retroactively, in order not to treat him unfairly.[22] Two more Chinese teachers were selected in accordance with the regulations laid down in 1862. Chang Hsü-sheng was made professor of Chinese in the French department, and Yang I-ming in the

[21] IWSM, TC 15, pp. 12–14.

[22] When W. A. P. Martin was appointed professor of English in 1864, his contract stipulated that he be paid 1000 taels per year and that he devote two hours per day to his duties at the school (*Cycle*, p. 297). The foreign teachers in all the modern schools in China were expected to work only six days each week, whereas the Chinese teachers worked every day except during vacation periods.

Russian department. In accordance with the regulations two proctors, Ch'eng-lin and Hsia Chia-hao, had been appointed to oversee the various activities of the T'ung-wen Kuan—particularly to see that the foreign staff refrained from preaching Christianity and that the subsistence allowances to students were honestly administered.[23]

From this time until the reorganization of the T'ung-wen Kuan in 1867 there were but two changes in the foreign staff: John Fryer, an Englishman who later became the head of the translation department of the Kiangnan Arsenal, replaced Burdon in 1863, and a year later when Fryer resigned to take a position in Shanghai, he was replaced as professor of English by W. A. P. Martin, an American.[24]

A Great Examination (triennial) should have been given the first English class in June of 1865, but the Tsungli Yamen announced on April 29 that it would be postponed until the French and Russian classes were ready for their examinations. The reason given for the postponement was that the English class had been delayed by changes in teachers and that it would be more convenient to examine all three classes at the same time. On December 22, the ministers of the Tsungli Yamen announced that they had conducted Great Examinations for all three departments between November 28 and December 7, assisted by Robert Hart, inspector-general of the Chinese Imperial Maritime Customs, and the foreign teachers of the T'ung-wen Kuan. Three examinations had been given each class: (1) translation of foreign official documents into Chinese, (2) translation

[23] Martin reports that during his first years at the T'ung-wen Kuan there was a placard in the classroom forbidding the teaching of the Bible but that it was removed after he assumed the presidency (*Cycle*, p. 325).

[24] 1879 *Calendar*, p. 34. Fryer was invited by Martin to rejoin the faculty in 1870, but he declined because of a commitment to the translation department and the Kuang fang-yen Kuan (Fryer to Martin, May 25, 1870, Fryer's Letter Journals, University of California [Berkeley] Library).

of the Chinese versions of treaties into English, French, or Russian, and (3) oral translation of Chinese sentences into a foreign language. The examinations disclosed that some progress had been made but that the students were far from proficient. None was deserving of promotion to the seventh official rank, as provided in the 1862 regulations. The best were to be rewarded with eighth or ninth rank but kept in the school for further study. Of the remainder, those having promise would be allowed to continue their studies and the rest would be sent back to their banners.[25]

On December 22 the Tsungli Yamen also submitted and obtained approval of a supplementary set of six regulations that were meant to correct some of the deficiencies disclosed during the first three years of operation of the school. The first of these new regulations provided that students should no longer receive the regular subsistence allowance from their banners but instead receive a student stipend of three taels per month from the T'ung-wen Kuan. It was further stipulated that after a student had won a salaried official rank this stipend should cease and any money saved thereby should be used to reward the students who led their classes in the monthly tests. The second regulation, intended to stimulate greater effort on the part of the students, stipulated that the quarterly and annual examinations should be conducted by functionaries of the Tsungli Yamen; it also set up a system of regular monetary rewards for achievement in the examinations. After each quar-

[25] IWSM, TC 37, pp. 30–31. Presumably only two members of the English class were given rank at this time, for it is known that Feng-i and Te-ming (later called Chang Te-i), who accompanied Hart to Europe the next summer, had official rank, and O'Brien reported eight members in this class without official rank in 1869. Although the French student who was sent with Hart had not received official rank, the two members of that class and the two members of the Russian class who accompanied the Burlingame mission in 1868 had official rank, showing that at least two of each of those classes must have been so rewarded after the 1865 examination (IWSM, TC 39, p. 2; TC 52, p. 6; NCH, Jan. 25, 1870).

terly examination the first two students in each department
were to be awarded prizes of three taels, and the next three,
one and one-half taels. After each annual examination the
prizes for the first two students in each department were to
be four taels, and for the next three, two taels.

The third regulation provided that the one teacher who had
been transferred from the old Russian School, Kuo-shih-ch'un,
should live at the T'ung-wen Kuan to keep track of the goings and comings of students and teachers and to control the
servants, a situation the proctors, serving only part time, had
been unable to manage.[26] The fourth regulation fixed limits on
student leave and provided that those who were wasting time
going to and from classes each day might live at the school.
The fifth regulation stipulated that new students should be
admitted provisionally, with an elimination examination at
the end of three months and another at the end of one year.
Monthly student stipends would begin only after the student
had attained full status by passing his first annual examination. The sixth regulation provided that those students who
won official rank should, like other officials, receive rice allowances for their families as well as the salaries stipulated
in the earlier T'ung-wen Kuan regulations. While these officials
continued to study in the school, the allowance should be
paid in silver at the rate of twelve taels per year for the seventh
rank, ten taels for the eighth rank, and eight taels for the ninth
rank. The Chinese members of the teaching staff should also
receive rice allowances. All these allowances, like T'ung-wen
Kuan salaries and stipends, were to be paid from the tonnage
dues transmitted to the Tsungli Yamen for educational pur-

---

[26] Martin says that Kuo-shih-ch'un had proved to be ignorant of Russian, and thus it was necessary to hire a native Russian to teach that
language (*Cycle*, p. 295). Presumably this appointment made it possible
to use him for something he could do.

poses rather than by the Board of Revenue which ordinarily paid the salaries and allowances of officials.[27]

The first opportunity given to T'ung-wen Kuan students to use their new language knowledge intensively came in 1866, when three of them were sent to Europe on a brief "mission of investigation." A year earlier the Tsungli Yamen had been asked to send two or three of the students from the Russian department to serve as interpreters with a Chinese boundary commission, but it had declined to do so on the ground that the students still were inadequately prepared for such duties.[28] However, when Robert Hart obtained leave of absence early in 1866 to return to his home in Ireland to be married and suggested that two or three of the more proficient students accompany him to observe conditions in Europe, the Tsungli Yamen agreed. Feng-i and Te-ming (who was known later as Chang Te-i), both students in the English department and holders of the eighth and ninth official rank respectively, and Yen Hui, a student in the French department, were appointed to go. Accompanied by three employees of the Maritime Customs—Pin-ch'un (an elderly Manchu official), E. C. Bowra (an Englishman), and E. de Champs (a Frenchman)—who served as advisers, the students left Shanghai with Hart on March 23. They spent three and a half months in England, France, and other northwest European countries, visiting factories, museums, and similar points of interest and being entertained by royalty and high officials. On the return trip Hongkong was reached on September 28, and the students reached Peking on October 26.[29]

[27] IWSM, TC 37, pp. 32–35.

[28] IWSM, TC 32, pp. 9–10 (May 9, 1865).

[29] For details and documentation, see Biggerstaff, "The first Chinese mission of investigation sent to Europe," *Pacific Historical Review*, 6 (Dec. 1937), 307–320.

Reorganization

In 1866 the Tsungli Yamen proposed expansion of the T'ung-wen Kuan by adding a scientific department to which only members of the traditionally educated elite might be admitted as students. This was an even more radical step than the setting up of a foreign-language school had been in the first place, for it appeared to imply recognition of shortcomings in the time-honored Chinese educational system; and it provoked a bitter controversy between conservative officials led by the Mongol Grand Secretary Wo-jen and the progressives in the Tsungli Yamen. Exactly when the decision was made is not known, but Robert Hart was commissioned to recruit teachers for the new department when he departed for Europe in March of 1866; clearly the matter was being considered by the Tsungli Yamen at least nine months prior to the date of the first formal request to the Throne.[30]

On December 11 the Tsungli Yamen submitted a memorial to the Throne proposing the creation of a department of astronomy and mathematics in the T'ung-wen Kuan to which Chinese and Manchus over twenty years of age who were holders of the *chü-jen* or *kung-sheng* degrees, as well as officials of the fifth rank or below who were still young and who had come up through the regular civil service examination system, might be admitted by special examination. The memorial declared that the manufacture abroad of machinery and arma-

[30] Stanley F. Wright says that Robert Hart threw himself enthusiastically into the work of strengthening and developing the T'ung-wen Kuan from the time he took up permanent residence in Peking in August 1865. Without citing a source for his information, he says that Hart argued the necessity for scientific education to produce Chinese leaders capable of developing the country along modern lines and that it was Hart who persuaded the Tsungli Yamen to broaden the curriculum of the school and to authorize him to engage suitable foreign professors to teach Western science (Wright, *Hart,* pp. 325–328). For a brief biography of Hart see Chap. I, note 46.

ments and even the movement of ships and armies were based upon astronomy and mathematics and that China must master these subjects if it was to be strong. "Chinese are not inferior to Westerners in either skill or intelligence. The achievement of knowledge and skill in mathematics, science, mechanics, and the exploration of natural resources will strengthen China." [31] The Tsungli Yamen considered the bannermen studying in the three language departments incapable of both becoming accomplished translators of foreign languages and mastering these new subjects and so directed that they continue to devote all their time to language study. The Tsungli Yamen obviously wished to recruit more promising students for the new department. The memorial urged that Western specialists be employed to teach in this new department and stated that the matter had been discussed with Robert Hart prior to his departure in March for Europe, in the expectation that he would look about for teachers while there. The purpose of this memorial was to outline the proposal and to secure Imperial permission to plan further. The Throne gave the requested sanction. [32]

On January 28, 1867, the Tsungli Yamen submitted another memorial on this subject, together with a set of six regulations for the proposed new department. This memorial was defensive in tone, frankly directed toward refuting the anticiated arguments of opponents. The proposed innovation, the Tsungli Yamen said, was not motivated by a love for the marvelous or

[31] Astronomy (*t'ien-wen*) and mathematics (*suan-hsüeh*) were old Chinese terms which appear to have been used in the name of the new department because they were expected to be more acceptable to traditionalists than a word such as science (*ko-chih*), which was new. The quotation made shows that the curriculum was intended to include more than astronomy and mathematics.

[32] IWSM, TC 46, pp. 3–4. A reasonably accurate translation of this memorial appears in *Papers Relating to Foreign Affairs, 1867–1868* (1868), pp. 473–474.

by admiration for Western learning but by a desire to master the knowledge that is basic to the building of ships and machinery, which China had recently decided were essential for national defense. Li Hung-chang and Tso Tsung-t'ang had already established machine shops and modern training schools, showing that it was not the Tsungli Yamen alone that was concerned with such things.

The view that it was disgraceful for China to learn from foreigners was regarded by the Tsungli Yamen as stupid. Moreover, to try to carry out a program of modernization of defenses without making use of foreign experts would be wasteful of government funds. European astronomy and mathematics had originated in China, the memorial said, but they had been greatly advanced in the West, and China could not afford to be behind other nations in such knowledge. The Emperor K'ang-hsi (1661–1722) had regarded Western learning so highly that he appointed Westerners to posts in the Imperial observatory; and he repealed a prohibition against the study of astronomy by private individuals. Moreover, Japan had sent men to England to study English, astronomy, and mathematics with the result that they could even write books on shipbuilding. The foreign office's memorial also sought to refute the widely held view that it is beneath the dignity of a scholar to concern himself with mechanical things, that these should be left to artisans. Historical precedents were cited to support the claim that principles must be understood by scholars if artisans are to be properly directed. Finally, the Tsungli Yamen urged that the list of eligibles for the new department be expanded to include all scholars of the Hanlin Academy below the rank of first-class compiler and all *chin-shih* of the fifth rank or below, as well as the *chü-jen* and *kung-sheng* stipulated earlier.[33]

[33] IWSM, TC 46, pp. 43–46. For a full translation of this memorial and the attached regulations, see Imperial Maritime Customs, *Reports on*

The first of the six regulations proposed for the new department stated that astronomy and mathematics are deep and subtle subjects that can be understood only by those who are capable of intensive study; hence the students must be restricted to men who have passed civil service examinations. After listing the various categories of degree holders who were eligible, it stated that candidates who were officials in Peking or the provinces and were recommended by their superiors, those not officials but certified by a fellow provincial who was an official in the capital, and bannermen certified by their banner should present themselves at the Tsungli Yamen for entrance examinations. The maximum entering age was set at thirty except for persons who had previously studied astronomy and mathematics and who wanted to enter the school merely to improve their knowledge of these subjects.

The second regulation required all students to live at the school, where food and lodging would be provided without charge. The students might leave the premises on legitimate errands, but their comings and goings must be recorded with the proctors. This rule was no doubt intended to prevent the absenteeism and dawdling that had plagued the language departments from the beginning. The fifth regulation, foreseeing that some students would not have independent means, stipulated that all the students in this department should receive in addition to board and lodging ten taels each month "to relieve them from anxiety about their private expenditures, to enable them to give their attention more undividedly to their work." This provision was clearly intended to attract students who might otherwise hesitate to enter the school.

The third, fourth, and sixth regulations dealt with examina-

_____

Trade at the Ports in China Open by Treaty to Foreign Trade for the Year 1866 (1867), pp. 158–161. A translation of the memorial also appears in the American *Foreign Affairs* volume cited in the previous note, pp. 474–476.

tions. After six months the students were to be examined monthly by the ministers of the Tsungli Yamen; in order to stimulate greater effort, those who demonstrated superiority were to be posted as "meritorious," those who proved to be inferior as "derelict." A Great Examination was to be given triennially, at the time of the regular civil service examinations, dividing the students into superior and inferior classes. The superior group was to be commended to the Throne, for possible probationary official appointments; the inferior group was to go on studying until the next triennial examination. Hope was expressed that the superior students would be rewarded with elevation in official rank, so that new students would be attracted in large numbers and those already enrolled would be stimulated to greater effort.[34]

On February 25 the Tsungli Yamen submitted a memorial requesting the appointment of one of its own ministers, Hsü Chi-yü, as director of the T'ung-wen Kuan. The memorial stated that whereas there was a Chinese professor in each of the language departments who taught and also served as an example to the students, the students in the new department of astronomy and mathematics were expected to be too advanced to require further study of Chinese subjects. Since they must have someone in the role of teacher who could lead and direct them and whom they could admire and respect and since it would not be proper for them to establish such a relationship with a foreigner, it appeared advisable to appoint the eminent scholar Hsü to serve as director and at the same time as an example for the entire T'ung-wen Kuan.[35] On the same day an

---

[34] IWSM, TC 46, pp. 46–48.

[35] IWSM, TC 47, pp. 7–8. Hsü Chi-yü (1795–1873), a *chin-shih* of 1826, had served with distinction in the Hanlin Academy, later in provincial offices, and ultimately in the governorship of Fukien. While financial commissioner and subsequently governor of Fukien, he had taken a great interest in foreign relations and had compiled a world geography entitled *Ying-huan chih-lüeh* (1850) which was widely read in China,

Imperial edict appointed Hsü Chi-yü director (*Tsung-kuan
. . . ta-ch'en*) of the T'ung-wen Kuan, the post to be held
concurrently with his position in the Tsungli Yamen.[36]

Meanwhile opposition to plans for the new department had
been developing, particularly to the proposal to draw its
student body from the civil service, even from such exalted persons as *chin-shih* and members of the Hanlin Academy. The
most powerful objector was Wo-jen, a Grand Secretary and
president of the Hanlin Academy, but the first openly expressed opposition appeared in a memorial from a censor
named Chang Sheng-tsao. Chang, although admitting that
China might benefit from some study of Western astronomy
and mathematics, deplored the proposed teaching of these
subjects to scholar-officials. The way to strengthen the country,
he wrote, is to strengthen morale. This is achieved by maintaining a government that fulfills all its proper functions; and
such a government is achieved by officials who know the
writings of Confucius and Mencius and are familiar with the
ideals of the sage kings of antiquity. Nothing is to be gained by
teaching them the principles basic to the manufacture of steamships and guns. Let the Board of Astronomy, he urged, recruit
intelligent boys (presumably without the classical education
required for the civil service examinations) to study astronomy
and mathematics in the T'ung-wen Kuan. And let the Board
of Works select skillful craftsmen and junior army officers to
learn how to build steamships and manufacture guns. Men
of education should not be so used, and he deplored luring
them into the new department by offering large allowances,
monetary prizes, and rapid promotion.[37]

---

particularly during the 1860's. He had been removed from office during
the period of extreme isolationism in the 1850's but was appointed to
the Tsungli Yamen in 1865. See biography by Tu Lien-che in Hummel,
pp. 309–310.

[36] IWSM, TC 47, p. 8.   [37] IWSM, TC 47, pp. 15–16.

An Imperial edict of March 5 rejected Chang's criticisms. It stated that science and mathematics are branches of knowledge with which scholars should be familiar; that they could in no wise be regarded as mere mechanical arts; that they could more readily be mastered by scholars, who have greater powers of application and greater intelligence, than by others; and that such studies would neither damage the traditional scholarly curriculum nor upset the public mind, as feared by Chang.[38]

This strong edict, however, did not deter the conservatives. On March 20 Wo-jen himself submitted a memorial in which he took the position that the foreign innovations proposed by the Tsungli Yamen were to be avoided at all cost, that tightening the ancient virtues and barring all things foreign would give China the strength necessary to resist Western aggression. This memorial, which expressed views held by most of the literati opponents of modernization during the second half of the nineteenth century, is worth quoting:

I have heard that the way to establish a state is to respect propriety and righteousness rather than power and scheming. The basic design is in men's minds not in their skills. Now if we pursue one of the secondary arts [mathematics] and also accept foreigners as teachers, we run the risk that the two-faced foreigners may not necessarily transmit their skills; even if the teachers teach with sincerity and the students study with sincerity, the products will be no more than mathematicians. In all history no one has been heard of who, relying on mathematics, was able to lift decline or to strengthen weakness. With the size of China, there is no need to worry about a lack of talent. If it is necessary to teach astronomy and mathematics, a wide search will necessarily disclose persons versed in these arts. Why should it be foreigners? Why must we learn from foreigners?

[38] IWSM, TC 47, pp. 16–17. For a full translation see *Papers Relating to Foreign Affairs, 1867–1868*, pp. 476–477.

What is more, the foreigners are our enemies. In 1860 they took up arms to force us to yield, insulting the national capital, alarming the altar of Imperial ancestors, burning the Imperial palace, and killing and injuring officials and people. It was the worst insult in the two hundred years of the present dynasty. Scholars and officials all felt resentment, and they have cherished their hatred until the present, although the government has had no alternative but to maintain peace. Yet how can we forget this hate and shame for a single day? Since the peace negotiations Christianity has flourished, and half of our ignorant and stupid people have been led astray. If reliable scholars will fully explain propriety and righteousness, perhaps it will be possible to hold on to the minds of the people.

If now it is recommended that the outstanding accomplished scholars nurtured by the state and held in reserve until they can be used change and follow foreigners, then truth will not be expressed and evil will therefore spread. It cannot but end after a few years by driving the Chinese people fully to yield to the foreigner. . . .

I have heard that foreign missionaries hate scholars who are unwilling to study their teachings. If scholars of the regular career service are ordered to study with them, it is to be feared that what they study cannot certainly be mastered and that the scholar will have already been subjected to bad influence and so will have fallen into their trap. It is to be hoped that the Emperor will decide independently to cancel the earlier decision at once, in order to care for the public well-being and stop unseen disaster. China would be most fortunate.[39]

The Tsungli Yamen answered Wo-jen's violent attack in a long memorial submitted on April 6. It began by declaring that its authors had originally held Wo-jen's views but that the experience of handling foreign relations had demonstrated their inadequacy. The memorial went on to remind the Emperor that when foreign troops had invaded Peking in 1860

---

[39] IWSM, TC 47, pp. 24–25. For another translation see Teng and Fairbank, pp. 76–77.

most of the officials (including Wo-jen, presumably) either fled or remained aloof, and Prince Kung and his associates were left to deal with the situation. After getting rid of the foreign armies the Tsungli Yamen had striven to strengthen China against further encroachment by such measures as the introduction of machinery, modernization of the army, a foreign-language training program, and the sending of officials to Europe to investigate foreign manners and conditions. Consultation with leading provincial officials disclosed the same belief held by the Tsungli Yamen that China must also manufacture its own arms and steamships and that such activities require a knowledge of mathematics. Hence the request for the establishment of a new department of astronomy and mathematics in the T'ung-wen Kuan. Because the ministers of the Tsungli Yamen shared Wo-jen's fear that uneducated youths might be led astray by the foreign teachers required in such a department, they had suggested that the students in this department be recruited from scholars and officials who had been properly educated.

This memorial then went on to say it made little sense to declare that the foreigners are enemies of China and at the same time that China could defend itself against their threat by means of propriety and righteousness. In conclusion, the ministers of the Tsungli Yamen asserted that they and a number of provincial officials had exhausted themselves seeking means to strengthen China; yet whenever a practical suggestion was made, it was attacked by ignorant critics. If Wo-jen had an ingenious scheme to restrain foreign countries without subjecting China to their control, the Tsungli Yamen would welcome it and do its best to carry it out.[40]

On April 12 Wo-jen submitted another memorial. After reiterating his previous arguments he finally said:

[40] IWSM, TC 48, pp. 1–4. For a full translation see Teng and Fairbank, pp. 77–79.

To sum up with respect to the teaching of mathematics by foreigners, if the Tsungli Yamen can guarantee that under its proposal mathematics can certainly be mastered, that machines can certainly be skillfully made, that Chinese scholars will certainly not be made use of by the foreigners, and that the foreign rascals will certainly be exterminated by China, the Emperor, officials, and people all will feel relieved, which certainly will be good. But if, on the contrary, these will not necessarily result, then it should not be done.[41]

On April 23 the Tsungli Yamen presented two more memorials on this matter. In the first, Wo-jen was bitterly criticized for misrepresenting the purpose of the new department and the manner of operating it. After the Imperial edict was issued following Chang Sheng-tsao's attack, the memorial said, applications for admission had continued to come in. But after Wo-jen espoused the criticisms, various officials secretly organized opposition, and as a result of the spread of baseless rumors and the arousing of suspicion there were no more applicants. Recognizing that it could not force people to attend the school, the Tsungli Yamen had decided to proceed to examine those who had already applied and to select from them students who should be admitted to the department of astronomy and mathematics. Strict care was promised in the operation of the new department, but as to guaranteeing the accomplishments demanded by Wo-jen, "we can only do what must be done and in the best way we know how." [42] In the second memorial the Tsungli Yamen took up Wo-jen's boast that in a country as large as China there must be competent astronomers and mathematicians who could be employed as teachers instead of foreigners. For more than twenty years, the ministers wrote, officials both in the capital and in the provinces had sought in vain for such talent. They expressed pleasure that Wo-jen actually knew of the existence of such

[41] IWSM, TC 48, pp. 11–12.   [42] *Ibid.*, pp. 12–14.

people and requested the Emperor to instruct him to recommend a few. They also requested that Wo-jen be ordered to set up another school of mathematics and astronomy, to be supervised by him.[43]

On the same day an Imperial edict was issued dealing with the contents of the two Tsungli Yamen memorials. Wo-jen's objections to the teaching of astronomy and mathematics in the T'ung-wen Kuan were peremptorily rejected on the grounds that the matter had been repeatedly urged by a number of high officials and been fully discussed by the responsible ministers. The Tsungli Yamen was instructed to examine the persons who had applied for admission and to admit to the new department those judged competent. Finally, Wo-jen was ordered to set up and direct a separate school in which the teachers would be the talented Chinese he supposedly knew about.[44]

On April 25 Wo-jen memorialized saying that he had merely set forth his own views regarding the relative unimportance of astronomy and mathematics and the danger of employing foreign teachers but that, since the Imperial mind was made up contrariwise, he had nothing further to offer. Since the T'ung-wen Kuan had already been established to provide such instruction, he could see no reason why it should be stopped or why he should set up a separate school, and he therefore asked to be relieved of the assignment. Moreover, he knew of no skilled astronomer or mathematician and so was unable to recommend any. The Emperor accordingly relieved him of these responsibilities.[45]

Although it is clear that Wo-jen remained unconvinced by the arguments of the Tsungli Yamen, he himself seems to have

[43] *Ibid.*, pp. 14–15.

[44] *Ibid.*, p. 15. There is a full translation of this edict in Imperial Maritime Customs, *Reports on Trade*, p. 162.

[45] IWSM, TC 48, pp. 18–19.

refrained from further open attacks on the T'ung-wen Kuan. The *Ch'ou-pan i-wu shih-mo* contains only one other such attack, a long memorial written by an expectant department magistrate named Yang T'ing-hsi which was transmitted to the Throne by the Censorate on June 30. Yang related the drought that prevailed during the spring and early summer of 1867 to Heavenly dissatisfaction with the existence of the T'ung-wen Kuan, elaborated on many of the points previously made by Wo-jen, and even suggested that the Tsungli Yamen was acting treasonably in advising the Throne that China should learn from the West and employ foreigners in the process. Yang was promptly reprimanded in an Imperial edict that called him ignorant and his memorial absurd. The edict also criticized "the narrow and hidebound opinions" of Wo-jen and the censor Chang Sheng-tsao and asked whether Hanlin scholars were only to write poems and not to concern themselves with the problems of the empire. Finally, the Tsungli Yamen was told not to allow loose talk to interfere with the carrying out of its duties.[46]

On July 3 the Tsungli Yamen announced that the entrance examination for the department of astronomy and mathematics of the T'ung-wen Kuan had been held on June 21. Of the ninety-eight persons who had originally applied, only seventy-two appeared for the examination and of these thirty were accepted.[47] In disappointment that their effort to enlist proper

[46] IWSM, TC 49, pp. 13–25.

[47] *Ibid.*, pp. 30–31. The 1879 *Calendar* (p. 32) gives the number as twenty-seven. M. J. O'Brien reported that thirteen studied English with him and about the same number studied French with Lépissier. O'Brien wrote that after Wo-jen's attack "no respectable Chinese would matriculate in it. No man young enough to still have hopes of advancement in any other career would cast in his fortune with that of the College. The few who came were men who had failed in the official career—broken down hacks to whom the stipend offered by the yamen proved dearer than their reputation. . . . They were looked upon by their literary brethren as renegades and traitors to the cause. They felt that they were

scholars to study in this department had been balked by conservative officials of the Wo-jen stripe, the ministers of the
Tsungli Yamen turned to the Canton and Shanghai T'ung-wen
Kuan for students. In a memorial dated October 12 they
pointed out that these two foreign-language schools had been
operating for three years and requested that a few of their
better students be ordered to Peking to study in the new department.[48] In due course this request was complied with, and
the two port schools thereafter from time to time sent their
best graduates for advanced study in the Peking T'ung-wen
Kuan.[49]

While in Europe in 1866 Robert Hart had engaged the services of professors of astronomy and mathematics, chemistry,
English, French, and military science for the T'ung-wen Kuan,
although of these only the professors of English, chemistry,
and French—M. J. O'Brien, Anatole Billequin, and E. L. Lépissier—actually took up their duties.[50] In 1867 W. A. P. Martin,

---

so themselves. One of them . . . admitted . . . that outside the yamen
. . . he represented himself as a copyist or clerk. He never acknowledged
himself to be a student of the College, such a position being, to use his
own expression, *han-ch'en,* disreputable" (NCH, Jan. 25, 1870).

[48] IWSM, TC 50, pp. 35–36.

[49] For descriptions of these two schools see Chap. I, pp. 36–43, and
Chap. III.

[50] Wright, *Hart,* pp. 327–328. These foreign professors were employed
at an annual salary of £600, which was roughly 1800 taels. After five
years the salary was to be increased to £800, and after ten years to
£1000 (*ibid.,* p. 335). Presumably the new professors were expected to
devote more than two hours per day to their duties in the school, in
contrast to the less-well-paid earlier appointees. O'Brien and Lépissier left
the school after a few years to join the Maritime Customs service (*ibid.,*
p. 328). Billequin, who continued to serve the T'ung-wen Kuan until
1896, was a French chemist later proclaimed by W. A. P. Martin the
"father of Chinese Chemistry" (Morse, *International Relations,* III, 475).
Baron Johannes von Gumpach, appointed professor of astronomy and
mathematics, was an eccentric who considered the level of teaching expected of him beneath his dignity and accordingly refused to teach during the two years he lived in Peking, spending his time quarreling with

who had been professor of English since 1864, was appointed professor of political economy and international law and departed for the United States to pursue advanced study of those subjects.[51] Li Shan-lan, an outstanding Chinese mathematician, was appointed professor of mathematics in 1869.[52]

Hart. In the end he brought a suit for misrepresentation and slander against Hart; this was decided in his favor by an anti-Hart British court in Shanghai but was ultimately rejected by the Privy Council in London to which the first judgment had been appealed. For a detailed discussion of the von Gumpach episode, see Wright, *Hart*, pp. 334–352. See also von Gumpach's violently anti-Hart book, *The Burlingame Mission* (1872).

[51] William Alexander Parsons Martin (1827–1916) was born and educated in Indiana; his father was a Presbyterian clergyman who pressed him toward a missionary career from childhood. A graduate of Indiana University, which emphasized rational scientific inquiry as well as faith in Christianity, the younger Martin became a missionary in Ningpo in 1850. More attracted to teaching than to preaching and too flexible in his attitude toward missionary work to please his fellow Presbyterians, he moved to Peking in 1863 to open a Christian chapel and school of his own. Meanwhile he had served as an interpreter for Thomas B. Reed and John E. Ward, American ministers to China in 1858 and 1859, and had made a translation of Wheaton's *International Law;* this attracted the attention of the Tsungli Yamen, which helped him to edit and publish the work. His relations with his mission having deteriorated further and his school being unsuccessful, he accepted the appointment with the T'ung-wen Kuan in 1864, and from 1869 he guided its destinies until his retirement in 1895 for reasons of health. Martin was, after Robert Hart, probably the most influential foreigner in the national capital during the last third of the nineteenth century. For a fuller biography see Peter Duus, "Science and salvation in China: The life and work of W. A. P. Martin," *Papers on China*, 10 (1956), 97–127.

[52] Li Shan-lan (1810–1882), having failed to progress beyond the first civil service degree, devoted his life to the study of mathematics—both Chinese and Western. He had already written several treatises on the subject before the age of forty, and he spent the 1850's in Shanghai where he assisted several missionaries with the translation of Western books on science. During the mid-1860's he served briefly on the talented staff of Li Hung-chang. In a memorial submitted to the Throne on Aug. 15, 1867, the Tsungli Yamen recalled that Kuo Sung-tao, the governor of Kwangtung, had a year earlier recommended two mathematicians, Tsou Po-ch'i and Li, and that they had been ordered to Peking but had been

On July 12, 1868, the Tsungli Yamen submitted a memorial to the Throne proposing a policy for the use of T'ung-wen Kuan graduates. It recalled that permission had been obtained earlier to grant the degrees of *sheng-yüan* or *chien-sheng* to students of the Shanghai T'ung-wen Kuan who had completed the three-year course, to admit them to the regular provincial civil service examination, and to send outstanding graduates to Peking to be examined for higher posts.[53] Although nothing quite like this was suggested for the Peking T'ung-wen Kuan, presumably because the students either had degrees already or were bannermen, it was now proposed that graduates of the Peking, Shanghai, and Canton schools who had passed their final examinations with distinction be assigned, if qualified, to professorships, presumably in the T'ung-wen Kuan from which each had graduated. Further demonstration of ability was to lead to recommendation for a higher post—those in the capital to be assigned to the Tsungli Yamen with the title of second-class secretary of a board, those in the coastal provinces to be assigned to offices dealing with foreign relations. Thus, said the Tsungli Yamen, what has been learned in these schools can be put to use for the benefit of the country. The Emperor approved.[54]

The T'ung-wen Kuan passed through a discouraging period between 1867 and 1870. The approximately thirty students selected in July 1867 for the new department of astronomy and mathematics (or scientific department, as it was called by

---

excused because of illness. They were now ordered again to come to the T'ung-wen Kuan. Li arrived in due course, but Tsou was presumably still ill, for he died in 1869. During his professorship Li at first held a nominal secretaryship in the Grand Secretariat but was later given the title of department director in the Board of Revenue and a secretaryship in the Tsungli Yamen with the fourth official rank. See biography by Fang Chao-ying in Hummel, pp. 479–480. See also IWSM, TC 44, p. 14; TC 50, pp. 8–9.

[53] See Chap. III, pp. 158–159.   [54] IWSM, TC 59, pp. 36–37.

Martin) proved to be disappointing. They evidently did not commence their studies, which at first were confined to a foreign language, until December, for their six-month examination was not given until the beginning of July 1868. As a result of that examination, which was conducted by officials of the Tsungli Yamen, all but ten were dismissed.[55] Five of those remaining were to continue their study of English and five French until sufficiently familiar with those languages to be able to take instruction from foreign teachers of science.[56] Three of the five students of English attended class so irregularly that they, too, were soon dropped. When Li Shan-lan joined the T'ung-wen Kuan faculty in July 1869 as professor of mathematics, the two science students who were still studying English and the three who remained in the French class were placed under his instruction, as well as four of the Shanghai T'ung-wen Kuan graduates admitted to the Peking school the year before and the two best students remaining in the original English class. Thus the department of astronomy and mathematics was finally launched, with a very small student body, each member of which had at least official rank if not a civil service degree and enjoyed a stipend of ten taels a month and a liberal table, quarters, and servants.[57]

[55] O'Brien, the professor of English after Martin's departure, was very critical of this examination which, he writes, was given without the knowledge of the T'ung-wen Kuan faculty. The examiners, who knew no foreign language, depended upon members of the advanced language classes and some phrase books to assist them. They appeared to be more interested in the Chinese style than in the accuracy of the translations of foreign-language passages that the students were asked to make. The two most promising members of the English class were dropped, he says, and two of the five in that class who survived the examination had been hopeless from the beginning (NCH, Jan. 25, 1870).

[56] IWSM, TC 59, pp. 35–36.

[57] NCH, Jan. 25, 1870. The two students transferred from the senior English class presumably had been among three who were granted the lowest official rank at the beginning of 1869. It is possible that a few students were transferred to the new department from the senior French

The senior classes in English, French, and Russian, which had begun in 1862 and 1863, evidently were not particularly successful either. O'Brien, writing about them in 1869, says that although their members were youngsters, in contrast with the middle-aged and elderly gentlemen recruited for the department of astronomy and mathematics and constituting the junior English and French classes, they were all sons of needy bannermen and "belonged to a very humble class, socially." It was no wonder that the progress of these students, intellectually unpromising to begin with, looked down upon by their countrymen for studying a foreign language under foreign teachers, and with few exceptions unrewarded with official rank or an increase in their three-tael-per-month salaries after years of study, was slow in English and French and that they devoted most of their time and energy to Chinese subjects which alone promised some hope of ultimate reward.[58] Six members of the three senior classes had previously been awarded low official rank and were abroad at this time with the Burlingame mission, but even they were not much to show for the six years of operation of the school. In fact, the ministers of the Tsungli Yamen themselves appear to have lost interest in the T'ung-wen Kuan by 1869, leaving to Robert Hart all efforts to keep it alive. Finally, Hart wrote to Martin, studying in the United States, that the authorities were dissatisfied with the working of the school and that it was likely to be disbanded, whereupon Martin hurried back to China.[59]

Martin reached Peking in September 1869 and was immediately asked by Hart to assume full direction of the T'ung-wen Kuan.[60] He agreed to accept the presidency provided Hart would not only guarantee the annual appropriation from the

and Russian classes also, though they were not mentioned by O'Brien in his letter to the *North-China Herald*.

[58] NCH, Jan. 25, 1870.   [59] Martin, *Cycle*, p. 241.

[60] Anson Burlingame wrote on April 10, 1867, that Martin was at that time "the senior professor, and by courtesy the head of the college" (*Papers Relating to Foreign Affairs, 1867–1868*, p. 473).

customs revenues of all funds required for the operation of
the school but would himself supervise all of its financial affairs. Hart acquiesced, and Martin reports that the bargain
was faithfully executed throughout the twenty-five years he
was in charge.⁶¹ The new president was duly appointed and
inaugurated on November 28, 1869, in the presence of several
ministers of the Tsungli Yamen, the American chargé d'affaires,
and the faculty and student body and immediately set about
to put the school on its feet.⁶² During the next two years the
T'ung-wen Kuan was thoroughly reorganized and assumed the
form that was to characterize it for more than a quarter of
a century.

There are two reports on the progress of the school as of
January 1872. On January 4 Hart wrote:

I am glad to say that the College is going ahead. We have now
over 70 Peking students, 12 Cantonese, and 7 from Kiangsoo and
Chekiang, about 100 in all; ⁶³ and Dr. Dudgeon has just been made
Professor of Anatomy and Physiology. The men are studying English, French, German,⁶⁴ Russian, Mathematics, Natural Philosophy
[i.e., physics], and Chemistry.⁶⁵

⁶¹ *Cycle*, p. 293.
⁶² *Ibid.*, p. 294; S. Wells Williams to Secretary of State Fish, Dec. 18,
1869, U.S. Department of State Archives, *China*, XXVII, no. 71. Martin
writes that before appointing him the ministers of the Tsungli Yamen
subjected him to an informal examination in mathematics. Who prepared
the questions handed to him for solution and who read the answers
Martin never knew (*Cycle*, p. 294).
⁶³ The 1879 *Calendar* (p. 32) says: "In the next two years [after 1868]
the number of students drawn from the Eight Banners of Peking, hitherto
limited to thirty, was doubled, and at the same time students were summoned from the schools for foreign languages in Canton and Shanghai,
while some were sent up from the provinces of the interior, and the
whole number raised to one hundred, which is the present limit."
⁶⁴ "A German class was formed about the same time [1871] and
placed under the charge of the Professor of Russian" (*loc. cit.*). C. Wae-
ber was acting professor of Russian and German from 1870 to 1872,
N. Titoushkin acting professor of German in 1873, and W. N. Hagen full
professor of German from 1873 to 1881 (1888 *Calendar*, p. 43).
⁶⁵ Hart to Campbell, quoted in Wright, *Hart*, p. 349.

On January 18 Martin wrote to F. F. Low, the American minister in Peking:

From the date of my appointment, a little more than two years ago, the College (as we prefer to call it) has been undergoing a gradual but thorough reorganization. . . . Mathematics are taught by a native Professor, whose influence does much to awaken a taste for such studies in the minds of his countrymen. Physics have been taught by the President; and since the last Spring we have had a professor of Chemistry lecturing and giving experiments to intelligent classes. Within the month past, a chair of Anatomy and Physiology has been added; and the Professor, (Dr. Dudgeon) is to enter on his duties with the opening of the coming Spring. . . . As to students, we have but a handful, only ninety-two, all told; but this is twice as many as Mr. Seward found in attendance at the time of his visit a year ago. The best of these have been brought up from the schools at the open ports, which are henceforth to be regarded as feeders for the central institution and affiliated to it.[66]

By the time the first triennial *Calendar* was issued in 1879 the pattern of the T'ung-wen Kuan was well established, not to be changed essentially during the remaining life of the school. With the almost complete disappearance of references to the T'ung-wen Kuan from published collections of official documents after 1870, dependence is largely upon the triennial *Calendars* and private accounts for information regarding its organization and operation thereafter.

Operation after 1870

After assuming the presidency, Martin tried to operate the T'ung-wen Kuan like an American college—both he and Hart customarily referred to it as "the College." The difficulty in maintaining the standards of quality to which Martin aspired will be brought out later.

[66] U.S. Department of State, Legation Archives, *China*, CCXLIII, 92–93.

Two curricula were available after the reorganization: one, of eight years, included the study of a foreign language; the other, of five years, did not include language study. The non-language courses were taught either in Chinese, English, or French; [67] those students who were enrolled in languages other than English and French generally studied their nonlanguage courses in Chinese together with the nonlanguage students. By suitable exercises, all foreign-language students were expected to keep up their knowledge of their own language; the younger ones were required to devote half of each day to the study of Chinese.[68]

In the eight-year curriculum most of the work during the first three years was given over to the study of a foreign language and, of course, Chinese. The first year was devoted to elementary reading, writing, and speaking of the foreign language; the second, to reading, grammar, speaking, and the translation of sentences; and the third to exercises in translation and speaking and to world geography and world history. During the fourth year arithmetic and algebra were studied and dispatches translated. During the fifth physics, geometry, and plane and spherical trigonometry were studied; practical

[67] Professor C. H. Oliver stated in 1889 that he taught his science courses entirely in Chinese (L. W. Pilcher, "The new education in China," *Chinese Recorder*, 20 [1889], 348). By 1898 physics and chemistry were being taught in German and Russian as well as in Chinese, English, and French (1898 *Calendar*, pp. 12–13, 17–18).

[68] 1879 *Calendar*, p. 18. According to Ch'i Ju-shan, who did not enter the T'ung-wen Kuan until the 1890's and who wrote about it in the 1950's, this instruction in Chinese was the same as that offered in private schools preparing candidates for the civil service examinations: chief emphasis was on the *Four Books*, with occasional lessons in the *Five Classics* and on calligraphy and the writing of essays. He agrees with what O'Brien wrote in 1869, that the beginning language students generally were quite young and were often neither intelligent nor diligent, with the result that their progress in both Chinese and the particular foreign language studied was very slow (*Chung-kuo i-chou*, nos. 237–238).

mechanics, differential and integral calculus, and navigation during the sixth; chemistry, astronomy, and international law during the seventh; and astronomy, geology and mineralogy, and political economy during the eighth. In addition, lectures were given to a selected class on anatomy and physiology, and throughout the last four years time was devoted by all students to practice in the translation of books.[69]

The five-year curriculum was as follows: first year, arithmetic, algebra, and a branch of Chinese mathematics called *chiu-chang suan-fa* (mathematical rules of the nine chapters);[70] second year, geometry, plane and spherical trigonometry, and a second branch of Chinese mathematics called *hsüeh ssu-yüan chieh* (analysis of the four elements);[71] third year, physics, chemistry, and theoretical mechanics; fourth year, differential and integral calculus, navigation, astronomy, and practical mechanics; and fifth year, international law, political economy, astronomy, and geology and mineralogy.[72]

The enrollment in the various courses taught in the T'ung-wen Kuan in 1879, 1888, 1893, and 1898, insofar as is indicated

[69] 1879 *Calendar*, p. 19; 1893 *Calendar*, pp. 39–40.

[70] Presumably this study was based on the Han dynasty work *Chiu-chang suan-shu*, "in its influence perhaps the most important of all Chinese mathematical books" (Joseph Needham, *Science and Civilization in China*, III [1959], 24–27, 41).

[71] Presumably this was based on a Sung dynasty book entitled *Ssu-yüan yü-chien* by Chu Shih-chieh (*ibid.*, pp. 41, 46, 125, 135).

[72] 1879 *Calendar* (Chinese text), p. 37; 1893 *Calendar*, p. 41. In 1882 Martin divided the school into two parts: "our Preparatory Department, containing an average of sixty students," and the "Scientific Department," with forty-five (letter in NCH, Aug. 25, 1882). This suggests that all students in the eight-year program passed from "Preparatory" into "Scientific" after three years. Ch'i Ju-shan makes a distinction between "Rear" and "Front" departments, the students in the former devoting much time to Chinese studies, those in the latter having a sufficient command of the traditional Chinese subjects to make their further study unnecessary (*Chung-kuo i-chou*, no. 237). Probably Martin and Ch'i are talking about the same thing.

in the *Calendars* of those years by the lists of students who took the Great Examinations, is given in Table 1. The total active enrollment of the school was 103 in 1879, 120 in 1888, 113 in 1893, and 133 in 1898. Of these all but eleven in 1879, six in 1888, five in 1893, and one in 1898 either were studying a foreign language, were new students, or were absent on leave.

Table 1. Enrollment in T'ung-wen Kuan courses *

	1879	1888	1893		1898	
English	38	35	53		32	
Elementary				23		23
Advanced				30		9
French	25	29	23		19	
Elementary				5		10
Advanced				18		9
Russian	15	17	13		22	
Elementary				2		15
Advanced				11		7
German	10	10	11		16	
Elementary				8		3
Advanced				3		13
Japanese					17	
Mathematics	33	19	25		30	
Mathematical physics	7	4	3			
Astronomy	6	5	7		11	
Chemistry	12	20	10		34	
Physics			20		4	
Medicine (Physiology)	8	9	7			
International law	9	8	12			
New students		20	8		26	
Absent on leave	4	3				

* Figures are based on the number of students taking the Great Examinations.

This remaining small number devoted themselves entirely to mathematics and science—presumably the only students who remained in the five-year curriculum.

Written tests were given in every class at the end of each month; and annual examinations were conducted during the last three days of the school year in the presence of the ministers of the Tsungli Yamen. Monetary prizes were distributed after each examination, and readjustments of the students' pay upward and downward were made on the basis of the results of the annual examinations.[73]

Once in three years a *ta-k'ao*, or Great Examination, is held, after which the successful competitors are rewarded by marks of official distinction.

Conspicuous merit entitles its possessors to the first step in the nine degrees of official rank.

Advancing a step further, they are appointed to the discharge of official functions in connection with some one of the Six Boards, or leading Departments in the Imperial Government.

These duties being at first only nominal, and demanding but a small portion of their time, they are required to continue their studies at the College, as "resident graduates."

In addition to their ordinary studies, they are expected to perform the duties of Interpreters to the Tsungli Yamen; to translate, or aid in the translation of useful books; and to hold themselves in readiness to be sent abroad to fill posts in the newly-organized Diplomatic and Consular Services of the County.[74]

Since the primary purpose of the T'ung-wen Kuan was to train men for government service, the students received government stipends.

During the first year, or a part of it, the student is on probation, and receives nothing beyond his food and lodging. At the end of this term he has [in addition to food and lodging] an allowance of three taels *per mensem*. If the student does well this allowance is doubled in two or three years, and respectable proficiency entitles him, after a similar period, to be advanced to the higher rate of ten taels.[75]

The turnover in the student body of the T'ung-wen Kuan was unusual in two respects: (1) there was a high proportion of

[73] 1879 *Calendar* (English text), p. 20.   [74] *Ibid.*, p. 14.
[75] *Ibid.*, p. 24; 1893 *Calendar*, p. 54.

failures among those admitted; and (2) because students were retained in the school until assigned to posts and returned to it as "resident graduates" between assignments,[76] some names appear on the records over many years. It has already been noted that twenty of the first thirty admitted to study astronomy and mathematics were dropped after half a year, and half of those remaining were dismissed during the next few months. Fifty-two of the 103 students listed in the 1879 *Calendar* are not mentioned in the 1888 *Calendar* either as students (including resident graduates) or as graduates assigned to official posts for which their training had fitted them, although five of their names reappear in the 1893 *Calendar*. Sixty-five of the 120 students listed in the 1888 *Calendar* are not mentioned in the 1893 *Calendar* either as students or graduates on active duty, though four of their names appear again in the 1898 *Calendar*. Forty-four of the 113 students listed in the 1893 *Calendar* are not listed in the 1898 *Calendar* as students or graduates serving in posts for which they had been trained.[77] The names of eighteen students listed in the 1879 *Calendar* appear as students in the 1893 *Calendar* (presumably all were

[76] In a foreign office memorial submitted to the Throne on June 24, 1886, the T'ung-wen Kuan was referred to as a place for storing talent. Specialists in foreign affairs were held there as "resident graduates" for later use, as needed (1893 *Calendar*, p. 77).

[77] These figures must not be taken as completely reliable, for it is almost impossible to identify those who may have changed their given names between issues of the T'ung-wen Kuan *Calendar*. Moreover, there appear always to have been some regularly enrolled students who failed to take the Great Examination, with the result that their names were not included in the *Calendar* lists. In the 1888 *Calendar*, for instance, the enrollment of the English department is given as forty-eight, but only thirty-five took the examination and had their names listed, and in the German department these figures were sixteen and ten. In the 1898 *Calendar* the names of six alumni are given which had not appeared in any of the three earlier calendars; one of these was Lu Tseng-hsiang (later, Lu Cheng-hsiang), who ultimately became the most eminent of all T'ung-wen Kuan graduates.

resident graduates), but none from the 1879 lists appear in the 1898 *Calendar;* and only four 1888 students are listed as students in the 1898 *Calendar.*

The work of the academic year was divided into two semesters, the first beginning three weeks after the Chinese New Year (that is, sometime between early February and early March), with the semesters separated from each other by vacation periods of from four to five weeks. A three-day vacation was allowed for the Spring Festival and another for the Autumn Festival; otherwise the students worked continuously, Sundays being recognized as holidays only for the foreign professors.[78]

Administration of the T'ung-wen Kuan was nominally the responsibility of all the ministers of the Tsungli Yamen (who sometimes numbered as many as ten),[79] although only two of them ordinarily were assigned special responsibility for the school. Actual control of students and employees was in the hands of two proctors and two assistant proctors; control of all academic activities rested with W. A. P. Martin, the president (*tsung-chiao-hsi*). Robert Hart, who held the title of inspector ex-officio, handled the finances of the school, as mentioned above.

The teaching staff always included three or four professors of Chinese to direct the students in the study of their own language and literature, a Chinese professor of mathematics (after the appointment of Li Shan-lan in 1869), and foreign professors of chemistry, astronomy, physics,[80] medicine (part-

[78] 1879 *Calendar,* p. 17; 1888 *Calendar,* p. 16.

[79] Hsü Chi-yü retired from active service in 1869 after two years as director. Although no specific evidence could be found, it appears that the ministers as a group reassumed responsibility at that time. The ministers of the Tsungli Yamen, called "Regents" in the English text, are collectively given the title *Tsung-kuan ta-ch'en* in the Chinese text of the 1879 and later *Calendars.* This is an abbreviation of the title given to Hsü in 1867.

[80] The physics chair was formally established in 1888, prior to which the subject was taught by the president (1893 *Calendar,* p. 84).

time instruction, really in physiology), English, French, Russian, German, and (in 1898) Japanese. The president taught international law (which course also included political economy). These professorships (*chiao-hsi*) were not always held by separate men—for example, Russian and German were taught by the same person for a number of years, and there were periods when language professors or Dr. Martin or even complete outsiders taught courses in the sciences. At the time of publication of the 1893 *Calendar* every one of these chairs was filled, but the teaching of international law ceased with the retirement of Dr. Martin in 1895. Finally, there were nearly always one or two resident graduates with the title of tutor (*fu-chiao-hsi*) assisting with the teaching of each subject.

It was earlier brought out that provision was made to reward with official rank and honors the faithful service of Chinese professors. At first the rewards to the foreign staff took the form of monetary bonuses. But in November 1885 the Tsungli Yamen requested and obtained official honors for President Martin and Professors Anatole Billequin (chemistry) and Charles Vapereau (French), Martin being granted the third official rank and the other two the fourth.[81] On July 2, 1893, the fourth official rank was awarded to Professors S. M. Russell (astronomy) and C. H. Oliver (physics) and the fifth rank to Herr V. von Grot (Russian).[82]

Because the buildings in the old Iron Money Bureau assigned to the T'ung-wen Kuan in 1862 were unsuitable for the expansion contemplated in 1865, new buildings were erected on the same site to house the school. Thereafter, from time to time, other buildings were added as needed. In 1896 Martin described the school buildings as

of one story, in the regulation style of Peking, with tile floors and little ornament. Each principal building has in front of it a paved

[81] 1885 *Calendar*, p. 39.   [82] 1893 *Calendar*, p. 74.

court, flanked by smaller houses or wings. The entire space is occupied by eight such quadrangles, and two rows of low houses. . . . The whole group resembles a barrack, or rather a camp.[83]

In 1873 commodious buildings were erected to house a printing office. There seven presses and four fonts of movable type were used to print not only the translations of foreign books made by the staff and students of the school but also some books for the government. "In 1876 buildings were erected for a Chemical Laboratory and Museum." [84] And in 1888 a fifty-foot astronomical observatory and a physics laboratory were built.[85] The school library was not large, possessing as late as 1898 only three thousand volumes of Chinese and foreign-language reference books, including one thousand volumes on Chinese mathematics.[86] Attached to the library was a reading room kept supplied with newspapers and magazines in various languages.[87]

In addition to instruction and study, two supplementary activities were carried on at the T'ung-wen Kuan: one, the supplying of interpreters and translators for the Tsungli Yamen; the other, the translation and printing of foreign books. As noted above, these two duties were stipulated for qualified students at least as early as 1879.

From the 1870's, resident graduates were occasionally called next door to the Tsungli Yamen to serve as interpreters. But in 1888 this procedure was regularized. On July 30 of that year the Tsungli Yamen memorialized and received permission to set up a translation office in the T'ung-wen Kuan consisting of one interpreter and one assistant interpreter for each of the

[83] *Cycle*, p. 307.   [84] 1879 *Calendar*, p. 33.
[85] 1893 *Calendar*, pp. 83–84.
[86] 1898 *Calendar*, p. 11. A number of books were presented to the school by the American minister to China in 1868, and 188 volumes by the French minister in 1872 (IWSM, TC 88, pp. 18–19).
[87] 1879 *Calendar*, p. 27.

four languages, to be selected from resident graduates who had seen service abroad. "Whenever foreign envoys come to the Tsungli Yamen to transact business, these officials can be summoned to interpret, and they can also be used to translate and to clarify Chinese and foreign terminology." The men assigned to the translation office were to receive extra pay and to be rewarded every three years with promotion.[88] In 1888 five resident graduates were appointed to this office, and in 1898 there were six. In 1895 a somewhat larger group, including the members of the translation office plus a few additional resident graduates—seventeen altogether—were designated to attend in rotation all conferences of the foreign office with foreign diplomats to check on translations.[89]

From fairly early in the history of the T'ung-wen Kuan the translation of Western books into Chinese was an important activity, and a printing plant, as just mentioned, was set up in 1873 to publish such translations for distribution by the Tsungli Yamen to officials throughout the empire. There were also some works published that had been written in Chinese by members of the T'ung-wen Kuan staff. As noted earlier, all students taking the eight-year course were required to spend some time during their last two years translating books, and the resident graduates presumably also devoted time to this type of work. On June 21, 1886, the Tsungli Yamen sought and obtained permission to appoint two resident graduates as editors to select and edit the works translated in the T'ung-wen Kuan. These were to be chosen from qualified persons of superior literary skill who were concurrently holding nominal posts in the capital, in accordance with the precedent of the Fang-lüeh Kuan.[90]

[88] 1893 *Calendar,* pp. 80–81.   [89] 1898 *Calendar,* p. 5.
[90] 1893 *Calendar,* pp. 76–77. The Fang-lüeh Kuan compiled "the records of military undertakings and achievements" (Brunnert and Hagelstrom, p. 45).

In 1896 the foreign office finally recognized that training could be carried only so far in the T'ung-wen Kuan and recommended that sixteen graduates be sent to Europe for more advanced study of foreign languages and mathematics—four each to England, France, Germany, and Russia. They were to live in the Chinese legations in the capitals of those countries and to carry on their studies under the supervision of the Chinese minister. At the end of three years those who had been successful in their studies would return to the T'ung-wen Kuan for examination by the Tsungli Yamen; following this they would, if deserving, be rewarded appropriately and presumably be assigned to official positions for which their advanced training would fit them. Each student, while abroad, was to have all his travel and study expenses paid by the Chinese government and receive in addition a salary of fifty taels per month. An edict received by the T'ung-wen Kuan in late May or early June 1896 ordered the sixteen students named therein to be ready to leave for Europe by June 11. Of these all but one had been listed as students in the 1893 *Calendar;* four were there as early as 1888, and two went back at least to 1879. These students were not to be employed at legation tasks, the intention of the assignment being to deepen their education so that they might serve their country better later on.[91] Eleven of the sixteen were actually studying abroad in 1898; two more occupied posts in China, so to all appearances they had not gone abroad at all. The names of the remaining three do not appear in the 1898 *Calendar;* presumably they had died, resigned, or were on leave.[92]

End of the T'ung-wen Kuan

After China's military defeat at the hands of Japan in 1895 there was widespread demand, both in official circles and outside, for reform, including some calls for a modern Chinese

[91] 1898 *Calendar,* pp. 12–16. [92] *Ibid.,* pp. 34–35.

educational system similar to those in Japan and the West. Out of this agitation came the so-called Hundred Days of Reform in 1898 sponsored by the young Emperor,[93] one product of which was a national university in Peking. On June 11 an Imperial edict ordered consultation between the Grand Council and the Tsungli Yamen regarding the establishment of a university, to be called the Ching-shih Ta-hsüeh-t'ang, which should also serve as a model for provincial universities.[94] On July 3, Sun Chia-nai, a president of the Board of Civil Office and formerly tutor to the Emperor, was placed in charge of the university project, and shortly thereafter he and the ministers of the Tsungli Yamen recommended that the new university be modeled on the T'ung-wen Kuan and that one section of the latter, probably the scientific department, be transferred to the university.[95] However, on August 30 the Emperor ordered postponement of the proposed transfer from the T'ung-wen Kuan, the matter to be re-examined after the university's organization had been determined.[96] Whether or not this reconsideration took place, the T'ung-wen Kuan continued to carry on with only minor changes, parallel to the new university, which was one of the few creations of the 1898 reforms that survived the reaction of September 26.[97] Meanwhile, on

[93] For discussion of this episode, see Meribeth E. Cameron, *The Reform Movement in China, 1898–1912* (1931), pp. 23–55.

[94] *Shih-lu,* KH 418, p. 15.   [95] *Shih-lu,* KH 424, pp. 8–9.

[96] *Ibid.*

[97] The new university, generally referred to in English as the Imperial University, was to consist of twelve departments: astronomy and mathematics, physics, chemistry, engineering, agriculture, medicine, law, English, French, Russian, German, and Japanese (*Wen-hsien ts'ung-pien,* vol. 25 [April 1935]). For a study of its origin and early history, see Renville Clifton Lund, "The Imperial University of Peking" (University of Washington Ph.D. dissertation, 1956). My original article on the T'ung-wen Kuan was in error in stating that all scientific instruction had been transferred from the T'ung-wen Kuan to the new university in 1898, and this error has been repeated by other writers, e.g., Wright, *Hart,* p. 332.

August 9, W. A. P. Martin, who had resigned his position with the T'ung-wen Kuan in 1895, was appointed dean of Western studies (*hsi-hsüeh tsung-chiao-hsi*) for the new university and awarded the brevet second official rank by the Emperor.[98]

In 1898 the T'ung-wen Kuan dropped its five-year curriculum, which had not required the study of a foreign language. Under revised regulations issued during that year, every T'ung-wen Kuan student was required to master one of the five foreign languages taught; after this was done, he might devote himself to any one of the nonlanguage subjects. Actually the eight-year curriculum published with the revised regulations was identical with the one that appeared in the 1893 and earlier *Calendars*. These regulations show that student laziness and frequent cutting of classes remained serious problems in the T'ung-wen Kuan.[99]

Although Lund says [100] that "a number of instructors were transferred to the university from the T'ung-wen Kuan," these must have been junior Chinese; only one foreign professor who had been with the T'ung-wen Kuan before 1898 was listed as a member of the university faculty in 1900—Dr. Robert Coltman, professor of surgery and medicine—and he also continued to teach in the T'ung-wen Kuan.[101] Martin, it will be remembered, had resigned from the T'ung-wen Kuan in 1895. The one transferred person mentioned by Lund, Yang Sheng, evidently was not a member of the T'ung-wen Kuan faculty; he is listed in the 1893 *Calendar* as a resident graduate studying English and international law and in the 1898 *Calendar* as a member of the staff of the Chinese legation in Germany. Ac-

[98] *Shih-lu*, KH 422, p. 6. Martin remembered in 1907 (Morse, *International Relations*, III, 475) that he had retired from the T'ung-wen Kuan in 1894, but the 1898 *Calendar* (p. 27) says 1895.

[99] "Ching-shih T'ung-wen Kuan kuan-kuei," *Chung-kuo chin-tai ch'u-pan shih-liao ch'u-pien* (1953), pp. 6–8.

[100] P. 121.

[101] *Chronicle and Directory for China . . . 1900*, p. 116.

tually the T'ung-wen Kuan appears to have been offering a broader range of courses in 1900 than the university. The T'ung-wen Kuan had foreign professors of natural history, astronomy and mathematics, chemistry, English, French, Russian, German, and Japanese. In contrast, the seven foreigners on the university faculty were listed as professors of English, French and gymnastics, Russian, German and military tactics, and Japanese. Dr. Coltman taught in both schools.[102]

Both the T'ung-wen Kuan and the Imperial University were badly damaged and forced to close by the Boxers during the summer of 1900.[103] On January 11, 1902, an Imperial edict ordered the reopening of the university and, at the same time, the transfer of the T'ung-wen Kuan from the jurisdiction of the foreign office to that of the university.[104] Within the university it was at first called the Fan-i k'e (department of translation), but during the spring and summer of 1903 it is reported to have been absorbed by the I-hsüeh Kuan, a special school or division specializing in foreign languages. The I-hsüeh Kuan, like other divisions of the university, was open by examination to graduates of the new middle schools. It had a five-year curriculum which bore a strong resemblance to that of the T'ung-wen Kuan, and in 1909 it was reported to have an enrollment of 360.[105]

Problems and Achievements

It is not easy to evaluate the accomplishments of the T'ung-wen Kuan, for only scattered and fragmentary judgments are

[102] *Ibid.* I do not know whether Martin was teaching courses in the university or not; nor do I know which Chinese professors were teaching in either school.

[103] *Chung-kuo i-chou*, no. 240; Lund, p. 153.

[104] THHL, KH 171, p. 1. One of the first acts of the new chancellor of the university was to dismiss on Feb. 7 the entire foreign faculty. See Martin letter, *Chinese Recorder*, 33 (1902), 143–144. This dismissal presumably applied equally to the foreign faculty of the T'ung-wen Kuan.

[105] Lund, p. 197; Harry Edwin King, *The Educational System of China as Recently Reconstructed* (1911), pp. 81–82.

available, and most of these come from biased sources. Martin and Hart, as one might expect, tended to judge the school in the best possible light, and the Tsungli Yamen naturally was inclined to defend its creature. Conservative officials and most other members of the literati regarded the school as highly unorthodox—even dangerous—and at best were unsympathetic in their criticisms. The fullest account, by a former student named Ch'i Ju-shan, although helpful, suffers from having been written more than half a century later; it contains obvious errors of fact that illustrate the difficulty of writing from memory long after the event.

As mentioned earlier, Martin and Hart always referred to the T'ung-wen Kuan as "the College." Through much, probably even all, of its history the school fell short of the present meaning of this term. But during the latter half of the nineteenth century there were numerous colleges, in the United States at any rate, that would not today be regarded as more than high schools. Therefore application of the term to the T'ung-wen Kuan was probably justifiable.

The most serious problem of the T'ung-wen Kuan from the beginning was that of recruiting promising students. Ch'i Ju-shan tells us that the study of a foreign language was generally regarded as treasonable during the early decades of the school —as evidence of surrender to a foreign country. He suggests that the social stigma attached to such study was so great that no family would willingly enter a son. To secure students, therefore, the Tsungli Yamen was compelled to draft them from the Eight Banner schools; even then, according to Ch'i, only boys who were stupid or whose families had no political influence were enrolled in the T'ung-wen Kuan.[106] The Wo-jen

---

[106] *Chung-kuo i-chou,* no. 237. Writing during the early years of the school, M. J. O'Brien said of the same students: "Foreign scholarship exposed them to the contempt of the literati, and to suspicion even on the part of their friends and relations" (NCH, Jan. 25, 1870).

attack in 1866, discussed above, so damaged the reputation of the school with the literati that no scholar had yet entered it a decade later, according to Ch'en K'ang-ch'i; [107] in fact, there is no evidence of entry by the children of Chinese officials before the 1890's.

It was pointed out earlier that unusually high stipends were offered in order to attract students; moreover, for the same reason, according to Ch'i, living conditions were luxurious and the enforcement of rules was lax. The school promised an easy road to official position for those who were unable to achieve it via the regular examination system, and this is said to have become its chief attraction.[108]

The first nonbanner students to enter the T'ung-wen Kuan were those transferred from the Kuang fang-yen Kuan in Shanghai for advanced study, but commencing in the 1870's there was a steady increase in the ratio of Chinese to bannermen. Fewer than 20 per cent of the students listed in the 1879 *Calendar* appear to have been Chinese; these included nine of the eleven enrolled in science and mathematics.[109] About 40 per cent of the students listed in the 1888 *Calendar* probably were Chinese, including sixteen of the twenty new students admitted that year. The corresponding percentages in the 1893 and 1898 *Calendars* were 52 and 79; five of eight new students in 1893 and twenty-four of twenty-six in 1898 were Chinese.[110] This shift suggests an improvement in the quality of the students; but it could also have resulted from an

[107] *Lang-ch'ien chi wen* (preface dated 1880), 1, p. 2.

[108] *Chung-kuo i-chou*, no. 237.

[109] In 1882 Martin wrote that fourteen of the forty-five students enrolled in the "Scientific Department" were Chinese. This appears to have included all of the advanced students, since the rest were in what he referred to as the "Preparatory Department" (NCH, Aug. 25, 1882).

[110] These figures are only approximate, for I have no means of distinguishing the names of Chinese bannermen—as distinct from Manchu and Mongol bannermen—from those of other Chinese.

increased awareness among Chinese who were seeking an easy road to official position of the opportunity offered by the T'ung-wen Kuan. Ch'i Ju-shan reports such a great increase in the demand by Chinese for admission in the late 1880's that the recommendation of an official or of an instructor or older student of the T'ung-wen Kuan was required for a while and that in the end entrance examinations were introduced.[111]

In 1889 the Tsungli Yamen submitted a memorial to the Throne answering charges made against the new diplomatic service by Yang Ch'en, a censor. Yang had declared that the interpreters in Chinese embassies abroad, most of whom were T'ung-wen Kuan graduates, were neither adequately educated in Chinese nor sufficiently familiar with a foreign language to serve effectively and, in addition, that they carried on intrigue with foreign officials to secure recommendations to the Chinese government that they be promoted to diplomatic rank. Moreover, he had charged that the foreign teachers in the T'ung-wen Kuan had been there so long that they had fallen into lazy habits and did not enforce discipline among the students. He urged the appointment, on recommendation by the Hanlin Academy and the Six Boards, of a Chinese president possessing character and virtue. In its memorial, the Tsungli Yamen denied that T'ung-wen Kuan students in overseas posts had asked foreign officials to recommend them, but there was no defense of the education these students had received. However, it did defend Martin as president of the school and pointed out the difficulty of finding a Chinese to serve in that position who was familiar with both Chinese and Western learning and who also could meet the proposed requirement regarding scholarship and character.[112]

[111] *Chung-kuo i-chou,* no. 239.

[112] WHTK, p. 10801. Charles Denby, American minister to China, reported in 1888 that he had recently examined the students of French

After China's defeat by Japan in 1895, the criticism of modern institutions such as the T'ung-wen Kuan tended to be in terms of their not going far enough, rather than going too far in the direction of Western education, as had been the case earlier. On February 7, 1896, the Tsungli Yamen again found itself answering charges made against the T'ung-wen Kuan by a censor, this time by one Ch'en Ch'i-chang. Ch'en had urged broadening the curriculum and encouraging degree holders to enter the school—as had the Tsungli Yamen nearly thirty years earlier. He had also charged superficiality of instruction, lack of diligence and discipline among the students, and the wheedling of the foreign instructors to secure passing grades on examinations. The Tsungli Yamen insisted that the T'ung-wen Kuan curriculum was already broad, that its students had been learning foreign languages, mathematics, and the sciences steadily if not rapidly, that in fact their progress had been regularly measured in examinations conducted by the ministers of the Yamen. However, the validity of Ch'en's criticisms was acknowledged by the statement that the faculty had been enjoined to give stricter examinations and the proctors to prevent cheating and to expel students who indulged in merrymaking and made no improvement in their studies. The new president, C. H. Oliver, was instructed to require students to work harder in their courses and to advance them only according to demonstrated merit, as was done in the West.[113]

The criticism of Li Tuan-fen, a vice-president of the Board of Punishments, was even sharper. In a memorial presented on June 12, 1896, he declared the instruction offered in the T'ung-wen Kuan and other modern schools to be superficial and impractical in the light of China's modern needs and proposed replacement by a system of provincial schools teaching

in the T'ung-wen Kuan "and found them very well advanced and instructed" (*Foreign Relations of the United States, 1889*, p. 73).

[113] *1898 Calendar*, pp. 6–11.

both Chinese and Western subjects which would culminate in a national university in Peking.[114] Sheng Hsüan-huai also criticized the "impractical" instruction of the T'ung-wen Kuan during the same year,[115] and Chang Chih-tung, in his *Ch'üan-hsüeh-p'ien*, expressed regret that neither the T'ung-wen Kuan nor the modern books published there appeared to have broadened the minds of officials.[116]

Ch'i Ju-shan also writes disparagingly of the Chinese instruction in the T'ung-wen Kuan. The Chinese professors were *chü-jen* or *kung-sheng*—that is, more than adequately educated to give such instruction—selected by special examinations from long lists of applicants, after an early period when few had applied for these positions. However, more were appointed than were needed, he says, with the result that they worked only part of the time; and when teaching they did not work hard at it, considering that the lazy and unpromising character of most of the students did not justify great effort.

Ch'i's criticism of the foreign professors is devastating, but, it would appear, unjustified. He implies that all were actually hired to work for the Maritime Customs and were used as teachers in the T'ung-wen Kuan only while learning enough Chinese to be able to take up their regular duties. He quotes a missionary as saying that not one member of the T'ung-wen Kuan faculty was a college graduate.[117] These charges may apply to temporary appointees who filled in while regular members of the faculty were away on leave, and it is true that there was an unusually large number of such substitutions during the mid-1890's when Ch'i was a student. But the leading members of the T'ung-wen Kuan faculty served for long periods. W. A. P. Martin was on the staff from 1864 to 1895, first

---

[114] THHL, KH 134, pp. 1–4. For a summary of his principal points, see Peake, *Nationalism*, pp. 25–28.

[115] THHL, KH 136, p. 12.   [116] Teng and Fairbank, p. 171.

[117] *Chung-kuo i-chou*, no. 238.

teaching English and from 1870 serving as professor of international law as well as president; Anatole Billequin was professor of chemistry from 1867 to 1896 and concurrently professor of physics from 1867 to 1888; Li Shan-lan was professor of mathematics from 1869 to 1882; Charles Vapereau was professor of French from 1871 to 1896; J. Dudgeon was professor of physiology from 1872 to 1895; C. H. Oliver was professor of English from 1879 to 1888, professor of physics from 1888 to 1900, and president of the T'ung-wen Kuan from 1895 until it was merged with the new university in 1902; S. M. Russell was professor of astronomy from 1879 to 1900; and Hsi Kan, himself a T'ung-wen Kuan graduate, was professor of mathematics from 1886 to 1898. With a few exceptions, the other regular foreign-language professors were on the staff for periods of from three to ten years.

Some of the regular foreign-language professors may not have been college graduates, but it could also be argued that their responsibilities did not demand a college degree. The teachers of science and mathematics, however, were unquestionably well-educated men. Martin was a graduate of Indiana University and had pursued graduate studies in the United States. Dudgeon had earned an M.D. at the University of Edinburgh. Oliver and Russell held B.A. and M.A. degrees from Queen's College, Belfast. Li Shan-lan was one of the leading Chinese mathematicians of the nineteenth century, and his student Hsi Kan was also well regarded—even by Ch'i Jushan.[118]

M. J. O'Brien wrote in 1869 of the poor quality of the students in the T'ung-wen Kuan and of their lack of interest in their foreign studies:

I soon ascertained that, with one or two exceptions, they pursued their English studies in a very perfunctory spirit, the greater part

[118] Martin, *Cycle*, p. 311; 1898 *Calendar; Chung-kuo i-chou*, no. 240.

of their time and energy being given to Chinese, . . . proficiency in Chinese being certain to give them a status and position in the country, while the career to be looked forward to as the reward of their foreign attainments was, at the best, uncertain.

He also noted that many of the students frequently missed their foreign-language classes. "On one occasion I remonstrated with one . . . and told him . . . he would never learn English at that rate. He replied . . . that it was a matter of absolute indifference to him whether he learnt English or not. . . . This was the spirit which animated the majority." O'Brien regarded the students as entirely capable of learning, but indifferent.[119]

Although the quality of students had improved by the 1890's, Ch'i reports that not more than half of those enrolled in his time attended classes and only from 20 to 30 per cent really studied. Those who worked hard could advance relatively rapidly, for the pace of instruction was extremely moderate. Much time was spent at the beginning of foreign-language study in learning the alphabet and simple words, Ch'i writes, and the first two or three months of the course in chemistry were devoted to explaining the use of equipment.[120] Martin has written that the students, being "quick of apprehension and patient in application . . . succeed well in scientific studies. . . . In languages they are not so ready . . . [and are] accordingly never require[d] . . . to apply [themselves] to more than one foreign language, . . . for them the mastery of one [being] a rare attainment." [121] By the end of the century the tendency among students appears to have been to neglect their Chinese studies. The revised T'ung-wen Kuan regulations issued in 1898 prescribed Chinese examinations for advanced students. Poor results were to send the student back to the "Preparatory Department" for more study of Chinese; and

[119] NCH, Jan. 25, 1870.   [120] *Chung-kuo i-chou*, no. 240.
[121] *Cycle*, p. 314.

preparatory students who had been cutting their Chinese classes were ordered to attend them regularly.[122] Ch'i remembers that those students who mastered a foreign language did so only after they had gone abroad. In spite of the enormous expenditure of money and time, says Ch'i, the T'ung-wen Kuan did not produce one real diplomat.[123] Ch'i feels that he himself wasted six years in the school; his only gain from the experience, he says, was what he learned about the West in numerous conversations in Chinese with his foreign teachers.[124]

The primary purpose of the T'ung-wen Kuan was to train men for the diplomatic service, men to be used either in Chinese legations abroad, in the Tsungli Yamen, or in provincial offices charged with foreign relations. Many of the graduates were thus employed, although others used their knowledge of Western subjects to teach in modern schools, and a few who were able to pass the regular civil service examinations gave up foreign affairs altogether.

As has been pointed out earlier, when a student had graduated but had not yet been assigned to an overseas or provincial post or when a graduate returned to Peking from overseas duty he remained in the T'ung-wen Kuan as a resident graduate. There he might be appointed to a tutorship, to an editorship, or to the translation office of the Tsungli Yamen. Or he might be expected to participate in T'ung-wen Kuan translating projects or other miscellaneous duties—two resident graduates, Chang Te-i and Shen To, even taught English to the Emperor for a time.[125] All except a few of the older resident graduates regularly took at least the triennial Great Examinations and so must have devoted a part of their time to study.

In the 1879 *Calendar* seventeen resident graduates are listed,

[122] *Chung-kuo chin-tai ch'u-pan shih-liao ch'u-pien*, pp. 6–8.

[123] This is a harsh judgment of those few graduates who ultimately did receive appointments as ministers to foreign countries. See the paragraphs following.

[124] *Chung-kuo i-chou*, no. 240.   [125] Martin, *Cycle*, pp. 316–317.

of whom seven held appointments as tutors in the T'ung-wen Kuan.[126] In the 1888 *Calendar* twenty-two resident graduates are listed, of whom seven were tutors.[127] The 1893 *Calendar* lists forty-three resident graduates, of whom two were editors of T'ung-wen Kuan publications (one of these was also professor of mathematics and the other a tutor in mathematics), five were members of the translation office, and ten were tutors.[128] The 1898 *Calendar* lists two editors (one was concurrently professor of mathematics, the other a tutor in chemistry), six members of the translation office (one of whom was also tutor in Russian), and nine other tutors, making a total of only seventeen resident graduates.

All diplomatic missions that went abroad were accompanied by graduates (or undergraduates, in the first two or three instances) of the T'ung-wen Kuan who were sent in the capacity of interpreters and diplomatic secretaries. The Burlingame mission (1868–1870) included six student-interpreters from the school,[129] and the Ch'ung-hou mission of apology to France (1870–1871) included two.[130]

After the appointment in 1876 of Kuo Sung-tao as Chinese minister to Great Britain, the first Chinese diplomatic representative ever sent to reside overseas, and the establishment of permanent Chinese legations in Berlin, Paris, Washington, Tokyo, and St. Petersburg during the next three years,[131] the

[126] Pp. 16, 9.   [127] Pp. 18, 9.   [128] Pp. 28–31, 4–5.

[129] See Biggerstaff, "The official Chinese attitude toward the Burlingame Mission," *American Historical Review*, 41 (July 1936), 687.

[130] See Biggerstaff, "The Ch'ung Hou mission to France, 1870–1871," *Nankai Social and Economic Quarterly*, 8 (Oct. 1935), 639; Martin, *Cycle*, p. 380.

[131] For a brief study of the establishment of these first legations see Biggerstaff, "The establishment of permanent Chinese diplomatic missions abroad," *Chinese Social and Political Science Review*, 20 (April 1936), 27–37. See also Immanuel C. Y. Hsü, *China's Entrance into the Family of Nations* (1960), chap. xii.

T'ung-wen Kuan was called upon to keep them supplied with interpreters; and it was this body of trained men who came to form China's permanent foreign service.

In 1879 there were sixteen T'ung-wen Kuan graduates stationed abroad: three in London, two in Paris, two in Tokyo, three in Berlin, four in St. Petersburg, and two with the legations in the United States, Spain, and Peru.[132] In 1888 there were twenty graduates abroad. Three of these were stationed in England, one in France, two in Russia, one in the United States, three in Japan (one as vice-consul at Nagasaki), and six in Germany; and there were two serving as interpreters with a mission of inquiry to England and France, one interpreting for such a mission to Russia, and one with a similar mission to Germany and Italy.[133] From 1891 to 1894 Wang Feng-tsao, a T'ung-wen Kuan graduate, served as Chinese minister to Japan; and in 1893 sixteen other graduates were stationed abroad in lesser capacities.[134] The 1898 *Calendar* lists nineteen graduates serving as officers in the Chinese legations in the United States, England, Germany, France, and Russia, including Ch'ing-ch'ang, who had recently been appointed minister to France. It also lists eleven graduates who were pursuing advanced study in Europe.

As the years passed and Chinese legations and consulates were established in all the important countries of the world, T'ung-wen Kuan graduates rose to high positions in this branch of their country's service. Besides Wang Feng-tsao and Ch'ing-ch'ang, just mentioned, Chang Te-i was minister to Great Britain from 1901 to 1905 [135] and Yin-ch'ang minister to Germany

---

[132] 1879 *Calendar*, p. 15.   [133] 1888 *Calendar*, pp. 16–17.

[134] *Ch'ing-shih kao*, 212, pp. 10–11; 1893 *Calendar*, pp. 34–35. This *Calendar* does not designate the specific overseas assignment except in the case of Wang.

[135] Hummel, p. 732. Ch'ing-ch'ang was minister to France from 1895 to 1899 (*Ch'ing-shih kao*, 212, pp. 11–14).

and Holland from 1901 to 1905 and to Germany from 1908 to 1910.[136] Yang Chao-yün was minister to Belgium from 1902 to 1905, Yang Tcheng minister to Austria-Hungary from 1903 to 1905 and to Germany from 1905 to 1907, Yang Shu minister to Japan from 1903 to 1907 and to Belgium from 1909 to 1910, Liu Shih-hsün minister to France and Spain from 1905 to 1912 and to Brazil from 1914 to 1916, and Lu Cheng-hsiang minister to Holland from 1905 to 1907 and from 1908 to 1911 and to Russia in 1911, after which he served as Chinese minister of foreign affairs several times between 1912 and 1920, as chief Chinese delegate to the Paris Peace Conference in 1919, and as Chinese delegate to the League of Nations in 1922.[137] Sa-yin-t'u was minister to Russia from 1907 to 1911, Wu Tsung-lien minister to Italy from 1909 until after the 1911 Revolution, and Liu Ching-jen minister to Holland in 1911 and to Russia from 1912 to 1918.[138]

T'ung-wen Kuan graduates were also assigned to provincial positions, most of which required special competence in the subjects they had studied. In 1888 twenty-one graduates held provincial posts, some as interpreters and foreign relations experts in treaty-port cities and provinces bordering Russia and some as teachers or officials connected with the new telegraph service and the modern military establishments of Tientsin.[139] The 1893 *Calendar* lists thirty-two graduates holding official positions as interpreters, foreign relations experts, teachers or technicians, or more orthodox prefects or magistrates, some of whom had achieved fairly high rank. The 1898 *Calendar* lists forty-seven graduates holding such official positions in the provinces.

[136] *Ch'ing-shih kao,* 212, pp. 15–17, 19–20.
[137] *Ibid.,* pp. 15–21; 1931 *Who's Who in China,* pp. 463–464, 282; 1925, pp. 563–564.
[138] *Ch'ing-shih kao,* 212, pp. 18–21; 1931 *Who's Who in China,* p. 273.
[139] 1888 *Calendar,* pp. 17–18.

The two T'ung-wen Kuan graduates who reached the highest positions in the national government, other than Lu Chenghsiang whose achievements have already been recorded, were Yin-ch'ang and Chou Tzu-ch'i. Besides his diplomatic career, mentioned above, Yin-ch'ang had a military career. He was made acting president of the Board of War in 1910 and commander in chief of Imperial forces for a time in 1911. Under Yüan Shih-k'ai he served as chief presidential military aide-de-camp and as chief of the General Staff, and following Yüan's death he held similar posts in the Peking government down to 1924.[140] Chou Tzu-ch'i, after serving in the Board of Foreign Affairs during the first decade of the twentieth century, held the posts of acting minister of finance and minister of communications at various times after the 1911 Revolution.[141]

The first T'ung-wen Kuan graduate to achieve a professorship in the school was Hsi Kan, who succeeded to Li Shan-lan's chair of mathematics in 1886.[142] Other graduates taught in the telegraph and military schools in Tientsin and in some of the new provincial schools opened after the Sino-Japanese War.[143]

An ancillary activity of the T'ung-wen Kuan was the translation of Western books into Chinese and their publication for distribution among government agencies. Although the translations made at the T'ung-wen Kuan were by no means as numerous as those issued by the translation department of the Kiangnan Arsenal, most of them were works of some importance and their free distribution in government circles no doubt contributed to the spread of modern ideas in China. As noted earlier, all students taking the eight-year course were required to devote some time during their last two years to the translation of books. However, perusal of a list of the translations actually published shows that credit for their production is

[140] 1925 *Who's Who in China*, pp. 938–939.
[141] *The China Year Book, 1914*, p. 563.
[142] 1888 *Calendar*, p. 43.   [143] 1893 and 1898 *Calendars*.

given to a few professors and about a dozen resident graduates. More than two dozen works altogether were published by the T'ung-wen Kuan before 1898, including five on international law, two on foreign laws, two on foreign history, one on political economy, and ten on chemistry, physics, mathematics, and astronomy.

The works on international law translated and published at the T'ung-wen Kuan were Wheaton's *Elements of International Law*, de Martens' *Guide diplomatique*, Woolsey's *International Law*, Bluntschli's *Droit international codifié*, and an article by Martin on the practice of international law in ancient China. The works on foreign law were the *Code Napoléon* and the *Penal Code of Singapore*, and those on foreign history were a *History of Russia* and Tytler's *Universal History*. The scientific works included Malaguti's *Chemistry*, Loomis' *Practical Astronomy*, and half a dozen works actually compiled or written by members of the staff. Martin, Billequin, and Wang Feng-tsao (the most eminent of the early graduates) each translated four or five of these publications.[144]

The T'ung-wen Kuan never succeeded in achieving the degree of influence in Chinese life hoped for it by a few foreigners such as Martin and Hart and by its Chinese (actually Manchu) founders, Prince Kung and Wen-hsiang. A major educational role for such an unorthodox institution was impossible during the nineteenth century because of the unfavorable intellectual atmosphere in which it was compelled to operate. In the face of the opposition, even scorn, of an overwhelming majority of the literati who dominated Chinese society and government, it was difficult to recruit promising students and no less difficult to place graduates in positions of influence.

When both its strengths and its weaknesses are considered, it seems to me that the T'ung-wen Kuan was anything but a failure. It manned China's new foreign service, both at home

[144] 1888 and 1898 *Calendars*.

and abroad, almost as rapidly as the service developed; it supplied teachers for its own use and for other modern government schools; and through its graduates and publications it contributed to the spread of modern ideas. Finally it was in the end the model for the new Peking university, which was to become within two decades the center of an epochal and vigorous cultural renaissance and within four decades one of the great educational institutions of the world.

III

Education and Training at

the Kiangnan Arsenal

Shanghai T'ung-wen Kuan

IN Chapter I it was noted that Feng Kuei-fen, an enlightened educator of Soochow and Shanghai, early advocated the establishment of schools in Shanghai and Canton to teach prospective officials foreign languages and mathematics so that China might be better prepared to deal with the Western powers. Upon learning of the proposal, made early in 1861, to establish the T'ung-wen Kuan in Peking, Feng wrote an essay entitled "On the establishment of a T'ung-wen Kuan in Shanghai," [1] in which he deplored the dependence of the Chinese government

---

[1] *Chiao pin-lu k'ang-i*, pp. 99–101. This essay is presumed to have been written in 1861 because the preface of the collection in which it was published is dated 1861.

upon the ill-educated and unscrupulous Chinese "linguists" who hung about the treaty ports and whose knowledge of Chinese was negligible and of foreign languages no better—the latter having been acquired in foreign business houses or missionary schools. He stated that the bannermen trained in the Peking T'ung-wen Kuan would be too few to meet the needs of the provincial governments, which also had constantly to deal with foreign officials. He therefore urged that intelligent and literate youths under fifteen years of age be recruited from the regions about Shanghai and Canton and sent to schools to be set up in those cities where foreign-language books and newspapers were plentiful and where there were many foreigners with whom the students might practice speaking. He proposed that foreigners be employed to teach the foreign languages and that Chinese scholars be appointed to teach the Chinese classics and Chinese history, literature, and the arts, in the expectation that after three years of study the better students would go on to the national capital to take the civil service examinations. Thus there would be placed in the official system men who knew foreign languages and were familiar with Western conditions, manners, and customs, with the result that China's position in international dealings would be greatly strengthened.

Since Feng Kuei-fen was at the time advising Li Hung-chang (superintendent of trade for the southern ports and governor of Kiangsu), it is to be presumed that he influenced the latter's memorial of March 11, 1863, urging that a T'ung-wen Kuan be established in both Shanghai and Canton.[2] In this memorial, which incorporated large sections of the Feng essay paraphrased in the foregoing paragraph, Li contrasted the practice of foreign governments, which used as interpreters their own

[2] *Kuang fang-yen Kuan ch'üan-an*, pp. 1–4 (cited hereafter as KFYK); IWSM, TC 14, pp. 2–5; partial translation in Teng and Fairbank, pp. 74–75. The memorial was presented to the Throne on March 28.

officials who had learned the Chinese language and had studied Chinese history and institutions, with that of the Chinese government. The Chinese government, he wrote, when dealing with foreign diplomats had to depend either upon the same foreign interpreters or upon Chinese "linguists" picked up in the treaty ports who through their own ignorance or in order to profit personally were the cause frequently of grave misunderstandings. In almost the same words as the Tsungli Yamen had used in proposing the original T'ung-wen Kuan, Li deplored official Chinese ignorance of foreign conditions and intentions. And he praised the establishment of the Peking T'ung-wen Kuan as a positive step forward, expressing the belief that it ultimately would produce talented men who by mastering Western knowledge would contribute to Chinese control of the behavior of the foreigners in China.

Li requested the Emperor to authorize the establishment of language schools in Shanghai and Canton similar to the one in Peking. He proposed to recruit youths under the age of fourteen who would be taught foreign languages by foreigners and given a classical Chinese education by selected Chinese degree-holders of character and learning. Upon completion of their training they should be allowed to take the regular civil service examinations and be assigned to provincial offices that needed personnel with this type of training. Li expressed the hope that instruction in foreign languages would ultimately provide a key to Chinese mastery of Western mathematics, physics, and technology, preparing the way for the construction of steamships and the manufacture of firearms in China. He asked that responsibility for the Shanghai T'ung-wen Kuan be assigned to the Shanghai customs intendant. And he stated that, if authorized to establish the school and to earmark a portion of the tonnage dues on shipping to cover salaries, food allowances, and other costs, he and the customs intendant would draw up plans. On April 11 Li's memorial was returned to him with an Imperial edict authorizing the Shanghai school.[3]

On June 15, 1863, Li Hung-chang and the customs intendant at Shanghai jointly reported that a site had been selected in the city of Shanghai for a local T'ung-wen Kuan and that materials and workmen for its construction had been obtained; moreover, since the provincial authorities were unable to supply the eight thousand taels it was estimated the school would require annually, it would be necessary for the customs to appropriate that amount from the shipping tonnage dues, as suggested in Li's earlier memorial. Finally, a set of twelve regulations for the operation of the new school was enclosed.[4]

This first set of regulations stipulated that applicants for admission to the Shanghai T'ung-wen Kuan must be not more than thirteen years of age (14 *sui*), of "superior intelligence and character," and recommended by reputable officials or gentry. Applicants, after registering at the school and submitting the required papers—including a family record going back three generations—would be sent to the Shanghai intendant for an entrance examination. A maximum number of forty students was set for the school, but a waiting list was to be maintained from which vacancies would be filled. The students were to live at the school, and their goings and comings, vacations, and leaves of absence because of mourning or sickness were to be strictly controlled. Provision was also made for admission to

[3] KFYK, p. 4; IWSM, TC 14, p. 5. The edict answering Li Hung-chang's memorial actually mentions only the Canton school; but since it refers to Li's memorial asking for authorization of both schools and was sent to him in Shanghai, it clearly was intended to apply to both schools. Li Hung-chang acted upon that interpretation, at any rate. The edict states that the students admitted to such schools must specialize in foreign languages. And it warns against allowing foreign teachers secretly to teach Christianity or otherwise deceive their students.

[4] KFYK, pp. 5–9.

the school of not more than ten special students selected from among junior officials awaiting assignment to office and adult members of the gentry.

The teaching staff was to comprise: a president (*tsung-chiao-hsi*), a Chinese "learned gentleman of superior character"; two "learned Englishmen" as English professors; and four holders of at least the first civil service degree as professors of Chinese. The appointment of a French professor was to be deferred. Four Chinese "thoroughly acquainted with foreign languages" were to live in the school to help explain the lectures of the foreign professors to the students.

The curriculum was to include English, mathematics, the Confucian classics, Chinese history, and Chinese composition —the first two to be studied every day and the others in whatever time remained and according to the individual needs of the students. All subjects except foreign languages were to be taught by the Chinese professors. Particular emphasis was laid on the study of mathematics, which was recognized as the basis of Western technological achievement; specialization in mathematics was to be not only permitted but encouraged. Oral tests would be given twice a month by the teaching staff, except that the special students (chosen from among junior officials and gentry) were to be examined only by the Shanghai intendant. Prizes of from four to eight taels would be awarded to the best students in order to encourage diligence. The course of study was for three years; at the end of this time students recommended by both their foreign and Chinese professors as capable of translating foreign books and possessing a good Chinese literary style would after examination by the superintendent of trade be awarded the first civil service degree (*sheng-yüan*) and become eligible for appointment as interpreters in the offices of the superintendent of trade or the commissioner of customs.[5] Graduates of outstanding ability might

---

[5] This provision apparently was never put into force.

be recommended by the superintendent of trade for the special provincial civil service examination in Peking. Students unable to translate entire foreign books were to be given the title of *i-sheng* [6] and dropped from the school. The special students, upon completing the three-year course, were also to be eligible for appointment as interpreters.

Administration of the school would be in the hands of a proctor selected from among the educational officials of the government of Shanghai and appointed for a three-year term. He was to be assisted by four deputies, also appointed for three-year terms, who would be in charge of keeping the students' records, checking on all persons entering or leaving the school, overseeing the care of buildings and equipment, and attending to other administrative matters. A picture of Confucius was to be presented to the school, and all students were required to participate in Confucian ceremonies twice a month under the direction of their professors (presumably not including the foreigners).

Annual salaries were set by the regulations as follows: foreign teachers 1500 taels each, the Chinese president 220 taels, and Chinese professors 120 taels each. The students were to receive one-tenth tael per day of attendance—approximately 33 taels per year if there were no absences. The Chinese staff and students were to be supplied with free board and room; and teachers and other employees who held official rank would receive in addition their regular official salaries.[7]

It is difficult to say with any certainty how far these regulations were actually applied. Only one professor of English was appointed at a time—during the first twenty-five years at any rate; the graduates appear not to have been rewarded with

[6] This title was ordinarily given to candidates for the first degree who failed to receive that degree because of a shortage of vacancies (R. H. Mathews, *Chinese-English Dictionary* [1943], p. 455).

[7] KFYK, p. 10.

official rank prior to the 1890's; and the salary of the only foreign professor during the 1860's varied from 110 to 125 taels per month—never more than 1250 taels per year. Some of the other stipulations, however, were rigidly adhered to.

I have not been able to ascertain the names of any members of the original Chinese staff. It seems likely that Chang An-hsing, educational commissioner for the district of Shanghai, who selected the site and supervised the construction of the school buildings, became the first proctor.[8] The first foreign teacher was Young J. Allen, an American missionary, who began instruction in English on March 28, 1864. Allen signed a six-month agreement with the customs intendant to teach six mornings each week at a salary of 125 taels per month, the arrangements having been made by a Mr. Dick, who was commissioner of customs at Shanghai. There were twenty-four students at first, and twenty-six more were admitted in July. Allen wrote in his diary that the first class had already picked up a smattering of English sounds from "one or two pretended linguists among them"; he set about at once to teach the basic principles of the English language and to move rapidly, as soon as these were mastered, through Webster's spelling book and the reading of short sentences to simple translations from Chinese into English. The customs intendant responsible for employing him was replaced by a Cantonese who reputedly disliked foreigners, and Allen's contract was not renewed at the end of the six months. Instead the English instruction was assumed by another Cantonese who was said to have little education in either Chinese or English.[9]

[8] KFYK, p. 6. In February 1867 the proctor was Ying Pao-shih, and in November 1867 Yeh Ch'eng-hsien (KFYK, p. 13).

[9] Allen's diary. I am most grateful to Dr. George R. Loehr, who has made available for my use material from his grandfather's diary. Allen, who was born in Georgia in 1836, graduated from Emory College in 1858, and reached Shanghai as a missionary of the Methodist Episcopal Church, South, in 1860. Because his mission had difficulty raising funds during

In February 1867 Young J. Allen was asked to resume the teaching of English in the Shanghai T'ung-wen Kuan. This time he signed a ten-month contract at 120 taels per month, committing himself to the school from nine to twelve each morning six days a week. On March 8 he reappeared at the school to find a total of thirty-three students, with seven more expected, thus filling the quota. He recorded that he "found the school in a miserably irregular and disorganized state." Setting about to reorganize the English department, he promptly ran into the resistance of the Chinese staff, who had been running the school to suit their own ideas and interests, and of some of the students who had accustomed themselves to dictating their own scholastic ranking regardless of achievement. Allen demonstrated that he "had a will as well as a way," however, and quickly established complete control over the English program. He discovered that the advancement of the students was "very indifferent," that they could neither spell nor read with any correctness. He divided the students into three classes: the first class he recorded as "progressing very well in grammar"; the second class he found "quite deficient . . . owing to the defective mode of their former teacher—a Chinaman"; and the third, he wrote, had "one or two promising young men" and at least one hopeless case that he recommended be discontinued at once.

---

and after the American Civil War, Allen found it necessary to support himself and his family by teaching in the Shanghai T'ung-wen Kuan as well as doing other things. From 1871 to 1881 he worked six days each week at the Kiangnan Arsenal, teaching in the English department in the mornings and working in the translation department in the afternoons; at the same time he edited and published the influential periodical *Wan-kuo kung-pao* (*Review of the Times*) and continued to carry on missionary work. In 1881 he gave up his government positions to become superintendent of his mission and president of its Anglo-Chinese College in Shanghai. He died in 1907 (Warren A. Candler, *Young J. Allen* [1931], pp. 108, 123, 148).

Allen appears to have taken his T'ung-wen Kuan position very seriously. Not only did he experiment with teaching techniques, trying out various types of phrase books and readers and using blackboard exercises, but he went further and undertook to introduce his students to Western science and even to insinuate the principles of Christianity into his teaching. He regularly lectured to his advanced class on scientific and technological subjects, demonstrating such instruments as the telegraph and the galvanic battery, and he took his students to visit the French gasworks, a modern flour mill, and the machine shops at the Kiangnan Arsenal. Like W. A. P. Martin, of the Peking T'ung-wen Kuan, and John Fryer, a later colleague in the Shanghai school, he believed that Western science would greatly help China, and he worked throughout his life to bring knowledge of it to the Chinese people. On March 4, 1867, just before he resumed his position in the Shanghai T'ung-wen Kuan, he wrote in his diary:

Engaged studying chemistry today with a view to making some experiments for the edification of the Chinese and in order to further interest them in matters pertaining to Western Science and religion. If I had the means at command would have me an interesting selection of experimenting apparatus with a view to interesting the more intelligent Chinese to whom I would explain the phenomena thus illustrated and endeavor to show them the folly and falsehood of many of their superstitious beliefs . . . and thereby broaden the way of access if possible for the approach of truth to their minds.

It is surprising that Allen makes no mention in his diary of a teacher of mathematics or of the instruction in mathematics in the school, for that subject must have been taught (by one of the Chinese teachers?) because the members of the first graduating class who were sent to Peking in 1868 demonstrated competence when examined there in that subject. For reading exercises for his students he "ordered some simple and easy books that the missionaries have translated with a view to teaching the elements of Christianity, such as the 'Peep of Day,' 'Henry and his Bearer,' and the 'Two Friends' "—stories that illustrated so-called Christian virtues without being outright religious tracts. "Should no objection be raised to their use," he wrote, "I hope they will not only be useful to teach them English but also the simpler truths of Christianity."

Allen soon discovered that the monetary prizes awarded periodically by the customs intendant to the students who led their classes provided a real incentive to study. He also learned that the customs intendant was examining the first class each Sunday afternoon by having them translate into Chinese the simpler and shorter communications which he himself had received during the preceding week from the American and English consulates. Since each of these documents was submitted in English with an accompanying Chinese translation, the intendant was able to check each student's translation against the one made in the consulate. Allen regarded this as a rather severe test. Finally, during the summer of 1867, he discovered that those of his advanced students who had already acquired the first civil service degree—of whom there evidently were a number—were devoting their time and energy to preparation for the triennial provincial examination for the *chü-jen* soon to be held in Nanking and that they therefore learned little English during the summer quarter.

In February 1868, during the Chinese New Year vacation that followed completion of the school year, Allen was reappointed for another year. This time the contract was for eleven months at a salary of 110 taels per month, but he was granted a two-week summer vacation and holidays at Christmas and the European New Year. There were about twenty-five students in the school when it reopened on February 26; unfortunately for the historian, Allen completely ignored the T'ung-wen Kuan in his diary during 1868 except to refer to reviewing for quarterly examinations in May and to note the ending of the school year on December 29.

On April 14, 1867, the customs intendant, Ying Pao-shih, informed the superintendent of trade, Tseng Kuo-fan, that he had completed the examination of the first class to finish the curriculum and that nine graduates who were already well educated in Chinese had demonstrated their ability to translate a foreign language, that is, English. Unfortunately, he reported, there had been no requests for interpreters from officials at the various ports, as had been anticipated when the school was established, and the problem was what to do with the graduates. He noted that the Tsungli Yamen had recently expressed its need for this kind of talent and suggested that the names and records of the graduates be sent to the capital for consideration by that office. It happened that the six best graduates already held the first civil service degree; the intendant therefore urged that after passing the tests of the Tsungli Yamen they be rewarded with secretaryships in the Grand Secretariat or clerkships in the National Academy in order to encourage other students.[10]

The first reply of the Tsungli Yamen was to the effect that the new department of astronomy and mathematics at the Peking T'ung-wen Kuan, to which such students would normally be sent, was not yet open; the graduates should, therefore, continue their studies in Shanghai until summoned.[11] However, in a memorial submitted to the Throne on October 12, 1867, the Tsungli Yamen noted the poor preparation of the students now in the new department of the Peking school—deploring especially their complete ignorance of a foreign language—and urged that the oustanding graduates of the Shanghai and the Canton T'ung-wen Kuan be called to the capital to study in the new department. The proposed action

[10] KFYK, pp. 11–12.   [11] KFYK, p. 13.

was promptly authorized by the Throne.[12] Accordingly, on November 22, the six best Shanghai graduates were ordered to Peking. One of the students, who was on mourning leave because of the death of his father, was allowed to postpone his departure until a later date.[13]

The five Shanghai graduates reached the national capital on April 1, 1868. They were lodged in the new department of astronomy and mathematics of the Peking T'ung-wen Kuan and were examined in both mathematics and English and declared competent. On July 12 the Tsungli Yamen, following the suggestion made a year earlier by Ying Pao-shih, nominated the two *sheng-yüan* among them to be secretaries in the Grand Secretariat and so eligible to take the provincial examination for the *chü-jen;* the three *chien-sheng* were nominated as clerks in the National Academy.[14] Thus they were rewarded with official positions which, having only nominal duties, enabled them to continue to study in the Peking T'ung-wen Kuan.[15]

Expansion of Educational Activities

Meanwhile, in the summer of 1865, Governor Li Hung-chang of Kiangsu and the Shanghai customs intendant Ting Jih-ch'ang had rented from Hunt and Company (a foreign firm) a machine shop in the Hongkew section of Shanghai for which additional foreign machinery was imported. This became the Kiangnan

[12] IWSM, TC 50, pp. 35–36.   [13] KFYK, pp. 13–14.

[14] IWSM, TC 59, p. 34. The *sheng-yüan* were Yen Liang-hsün and Hsi Kan; the *chien-sheng* Wang Feng-tsao, Wang Yüan-kun, and Wang Wen-hsiu.

[15] Yen was allowed to return home on a plea of filial responsibility and to seek official employment in his native province (IWSM, TC 60, p. 20). He taught at his alma mater until April 1876, when he was sent to a position in the Navy Yard School at Foochow; he remained there only one year and died shortly thereafter (CCTI, 17, p. 16).

Arsenal,[16] one of the earliest projects of the Chinese government to introduce Western machinery, armament manufacturing, and modern shipbuilding.[17] In the summer of 1867, under orders of Governor-general Tseng Kuo-fan, a plot of more than ten acres of land was purchased on the Hwangpoo River just outside the south gate of the "Chinese City" of Shanghai, and there buildings were erected into which the Kiangnan Arsenal was moved. In reviewing the history of the arsenal in a memorial submitted to the Throne in the autumn of 1868, just as he was being transferred to the governor-generalship of Chihli, Tseng discussed, among other things, steps that had been taken at the arsenal to begin the translation into Chinese of Western books on mathematics, science, and technology. He now proposed the formal establishment within the arsenal of a translation department which should also include a school to train intelligent Chinese youths as translators; this action was authorized by the Throne on November 1.[18]

As will be brought out later, the translation department of the Kiangnan Arsenal came to play a major role, during the next forty years, in the introduction of Western scientific and technical knowledge into China. It is not known whether the school to train translators actually began operation, but in November 1869 the Shanghai customs intendant asked the incumbent superintendent of trade, Ma Hsin-i, for permission to move the Shanghai T'ung-wen Kuan (the name of which, probably at this time, was changed to Kuang fang-yen Kuan) to the Kiangnan Arsenal and to amalgamate it with the translation department's school, since the aims of the two appeared

[16] Closer translation of the official name, Kiangnan chi-ch'i chih-tsao chü, would be Kiangnan Machine Manufacturing Bureau.

[17] IWSM, TC 35, pp. 1–6; NCH, Aug. 16, 1867. For a summary of the early history of the Kiangnan Arsenal see Gideon Chen, *Tseng Kuo-fan, Pioneer Promoter of the Steamship in China* (1935), pp. 43–52.

[18] IWSM, TC 61, pp. 29–31.

to be identical.[19] On December 16 the arsenal authorities were notified that the consolidation had been authorized.[20]

On April 3, 1870, the directors of the arsenal reported to Ting Jih-ch'ang, now governor of Kiangsu and superintendent of trade, that the buildings intended for the use of the school and the translation department had been completed on the new site in January and had been occupied since the end of February. Thereafter the Kuang fang-yen Kuan remained with, but separate from, the translation department, under the administrative control of the Kiangnan Arsenal. The buildings had been paid for from revenues collected by the Maritime Customs, but the school would continue to be supported from the ship tonnage dues.[21] The directors enclosed two sets of regulations covering the curriculum and activities of the Kuang fang-yen Kuan, the translation department, and the other training facilities of the arsenal. These documents give a picture of the broadly expanded educational program contemplated at the time.[22]

Yung Wing, a Yale-educated Chinese who had been sent to the United States by Tseng Kuo-fan in 1863 to buy machinery for the Kiangnan Arsenal and who appears to have proposed to Tseng Kuo-fan the Chinese Educational Mission to the United States mentioned in Chapter I, claims to have suggested

[19] KFYK, pp. 17–18. The literal meaning of Kuang fang-yen Kuan is School for the Diffusion of Languages.

[20] KFYK, p. 18.   [21] KFYK, pp. 19–20.

[22] KFYK, pp. 20–39. Except when other references are cited, the two documents covering regulations are the source of all statements from this point to page 173. John Fryer wrote to his Uncle George and Aunt Mary Ann on Nov. 1, 1869, that "a College has been erected which will accommodate about fifty students who will be instructed in engineering, navigation, military and naval affairs together with chemistry, mineralogy and other such subjects" (Fryer's Letter Journals). A brief summary of the new program appeared in the Jan. 11, 1870, issue of the *North-China Herald*.

this broadening of the Kuang fang-yen Kuan. During Tseng's inspection of the arsenal in 1867, Yung writes:

I succeeded in persuading him to have a mechanical school annexed to the arsenal, in which Chinese youths might be taught the theory as well as the practice of mechanical engineering, and thus enable China in time to dispense with the employment of foreign mechanical engineers and machinists, and be perfectly independent. This at once appealed to the practical turn of the Chinese mind and the school was finally added to the arsenal.[23]

But the progressive scholars Hsü Shou and Hua Heng-fang, who had been associated with Tseng's shipbuilding and other modernization activities from the early 1860's, who had introduced Yung Wing to Tseng Kuo-fan in the first place, and who were now active in the translation department of the Kiangnan Arsenal, probably deserve even more credit for the proposal.[24]

The 1870 regulations made provision for education or training of several kinds and on different levels, the emphasis in all cases being on practical knowledge. First, there was to be on-the-job training, where workmen in the machine shops, shipyard, and arms factory of the arsenal would be taught by foreign (and later by Chinese) engineers and machinists how to operate modern machinery. Secondly, there were to be evening classes at the school where workmen from the arsenal and the crews of ships might improve their technical knowledge. Thirdly, there was to be an expansion of the curriculum of the Kuang fang-yen Kuan to include several scientific and engineering departments. Finally, there was the translation department. As stated in one of the regulations, there were several roads to knowledge: there were to be "those who study in the school, those who learn while working in the shops, those who train aboard ship, and in the future there will be those who go abroad for advanced study."

[23] *My Life in China and America* (1909), pp. 168–169.
[24] *Ibid.*, pp. 137–152; Chen, *Tseng Kuo-fan*, pp. 40–42, 89–91.

There is little information about the program of on-the-job training beyond the statement that it was to be offered and the obvious fact that the arsenal was operated by Chinese machinists and other skilled craftsmen almost all of whom must have acquired their skill right there. Tseng Kuo-fan reported to the Empresses Dowager in 1869 that six or seven French and English mechanics were working side by side with Chinese workmen in the Kiangnan Arsenal at that time.[25] This use of skilled foreigners as instructors in the shops of the arsenal was no doubt continued. At any rate foreign engineers and technicians continued to be employed by the arsenal.[26]

Whether or not the evening classes were actually instituted is not clear. The plan called for two classes, one on machinery and shipbuilding and the other on navigation and naval maneuvers, to be held daily from 6 to 9 P.M. for arsenal workmen and for pilots, sailors, and mechanics from ships—undoubtedly the ships built by and operated from the arsenal—who had mastered their crafts and were considered capable of understanding the lectures. The lectures were to be given by foreign engineers from the staff of the arsenal, and advanced language students were to be assigned as interpreters for the benefit of those who could not understand the foreign language spoken by the teachers.

The plans for the reorganized Kuang fang-yen Kuan called for a much broader curriculum than that of the original Shanghai T'ung-wen Kuan. The first year, the lower-division curriculum was the same for all students except that those who were being trained as interpreters were to study a foreign language. The upper division was to offer seven possible fields of specialization, of which foreign languages and cultures was only one.

[25] Chen, *Tseng Kuo-fan*, pp. 49–50.
[26] See, for example, *Chronicle and Directory for China . . . 1877*, p. 287; *1882*, p. 344; *1889*, p. 422.

The emphasis that had been given to traditional Chinese studies in the Shanghai T'ung-wen Kuan was to continue, especially in the lower division. Those selected as students were required to have been well prepared in the traditional subjects before entering, and it was anticipated that they would be able to pass the regular civil service examinations after graduation. Study of the classics was prescribed and also Chinese history, philosophy, and composition. More than mere reading was expected. The basic works and standard commentaries were to be studied with care and each student's reflections on his reading written down in notebooks to be submitted periodically to the faculty for criticism and evaluation. All students were expected to attend the classes taught by the Chinese professors, and all-day essay-form examinations were to be given once each week.

The *Ch'un-ch'iu* and *Tso chuan* were the classical texts to be studied, together with various standard commentaries on them that were listed in the regulations. Under history, study of the twenty-four dynastic histories was dispensed with as being too long and cumbersome, but the *Tzu-chih t'ung-chien* of Ssu-ma Kuang was to be required reading, being preferred over the shorter and more popular *T'ung-chien kang-mu* of Chu Hsi. Twenty pages of the *Tzu-chih t'ung-chien* were to be studied each day, and upon completing it the students were to turn to the standard supplements that bring the narrative down to the end of the Ming dynasty. A few historical commentaries and other historical works were also listed for study. Various Sung philosophical works were to be studied, beginning with the *Hsiao-hsüeh* and *Chin-ssu lu* of Chu Hsi, continuing through Chu Hsi's collected works, and culminating in the *Hsing-li ching-i,* an eighteenth-century collection of the writings of the Sung school of Confucianism. Finally, great stress was laid on literary composition. Students who could not express their ideas clearly were to be drilled in writing the "eight-legged" essays demanded in the civil service examinations. In the weekly examinations mentioned earlier great attention was to be paid to literary form and expression.

Mathematics not only was one of the "six arts" of traditional Chinese scholarship but was also recognized as basic to Western technological advancement. Therefore it was given a major place in the curriculum of the Kuang fang-yen Kuan. The regulations stipulated that all students in the lower division must study both Chinese and Western mathematics daily because mastery of this subject was essential for China's future development. So important was it considered that students demonstrating unusual proficiency in mathematics were to be excused from the weekly examinations in other subjects to allow more time for its study. The mathematics covered in the regular lower-division curriculum was to include algebra, geometry, trigonometry, astronomy, mechanics, and ten Chinese mathematical manuals collected under the title *Suan ching* (or *Suan-ching shih-shu*).[27]

Lower-division students were also to be required to study "the universal principles" and international law of the non-Chinese world, as well as geography and drawing. Finally, those destined for careers as interpreters were to begin their study of a foreign language. In the regulations particular stress was laid on the relationship of drawing to the study and practice of technical subjects; three unusually competent Chinese draughtsmen had already been appointed as teachers. Although English had been taught from the beginning of the school, French apparently was not introduced until the move to the new arsenal site. German was taught for a few years during the 1870's.

The regulations indicate that the work of the lower division was to be completed within one year. They provided that examinations be given at the end of the first year to determine

[27] See Needham, III (1959), 18 ff.

which students should be advanced to the upper division and which continued at the lower level.

The upper division was to be divided into seven fields of concentration: (1) mineralogy and metallurgy, (2) metal casting and forging, (3) manufacturing of objects of wood and iron, (4) design and operation of machinery, (5) navigation, (6) naval and land warfare, and (7) foreign languages, customs, and institutions. Besides their advanced courses all students in the upper division were expected to continue the studies begun in the lower division. The two divisions together were to be completed in three years although a student might remain two additional years for specialized training.

The old Shanghai T'ung-wen Kuan rules appear to have been continued in part in the reorganized Kuang fang-yen Kuan. The total enrollment was to be forty, with a waiting list of twenty to be drawn upon to replace students who failed to live up to the requirements. At the time of entry students were to be about thirteen years old, and they must be recommended by officials or other members of the gentry. Upon successful completion of the course graduates were supposed to become *sheng-yüan* (actually *fu-sheng*—the lowest in rank of the holders of the first regular civil service degree) and appointed interpreters or given responsibility for foreign affairs —almost certainly in Kiangsu and adjoining provinces. It was proposed that graduates who were outstanding in mathematics, manufacturing (engineering?), or foreign languages be transferred to Peking by the superintendent of trade for special examinations making them eligible for the provincial examination and the *chü-jen* degree or at least that they be granted official titles and assigned either to the Tsungli Yamen or to one of the modern arsenals being set up in the provinces.

The 1870 regulations also stipulated the building up of a strong library in Chinese and foreign languages for use of the school and the translation department and the purchase of scientific instruments of all kinds for teaching purposes. Extensive use of diagrams and charts was recommended, and provision was made for the publication of scientific and technical papers. The proposed regulations were approved by Li Hung-chang, Ma Hsin-i, Ting Jih-ch'ang, and Tseng Kuo-fan, to whom they had been referred for comment, except that Tseng did not see why the graduates should take the provincial examinations—their skill and training, in his view, necessarily being different from those of the regular *chü-jen.*

The translation department of the Kiangnan Arsenal "was established toward the close of the year 1867 mainly through the instrumentality of Mr. Hsü [Hsü Shou] and Mr. Hwa [Hua Heng-fang], natives of Wu-seih [Wusih] and who at that time were on the staff of officials at the Kiang-nan Arsenal." [28] Hsü Shou and Hua Heng-fang, together with Hsü's son Chien-yin, had for some time been reading and discussing various earlier translations of Western writings on mathematics and science in their native city, and the two older men had been associated with Tseng Kuo-fan's first venture in steamship building at Anking in the early 1860's.[29] In 1867 the three men settled in Shanghai in order to carry on their studies near foreigners who could help them. There they became the chief Chinese translator-writers in the new translation department of the arsenal.

These three men were probably the leading Chinese students

[28] John Fryer, "An account of the department for the translation of foreign books at the Kiangnan Arsenal, Shanghai" (reprinted from the *North-China Herald* of Jan. 29, 1880), p. 1. The material here given, unless otherwise indicated, is derived from this pamphlet and from the 1870 Kuang fang-yen Kuan regulations cited above. Fryer's article, "Science in China," in *Nature*, vol. 24 (1881), contains nothing of significance that did not appear earlier in the *North-China Herald*. For additional biographical information about and portraits of the two Hsüs and Hua, see Chen, *Tseng Kuo-fan*, pp. 87–91, and Yang Mo, *Hsi chin ssu-che shih-shih hui-ts'un* (1910).

[29] Chen, *Tseng Kuo-fan*, pp. 40–41.

of Western science and technology of their time. Among them they worked out a "plan for the translation and publication of a series of treatises in the various branches of Western learning. . . . In this manner they hoped not only to instruct themselves, but to diffuse the knowledge they had acquired with so much pains, among their fellow countrymen." The translation project was launched with the employment by the arsenal of John Fryer, who was at the time editing a Chinese newspaper published in Shanghai by the *North-China Herald,* to collaborate with Hsü Chien-yin in the translation of Burchett's *Practical Geometry.*[30] Shortly thereafter Alexander Wylie[31] joined Hsü Shou in the translation of Mains's *Manual of the Steam Engine,* and D. J. Macgowan[32] joined Hua in

[30] John Fryer was born in Hythe, Kent, England, on Aug. 6, 1839, and educated at Highbury College, London. He went to Hongkong in 1861 as a missionary of the Church of England. He served there as principal of St. Paul's College for two years, after which he was professor of English in the Peking T'ung-wen Kuan in 1863–1864. Thereafter he moved to Shanghai, where he was headmaster of the Church Mission Society's Anglo-Chinese School prior to accepting a position with the Kiangnan Arsenal. Besides his duties in the translation department of the arsenal, Fryer edited and published the *Ko-chih hui-pien* (*Chinese Scientific Magazine*) between 1875 and 1892; he was largely responsible for the organization and operation of the Shanghai Polytechnic Institution and Reading Room; he owned and managed the Chinese Scientific Book Depot; and he was a leader in missionary educational circles. In 1896 he left Shanghai to accept the Louis Agassiz professorship of Oriental languages and literature at the University of California in Berkeley. There he taught courses in the Chinese language and literature until his retirement at the age of seventy-five in 1914. He died in Berkeley on July 2, 1928 (Richard G. Irwin, "John Fryer's Legacy of Chinese Writings," unpublished MS, 1950, pp. 2, 5; Biggerstaff, "Shanghai Polytechnic Institution and Reading Room," *Pacific Historical Review,* 25 [1956], 131 ff.).

[31] Wylie, who died in 1887, was an English missionary noted for his knowledge of Chinese literature and for his translations into Chinese. He served for some years as editor of the *Chinese Recorder* (Samuel Couling, *The Encyclopaedia Sinica* [1917], p. 610).

[32] Macgowan (1814–1893) was an American who served successively as a medical missionary, a free-lance lecturer and writer, and a member

the translation of Lyell's *Geology*. These first translations were prepared in the homes of the foreigners concerned, but it was soon clear that such an arrangement was unsatisfactory and, as stated above, quarters for the department were built at the arsenal. Even before those were completed, Fryer was employed to give full time to the translation department,[33] and later Carl T. Kreyer, an American ex-Baptist missionary, was added to the staff.[34] After the Kuang fang-yen Kuan was moved to the arsenal, Young J. Allen, who served as professor of English in that school, was also asked to devote a part of his time to the translation department.[35]

Several articles in the set of sixteen regulations issued in 1870 applied to the translation department. Article 7 ordered the translation of a Western navigational almanac and Article

---

of the Maritime Customs service. He was a distinguished scholar in the Chinese field (*ibid.*, p. 821).

[33] Fryer wrote to his father and sister on May 9, 1868, that he had been appointed "Translator of Scientific Books" at the arsenal at a salary approximating £ 800 per year and was to take up his duties on May 20. On July 11 he wrote to a Cousin Susy that it was a relief to be free from the dull monotonous task of a pedagogue (he had been teaching Chinese boys in the Anglo-Chinese School) and that his new position was useful as well as respectable. "I always loved science," he wrote, "but never have had time or opportunity to cultivate it. . . . I have begun by studying and translating three subjects at once. In the morning I take coal-mining in all its details, in the afternoon I dig into chemistry and in the evening acoustics. The Chinese who are working with me are some of them really clever. . . . There are now three [foreign] translators on the staff, but I am Senior and my salary is highest" (Fryer, Letter Journals). I am indebted to George F. Drake, at the time a student at the University of California, for calling these journals to my attention and for sending me an analysis of their contents and a copy of the Cousin Susy letter quoted here.

[34] Fryer's letter of Dec. 7, 1869, to his brother (Letter Journals). Kreyer was to be paid 200 taels per month.

[35] Allen reported in 1875 that he had ceased teaching in the school when it was moved to the arsenal in 1870 but had been reappointed to the school and appointed to the translation department in March 1871 (Candler, p. 108).

8 the translation and lithographing of Chinese coastal charts prepared in Europe—both for use on Chinese vessels. Article 9 called for a broad translation program to include books on armaments, military training, shipping and other transportation, dredging, coal and iron mining, the circulation of money, and other subjects relating to the people's livelihood. The emphasis, said Article 9, should be on the practical application of mathematics and modern science. Works on diplomatic negotiations were also needed. Russian, French, and German authorities should be translated as well as English. Article 10 stipulated that foreign newspapers should be scanned and articles throwing light on foreign conditions and developments translated. Finally, Article 13 stipulated that the translation department should print its translations, and also reprint important earlier translations, for wide distribution.

Operation of Educational Departments after 1870

I have found no evidence that the full program of educational activities at the Kiangnan Arsenal outlined in the 1870 regulations was ever carried out. In 1881, more than a decade later, the directors of the arsenal reported to the superintendent of trade that there were at that time six teaching departments operating. The first three, English, French, and mathematics, made up what continued to be called the Kuang fang-yen Kuan. The remaining three, military science,[36] naval architecture, and marine engineering,[37] constituted what must have been a kind of technical school. These two schools, though located in and administered by the arsenal, appear to have remained separate from each other, as did the translation department. For one thing, the Kuang fang-yen Kuan continued to receive its financial support (over 500 taels per month in

[36] This may have been the ordnance department (P'ao Hsüeh-t'ang) that was established in 1874 (*Kiangnan chih-tsao-chü chi* [1905], 2, p. 1).
[37] Fryer, "An account," p. 16.

1881) from the Shanghai shipping dues, whereas the technical training departments received their funds (about 300 taels each month) from the maritime customs revenues.[38]

The Kuang fang-yen Kuan continued to concentrate on foreign languages and mathematics, and it fed some of its best graduates into the Peking T'ung-wen Kuan. The 1881 report, mentioned above, states that there were at that time thirty-nine students in the English and French departments—the former divided into two classes and the latter having only one class—and six in the mathematics department. The English curriculum was said to require five years to finish at this time, and it seems probable that those in French and mathematics were of equal length. However, references are found both before and after 1881 to the Kuang fang-yen Kuan as offering a three-year program.

There is relatively little information about the technical teaching departments of the arsenal. In 1881 forty-six students were enrolled in them. Besides the *Four Books* and *Five Classics* of the traditional Chinese curriculum, the students were reported to be studying drafting, mathematics, military science, gunnery, and a foreign language.[39] Fryer complained that, although these technical students began with no knowledge of a foreign language and were taught by foreigners who knew no Chinese, no use was made of the many technical books that had been written or translated into Chinese and published by the translation department of the same Kiangnan Arsenal.[40] In 1879 three foreigners were teaching in this division of the arsenal school: J. M. Allan, who taught engineering science; L. Bretschneider, military science; and John Rennie, shipbuilding.[41]

In 1881 the military science department was transformed

[38] KFYK, pp. 51–52, 53.   [39] KFYK, p. 52.
[40] "An account," p. 16.
[41] *North China Desk Hong List, 1879,* p. 18.

into an artillery battalion (P'ao-tui ying), which evidently was a training unit since it was made up in part of gunnery trainees (p'ao hsüeh-t'u). At some unidentified time the remaining technical departments were either replaced by or transformed into what was called the drafting division (Hua-t'u fang), which trained young men to design machinery for the various operating divisions of the arsenal. The drafting division ordinarily consisted of more than ten students, who studied Chinese, a foreign language, mathematics, and drafting, and twenty young apprentices drawn from various shops of the arsenal.[42]

The teachers of foreign languages in the Kuang fang-yen Kuan were drawn mainly from the staff of the translation department of the arsenal. Young J. Allen's primary responsibility was to the school, in which he taught English, although he also did some translating. John Fryer's responsibility was primarily to the translation department although he also taught French in the school. Carl T. Kreyer, besides his work in the translation department, also taught German in the school for several years during the 1870's, but after his resignation to accept a position as interpreter for the Shanghai intendant, that language was dropped. In 1879 the Shanghai intendant, in answer to an inquiry that had originated with the Tsungli Yamen, informed the superintendent of trade that there was no likelihood that instruction would soon be offered in either German or Russian.[43] By 1881 there was no foreigner teaching in the school. English was being taught by Shu Kao-ti (referred to by Fryer and other foreigners as Dr. V. P. Suvoong), a native of Che-

[42] *Kiangnan chih-tsao-chü chi*, 2, pp. 1, 3, 43. As early as 1875 Li Hung-chang reported to the Throne that several tens of apprentices in the Kiangnan Arsenal had been selected to live in the Kuang fang-yen Kuan to study both Chinese and Western subjects (Li Hung-chang, 26, p. 15). They were no doubt assigned to the technical teaching departments.

[43] KFYK, pp. 46–47

kiang who had spent more than ten years in the United States, during which time he had secured an M.D. degree, and who had become one of the principal translators in the translation department; mathematics was taught by Liu I-ch'eng, a Kiangsu scholar; and French by Ku Wen-tsao, a native of Shanghai who had studied at the Foochow Navy Yard School. Ku evidently was not satisfactory, for the Chinese minister to France had been requested to engage a French teacher.[44] The minister must have been successful, for a French lawyer named Boyer came to teach French and international law in the school; after a brief sojourn he was succeeded for an undetermined period by another Frenchman named Alphonse Bottu.[45] In 1895 English was being taught by Shu Kao-ti and Feng-i, the latter an early graduate of the Peking T'ung-wen Kuan, and French by a Mr. Yü.[46] Shu Kao-ti was teaching English in 1900, and he continued to do so until 1905, when the school seems to have been discontinued. Yu Hsiao-k'ai (Yeou Hsio Kaë) taught French for a while at the end of the

[44] KFYK, pp. 51–52.

[45] Kan Tso-lin is my authority regarding the appointment of Boyer. Kan says that Bottu taught in the school only two years before resigning to take a position in the Shanghai French Concession (*Tung-fang tsa-chih*, vol. 11, no. 6 [Dec. 1914], 24). Lu Cheng-hsiang, who attended the Kuang fang-yen Kuan between 1884 or 1885 and 1891, implies that he studied with Bottu during much of that time (Lou Tseng-tsiang, *Souvenirs et pensées* [1945], p. 22). The *Chronicle and Directory for China . . . 1882* (p. 344) lists one Koo Shewti (possibly a different version of Ku Wen-tsao?) as teacher of French in that year. Bottu is listed as professor of French in the 1889 issue of the same directory. Unfortunately I have not had access to the intervening issues. I am indebted to Dr. T. L. Yüan for calling the Lou book to my attention. Both Kan and Lu indicate that Bottu was an unusually successful teacher.

[46] Fryer, *Educational Directory*, p. 84. Kan Tso-lin may be right in saying that a Mr. Bebelmann taught French for a year or so after Bottu's departure in the 1880's, but he is clearly wrong in saying that French instruction ended thereafter.

century and was replaced by Wu Tsung-lien (On Tsong Lien),
who taught it for a year or two.[47]

It was noted earlier that the Shanghai T'ung-wen Kuan had
trouble placing its graduates, and this problem continued to
plague the Kuang fang-yen Kuan. Although I have found only
one reference to the actual employment of graduates other
than those sent to Peking for advanced training, it is difficult
to believe that at least the best of those remaining were not
used locally by the Chinese government as interpreters or
specialists in foreign affairs. The one reference is in a document written by the Shanghai customs intendant on August
9, 1890, which lists six graduates recommended to Peking in
1888 who were not promptly called and had taken positions in
customs offices in various parts of the country.[48]

In a statement of the directors of the arsenal dated in 1881
it was disclosed that a number of students who had completed
the course prior to 1879 had not been able to find suitable
positions and had therefore remained in the school, where
they devoted all their time to studying Chinese subjects in
preparation for the regular civil service examinations, and
that most of them had forgotten the foreign languages they
had been taught. Since it was not the purpose of the Kuang
fang-yen Kuan to train persons for the regular civil service,
those of this group who had kept up their foreign languages
had finally been assigned to translation work—possibly in
the translation department of the arsenal—and the rest had
been dismissed from the school to make room for new stu-

[47] *Chronicle and Directory for China,* 1900 to 1906 issues. Yu was one
of the six graduates of the Foochow Navy Yard School who studied
French and international law in France from 1886 to 1892. Wu was sent
to Peking in 1879 after graduating from the Kuang fang-yen Kuan and
later graduated from the T'ung-wen Kuan (1931 *Who's Who in China,*
p. 452).

[48] Kaiping, Yünnan, Kwangtung, and Korea—still a Chinese tributary
—are mentioned (KFYK, p. 67).

dents.[49] Evidently shocked to learn of this waste, the governor-general of Liang-chiang, Liu K'un-i, on May 13, 1881, ordered the officials responsible to keep his office informed of those students in the arsenal schools who distinguished themselves in the study of Western languages, mathematics, and military and naval science so that their knowledge might be utilized for the benefit of the state. Such talent, he said, should be carefully nurtured and not allowed to be scattered. He particularly deplored the loss of the services of such trained Chinese to foreigners, who apparently were ready to offer employment to graduates who did not find government positions.[50]

The reward for outstanding achievement in the Kuang fang-yen Kuan was an appointment to the Peking T'ung-wen Kuan for advanced study. But this reward was not often given. The first group of five graduates sent to the capital in 1868 has already been mentioned. Other small groups went in 1871, 1879, 1888, 1891, and sometime after May 1894.

In the summer of 1871, in compliance with a request from the Peking T'ung-wen Kuan, the Kiangnan Arsenal dispatched seven graduates of the English department, six of whom already possessed the *sheng-yüan* degree and one the *chien-sheng*.[51] There was not another call until 1879, when Peking expressed interest in graduates of the French department. This was the principal language of diplomacy, said the Tsungli Yamen, but there were few students of French in the T'ung-wen Kuan and more were badly needed. The Shanghai customs intendant reported that there were at the time only four students in the French department of the Kuang fang-yen Kuan, of whom only two had completed the course. These two were promptly examined by the intendant, granted travel funds and extra salary, and ordered to sail for the north in October.[52]

[49] KFYK, p. 52.   [50] KFYK, p. 53.
[51] KFYK, pp. 42–45. Chu Ke-jen, Wang Tsung-fu, Yang Chao-ying, Li Tzu-hsiang, Hsü Kuang-k'un, Chin Jen-shu, Yang Chao-chün.
[52] KFYK, pp. 46–50. Wu Tsung-lien and Huang Chih-yao.

Seven years later, on December 23, 1886, the arsenal submitted to the customs intendant another list of Kuang fang-yen Kuan graduates—five in English, six in French, and four in mathematics—which was forwarded to the Tsungli Yamen with the request that they be called to the capital. Nothing having come of this proposal, the intendant wrote to the superintendent of trade on April 10, 1888, asking him to press the Tsungli Yamen to act. He again urged that all fifteen graduates be called, but at the same time he drew special attention to the four from the mathematics department, recalling that the Tsungli Yamen had the year before secured Imperial sanction for scholars who had mastered mathematics to be sent to the Peking T'ung-wen Kuan, where they would be examined by the Tsungli Yamen and then allowed to take the provincial civil service examination.[53] He pointed out that this was the year of the triennial provincial examinations and that these students could reach Peking in time to be examined if there was no further delay.[54]

In a memorial submitted to the Throne on May 15, the Tsungli Yamen reported a request of the superintendent of trade for the southern ports that Kuang fang-yen Kuan graduates in mathematics be brought to the Peking T'ung-wen Kuan and allowed to take the provincial examination. The Tsungli Yamen acknowledged the legitimacy of this request, saying that the superintendent of trade for the northern ports had been permitted under the new rules concerning examinations in mathematics to send graduates of the Tientsin Naval Academy to the Yamen for examination. Those mathematics graduates of the Shanghai school who had already won the first civil service degree and had a superior literary style were therefore to be sent to the Tsungli Yamen for testing preparatory to taking the examination for the *chü-jen* degree. As there was no room for these students in the T'ung-wen Kuan, according to the Tsungli Yamen, they would not be assigned to that

[53] See Chap. I, pp. 28–29.   [54] KFYK, pp. 60–61.

school.[55] The directors of the Kiangnan Arsenal were informed of this decision on June 9, 1888, and on July 27 it was announced that the four mathematics graduates, all of whom had previously earned the degree of *sheng-yüan,* had received their papers and would leave shortly for the capital.[56]

The students of English and French were not forgotten, however. A year later, on May 16, 1889, the Tsungli Yamen took note of the appeal it had received from Shanghai in December 1886 and gave instructions that a few Kuang fang-yen Kuan students of English and French who were skilled at translating should be sent to the T'ung-wen Kuan. One or two good translators of Russian and German would be welcome, too, it said, but no mathematicians were wanted at this time.[57] The order evidently proved embarrassing to the arsenal authorities, for there was no response for more than a year. Finally, on August 9, 1890, they wrote to the Shanghai intendant that they had three graduates in English and four in French ready to send. In the time since the original list of eleven graduates in English and French had been submitted, they said, two had died and six had taken positions elsewhere. They pointed out that neither Russian nor German was taught in the Kuang fang-yen Kuan.[58] The members of this group were ordered to report to the intendant on August 22 for final testing, and they were all sent to Peking the following year.[59]

In 1893 the arsenal authorities and the customs intendant

[55] KFYK, p. 63.

[56] KFYK, p. 66. Chu Cheng-yüan, Hu Wei-te, Yeh Yao-yüan, and Li Hsi-en were the four. It seems likely that they proceeded to Peking and took the provincial examination there, but I have found no record of it, and none of the four is listed as a student or graduate of the T'ung-wen Kuan. One of them, Hu Wei-te, probably won the *chü-jen,* for he advanced rapidly in the government, as will be noted later in this chapter.

[57] KFYK, pp. 61–62.   [58] KFYK, p. 67.

[59] KFYK, p. 68. Chu Ching-i, Yang Shu-wen, and Ch'en I-fan were the English graduates; Liu Ching-jen, Liu Shih-hsün, Lu Tseng-hsiang (known later as Lu Cheng-hsiang), and Chai Ch'ing-sung the French. All seven names appear in the 1893 or 1898 T'ung-wen Kuan *Calendar.*

raised with the superintendent of trade the matter of adequate rewards for the graduates of the Kuang fang-yen Kuan. They recalled that it had been stipulated when the school was established in 1863 that the better students, upon completing the course, would be summoned to Peking by the Tsungli Yamen to be examined and to continue their studies in the T'ung-wen Kuan. Yet during the intervening twenty-eight years, they said, only a few more than twenty (actually twenty-five) had been sent to the capital in only four groups (actually five, though the four mathematicians sent in 1888 and the seven language trainees sent in 1891 may have been counted as only one group). Now word had come from the Tsungli Yamen that the Peking T'ung-wen Kuan was overcrowded and that no more students should be sent from Shanghai. Under these circumstances, what was to be done to encourage these students? They were naturally disappointed to be left to languish in the school after devoting three years to learning a foreign language (the five-year curriculum introduced in 1881 evidently had been abandoned). As they grew older, they felt increasingly frustrated; some accepted other positions, thus wasting their training and balking the purpose for which the school had been founded. The attention of the superintendent of trade was called to the Canton T'ung-wen Kuan, whose graduates were reported to be examined locally at the end of their three-year period of training and given a first degree —either a *fan-i sheng* or a *chien-sheng* [60]—and so were eligible to take the provincial examination for the *chü-jen*. The authorities of the Kuang fang-yen Kuan asked that the same procedure be authorized for the graduates of the Shanghai school.[61]

[60] The first of these had been invented for bannermen; the second may have been the *en-chien-sheng* that was occasionally bestowed upon students in the banner schools (Chung-li Chang, p. 13).

[61] KFYK, pp. 69–70.

A request for information regarding the current practice at the Canton school addressed to the Kwangtung authorities by the superintendent of trade elicited a report that examinations had in fact been given by the governor-general, intendant of customs, and commanders of the Canton banner garrison regularly every three years since the opening of the school, most recently in 1892, and that one of the first degrees (*sheng chien* was the term used) had been awarded each time to the better students, permitting them to enter the provincial civil service examination even while continuing their studies in the school. Moreover, the teachers and those students who were most promising as officials were formally recommended to the Emperor for rewards, and they were to have their names registered for official positions.⁶² Upon receipt of this information the superintendent of trade for the southern ports petitioned the Tsungli Yamen to extend the same privilege to graduates of the Kuang fang-yen Kuan. This request was acceded to in a reply received by the superintendent on August 10, 1893, which merely stipulated that the students so rewarded be selected with care in order not to fill the official system with incompetents. There is no clear indication whether the *fan-i sheng* or the *sheng-yüan* degree was to be granted in addition to the *chien-sheng*.⁶³

On February 2, 1894, the arsenal authorities notified the Shanghai intendant that fifteen more Kuang fang-yen Kuan students had completed the three-year course and asked that

⁶² KFYK, p. 71.

⁶³ KFYK, pp. 72–73. The general term *sheng chien* was the only one used in the discussion relating to the Shanghai school. This term was used interchangeably with *fan-i sheng* and *chien-sheng* in describing the degrees awarded to Canton T'ung-wen Kuan graduates; but it was also used elsewhere as an abbreviation for the *sheng-yüan* and *chien-sheng* degrees. Since none of the Shanghai students were bannermen (whereas all the Canton students were), it would seem to have been improper to award them the *fan-i sheng* degree that had been created for bannermen.

they be examined and recommended for the first degree (*sheng chien* was again used) following the precedent of the Canton T'ung-wen Kuan.[64] Thirteen were examined, four in English, six in French, and three in astronomy and mathematics,[65] but there is no indication of how many degrees were actually awarded. At least three of the French graduates in this class must later have been sent to Peking, for their names appear among the students listed in the 1898 T'ung-wen Kuan *Calendar*.[66]

The last document in the *Kuang fang-yen Kuan ch'üan-an*, the collection from which most of my material on the Shanghai arsenal schools is derived, is a set of ten "recently modified and simplified regulations" of the Kuang fang-yen Kuan that appears to have been appended to the May 27, 1894, communication of the Shanghai customs intendant to the directors of the arsenal. A new department of astronomy was said to have been added to the three older departments of English, French, and mathematics, although I have found no later reference to it. The original limit of forty students, with a waiting list of ten, was retained for the three older departments; no figure was given for the number that might enroll in the new one. The students in all four departments were expected to devote themselves to Western learning and mathematics during the first four days of each week and to traditional Chinese subjects the remaining three days, studying eight hours each day. Those discovered neglecting their Western studies and studying only Chinese subjects were to be transferred to traditional schools. Provision was made for three-month and six-month trial periods for new students; at the end of the first the unpromising ones would be dropped, and at the end of the second the surviving students' stipends would be increased. Monthly quizzes were to be given in the school, and examinations were to be conducted

[64] KFYK, p. 15.   [65] KFYK, p. 77
[66] Ch'en Szu-ch'ien, Hsü Shao-chia, and Tai Ch'en-lin.

by the customs intendant and directors of the arsenal three times each year as in the past. The students who ranked high in these were to be rewarded, and any listed at the bottom of the class three times would be dismissed. Leaves of absence were to be strictly limited, and immorality, quarrelsomeness, laziness, and truancy would be punished after the first offense and result in dismissal after the second.

The Tsungli Yamen was to continue to receive the names of recommended graduates of the English and French departments for examination and admission to an additional three-year course in the Peking T'ung-wen Kuan. Upon completion of the course, the graduates would be assigned to diplomatic posts abroad or in the provinces. It is puzzling to find no mention here of the granting of a first civil service degree to the graduates of these departments as authorized during the previous summer, but this set of regulations may actually have predated that action. These regulations seem to indicate that students had to hold a first civil service degree to be eligible to enter the mathematics department. In any event, it was taken for granted that all mathematics students had the first degree, and the regulations stipulated that they were to be sent to the Tsungli Yamen each triennial examination year to take the provincial examination in the national capital. No provision was made in these regulations for graduates of the new astronomy department, but since they were grouped with the mathematicians by the Shanghai intendant in his 1894 list, it may be supposed that they were to be similarly treated.[67]

Attached to these regulations is a table of salaries which provided for the following teaching and administrative staff: one director, one examiner, three professors of Chinese, one professor of English and translator, one tutor in English and assistant translator, one professor of French and translator, one professor of mathematics, one tutor in mathematics, one pro-

[67] KFYK, pp. 77–79.

fessor of astronomy and translator, one tutor in astronomy and assistant translator, and one librarian. It should be noted that some of the professors and tutors were expected to divide their time between the Kuang fang-yen Kuan and the translation department of the arsenal, as had been customary from the time the school was moved into the arsenal.[68]

In what seems to have been 1898 a proposal that the Kuang fang-yen Kuan be combined with the artillery battalion to form a Kung-i Hsüeh-t'ang (School of Technology) within the Kiangnan Arsenal was considered by its director, Lin Chih-tao. He said that the arsenal had for more than thirty years been a center of technological development in China and that he therefore regarded it as an appropriate location for a technical training school comparable to the schools of technology that had been established in Japan. Because of the special status of the Kuang fang-yen Kuan under the Shanghai customs intendant, he declared, it could not be absorbed by the proposed school; however, such a school could be created by consolidating the artillery battalion and the drafting division, both of them supported by funds over which the arsenal exercised control.

Director Lin thereupon outlined a plan for a Kung-i Hsüeh-t'ang that would add courses in chemistry and mechanics to the instruction already being offered in Chinese, English, mathematics, and drafting by the drafting division. Five Chinese specialists in modern technical subjects were to be appointed to the teaching staff, with provision for the employment of foreigners to give advanced instruction when expansion would make it possible. Fifty students could be supported by the available funds, and control of the new school would be assigned to the director of the Kuang fang-yen Kuan. The equipment of the operating departments of the arsenal would be made available for teaching purposes, and other

[68] KFYK, pp. 79–80.

equipment such as chemical instruments, machine models, charts, and so on would be purchased. The translation department would be encouraged to step up its activities in order to supply books needed by the new school. Liu K'un-i, governor-general of Liang-chiang, approved the proposal, and the school was established.[69]

The translation department of the Kiangnan Arsenal maintained an active and independent existence even though it shared a building and some of its staff with the Kuang fang-yen Kuan. I have not been able to ascertain the exact number of books that were translated from foreign languages or written in Chinese and published by this department because late lists of publications do not include all the titles that appeared in earlier lists. The latest list I have seen is undated, but it probably was issued about 1910 since it contains 26 titles that were not listed in the *Kiangnan chih-tsao-chü chi* published in 1905.[70] This later catalogue lists 200 titles, plus a quarterly periodical and two arsenal catalogues. Of the 200 titles, 27 were reprints of works not originally prepared in the translation department, but the remaining 173 either were translations of foreign-language books, maps, and charts (including a few translations from Japanese and Korean) or were original works written by members of the staff of the translation department. An 1880 list [71] includes 22 titles omitted from the *Shanghai chih-tsao-chü i-yin t'u-shu mu-lu,* and there may have been works published after 1880 which do not appear in the latter list because they had either gone out of print or been superseded. The difficulty of supplying completely accurate data on publications of the Kiangnan Arsenal is further complicated by occasional

[69] *Kiangnan chih-tsao-chü chi*, 2, pp. 42–45. This document is undated, but the context would seem to place it about 1898.

[70] *Shanghai chih-tsao-chü i-yin t'u-shu mu-lu*, 14 pp. My copy was transcribed from a block-print edition in the Kiangsu Provincial Sinological Library in Nanking.

[71] Attached to Fryer, "An account," pp. 22–25.

changes in the titles of books and more often by the combining under a single title in one list of two or more works listed separately in another. Finally, there were a few works translated at the arsenal which for some reason never were published.[72]

The most prolific producer in the translation department of the Kiangnan Arsenal was John Fryer, who translated or himself wrote in Chinese at least eighty-seven works that were published by the arsenal between 1871 and 1902.[73] At least thirty-seven works are attributed to Carl T. Kreyer as translator in the lists that I have examined, fifteen to Young J. Allen, fourteen to Shu Kao-ti,[74] and ten to Alexander Wylie. Sixteen other translators, most of them Chinese, are credited with from one to five works each; and no name at all is attached to a dozen or more works written or translated at the arsenal.

The method of translating or compiling the works published by the arsenal is of some interest. According to Fryer, the translator, if a foreigner or a Western-educated Chinese like Shu Kao-ti, having first mastered the subject of the work to be translated or written, would sit down with a Chinese "writer" and dictate to him

sentence by sentence, consulting with him wherever a difficulty [arose] as to the way the ideas ought to be expressed in Chinese, or explaining to him any point that [happened] to be beyond his comprehension. The manuscript [was] then revised by the Chinese

[72] Richard G. Irwin lists two manuscripts of this description which are in the East Asiatic Library of the University of California at Berkeley ("John Fryer's Legacy of Chinese Writings," pp. 16, 17).

[73] Irwin, p. 5, points out that Fryer maintained an active connection with the arsenal as translator for seven years after taking up his professorship at the University of California in 1896. Dr. Irwin has prepared a bibliography of Fryer's writings in Chinese which includes a total of 138 items, of which 79 were published by the arsenal. My figure of 87 includes all works attributed to Fryer in the *Shanghai chih-tsao-chü i-yin t'u-shu mu-lu,* plus works not in that list but included in the 1880 list cited in note 71.

[74] Referred to by Fryer and the *Chronicle and Directory for China* as V. P. Suvoong and by Tsuen-hsuin Tsien as Hsü Feng.

writer, and any errors in style, etc., [were] corrected by him. In a few cases the translations [were] carefully gone over again with the foreign translator, but in most instances such an amount of trouble [was] avoided by the native writers, who, as a rule, [were] able to detect errors of any importance themselves, and who . . . [took] great pains to make the style as clear and the information as accurate as possible.[75]

The Chinese writers in the beginning were Hsü Shou, Hua Heng-fang, and Hsü Chien-yin, but there were frequent changes and dozens of Chinese served in this capacity during the life of the translation department, some of them becoming leading authorities in the new subjects they helped introduce. In time, not a few of the Chinese writers themselves translated or compiled works that were issued either by the arsenal or by other publishers.

The intention when the translation department was first established was

to prepare an encyclopaedia that should bear some resemblance to the "Encyclopaedia Britannica." It was soon found, however, that many of the treatises in the eighth edition of that valuable work were too elementary and too far behind the times. It became necessary therefore to translate from more modern and complete publications. Various high officials asked to have works translated for them on special subjects. Several treatises not considered sufficiently complete had to be supplemented by larger ones, and hence the idea of an encyclopaedia gradually [was] almost lost, while a miscellaneous collection of translations and compilations embracing but a comparatively limited range of subjects [was] the result. In most cases each translator and Chinese writer seems merely to have selected such subjects as suited him best without regard to the symmetry or harmony of the entire collection.[76]

Of the 173 translations and compilations of the Kiangnan Arsenal listed in the *Shanghai chih-tsao-chü i-yin t'u-shu mu-lu*, 37 are classified under military and naval science; 31

[75] Fryer, "An account," p. 12.   [76] *Ibid.*, p. 11.

under engineering; 12 each under agriculture and medicine; 10 each under chemistry and mining; 7 each under mathematics and ships and shipping; 6 each under science, history, and drafting; 5 each under international law and electricity; 3 each under geology, geography, government, commerce, and education; and 2 each under physics and astronomy. One of the earliest Chinese news periodicals, the *Hsi-kuo chin-shih hui-pien*, was published by the translation department from 1873 to 1899, although its circulation was confined to government officials. It contained only foreign news and was first edited by Carl T. Kreyer; the editorship was taken over by Young J. Allen in 1878 and subsequently by John Fryer. It was issued weekly, but the numbers were bound together quarterly, making four volumes each year.[77]

The translation department had its own printing facilities, using old-fashioned wooden-block printing which was both inexpensive and convenient because the blocks could be stored and additional copies run off quickly by hand as required. In contrast to the translations of the Peking T'ung-wen Kuan, which were distributed without cost to various government offices, most of those of the Kiangnan Arsenal were offered for sale.[78]

The *Kiangnan chih-tsao-chü chi* sets forth in tabular form the provisions for staff, curricula, students, and budgets of the two schools and translation department of the Kiangnan Arsenal as of 1905.[79] The Kuang fang-yen Kuan was authorized to offer instruction in English, French, mathematics, geography, and Chinese subjects. Provision was made for three professors of Chinese subjects and for four professors of Western subjects.

---

[77] Allen letter to Alpheus W. Wilson, quoted by George R. Loehr, "Young J. Allen and mandarins," *Emory University Quarterly*, 4 (June 1948), 105–106; Roswell S. Britton, *The Chinese Periodical Press* (1933), p. 62; Fryer, "An account," p. 24.

[78] Fryer, "An account," pp. 12–13.   [79] Ch. 2, p. 14.

There was a limit of forty students in the regular curriculum and forty in the supplementary curriculum (*fu-k'e*)—whatever the latter may have been. Each required four years to complete; all students were to be between fourteen and nineteen years of age. The annual budget was 9000 taels, with two-thirds of the funds derived from the Shanghai shipping dues and one-third from the resources of the arsenal. The Kung-i Hsüeh-t'ang was divided into chemical engineering and mechanical engineering departments; the curriculum of the former included Chinese, English, and mathematics, that of the latter the same plus drafting. Two professors of Chinese subjects and six of Western subjects were authorized, and the annual budget was more than 9000 taels. A total of fifty students was allowed, and the curricula required four years to complete. The translation department was allowed two translators and three "writers"; it had no fixed budget.

In 1905 Governor-general Chou Fu of Liang-chiang evidently combined the Kuang fang-yen Kuan with the Kung-i Hsüeh-t'ang to form the Kung-yeh Hsüeh-t'ang (School of Technology), carrying out the move that had failed in the late 1890's.[80] Not long afterward the Ministry of War reorganized the Kung-yeh Hsüeh-t'ang to form three military technical schools: a higher school (Ping-kung shih-men Hsüeh-t'ang), a middle school (Ping-kung Chung-hsüeh-t'ang), and a primary school (Ping-kung Hsiao-hsüeh-t'ang).[81]

Shu Kao-ti (Suvoong) and E. T. Williams, the latter an American missionary who later joined the staff of the American

[80] Ting Chih-p'in, *Chung-kuo chin ch'i-shih-nien lai chiao-yü chi-shih* (1935), p. 16, and Hu-Huai-shen, "Shanghai hsüeh-i kai-yao," *Shanghai-shih t'ung-chih-kuan ch'i-k'an,* no. 2 (1933), p. 507, say that the Kuang fang-yen Kuan was changed into the Kung-yeh Hsüeh-t'ang. Chang Po-ch'u, in "Shanghai ping kung-ch'ang chih shih-mo," *Jen-wen yüeh-k'an,* 5 (June 15, 1934), 2, says that the Kung-i Hsüeh-t'ang became the Kung-yeh Hsüeh-t'ang.

[81] Hu, *loc. cit.;* Chang, *loc. cit.*

legation in Peking, were the translators operating the translation department in 1900 and 1901.[82] After 1901 Shu appears to have carried on the task alone at least as late as 1913; the translation department was still in existence after the fall of the Ch'ing dynasty.[83]

Accomplishments

The quality and achievements of the graduates of the Kuang fang-yen Kuan are difficult to judge because information is available for only a few of them. The lists of graduates I have found are those of the comparatively small number who were sent to Peking for advanced study. It was noted earlier that no such demand for interpreters and foreign affairs experts developed in nearby provincial and local governments as had been anticipated when the school was established and that some graduates had no alternative but to take positions with the Maritime Customs or to seek employment with foreign companies. Throughout the history of the Shanghai school there was discouragement among students, graduates, and the officials of the arsenal over the unavailability of official positions for most of those who completed the curriculum. In 1893 A. P. Parker, quoting an article in the *Shen-pao*, wrote that Kuang fang-yen Kuan graduates had been "suffered to drift about among higher officials without permanent employment or hope of promotion, with no prospects but a monthly stipend of three or four taels," and the result was that the students in the school could see little hope for advancement and therefore lost interest in their studies.[84]

Of the twenty-five graduates sent to Peking between 1867

[82] *Chronicle and Directory for China* . . . *1900*, p. 194; *1901*, p. 208; Kan Tso-lin, p. 24.

[83] *Chronicle and Directory for China*, 1902 to 1913 issues. Fryer was listed as a member of the staff on leave of absence until 1908.

[84] "The government colleges of Suchow," *Chinese Recorder*, 24 (Dec. 1893), 582.

and 1890 for advanced study at the T'ung-wen Kuan and/or an opportunity to take the special provincial civil service examination given there, a surprisingly large number rose to positions of importance. Of the 1867 group, Hsi Kan succeeded to Li Shan-lan's chair in mathematics at the Peking T'ung-wen Kuan in 1886 and served as the only Chinese professor in that faculty other than those teaching traditional Chinese subjects until Wang Chi-t'ung was promoted in 1895; and Wang Feng-tsao was Chinese minister to Japan from 1891 to 1894.[85] Wu Tsung-lien, of the 1879 group, was minister to Italy from 1909 to the end of the dynasty.[86] Hu Wei-te of the 1888 group was minister to Russia from 1902 to 1907, minister to Japan from 1908 to 1910, junior vice-president of the Board of Foreign Affairs in 1910, acting minister for foreign affairs in 1912, and minister to France, Spain, and Portugal later the same year.[87] Of the 1890 group Liu Ching-jen was minister to Russia from 1911 to 1918; Liu Shih-hsün was minister to France from 1905 to 1912, minister to Brazil from 1914 to 1916, and vice-minister for foreign affairs in 1913, 1916–1917, and 1920–1922; and Lu Cheng-hsiang was minister to the Netherlands from 1905 to 1907, minister for foreign affairs in 1912–1913, 1915–1916, and 1917–1920, and Chinese representative at the League of Nations in 1922.[88] Of the last group ordered to Peking (in 1894), Tai Ch'en-lin, who was appointed minister to Spain in 1916,[89] appears to have been the only one to attain a high diplomatic post.

It is my belief that the students of the Kuang fang-yen Kuan were of higher quality than those who entered the Peking or the Canton T'ung-wen Kuan because more of them rose to

[85] *Ch'ing-shih kao*, 212, pp. 10–11.   [86] *Ibid.*, pp. 20–21.
[87] *Ibid.*, pp. 15–22; *The China Year Book, 1914*, p. 570.
[88] 1925 *Who's Who in China*, pp. 531–532, 546–547, 563–564; *Ch'ing-shih kao*, 212, pp. 17–18.
[89] *The China Year Book, 1919–1920*, p. 545.

relatively high position than did the students of the other schools.[90] It is possible that the more cosmopolitan atmosphere of the foreign-influenced city of Shanghai made it easier for an unorthodox school to attract good students. John Fryer wrote in 1867 that so many lads were seeking an English education at that time in Shanghai that the local T'ung-wen Kuan could pick the best.[91] Although Lu Cheng-hsiang says that when he entered the Kuang fang-yen Kuan in the early 1880's students there were still regarded as traitors who used a foreign language to betray their country to foreigners, he nevertheless entered.[92] Lu came from an educated Christian family; no doubt he and a number of his fellow students were much better prepared for their studies than the bannermen who filled the Canton T'ung-wen Kuan and the preparatory division of the Peking school.

Some graduates of the Kuang fang-yen Kuan must have found positions in Liang-chiang provincial offices, but with the exception of Wang Tsung-fu, who was listed as an interpreter to the Shanghai intendant in the 1888 T'ung-wen Kuan *Calendar*, I have found no names. One may assume that some of the graduates who were not sent on to Peking contributed to the spread of modern ideas in the Shanghai region, which was and continued to be through the first third of the twentieth century the most modern part of China. It is also likely that some of the graduates of the technical training departments of the arsenal, such as the drafting division and the later Kung-i Hsüeh-t'ang, made a contribution to the modernization of China. Most of the latter group undoubtedly found employment in the machine shops or the shipbuilding department of the Kiangnan Arsenal itself or in government arsenals else-

[90] Only five or six T'ung-wen Kuan graduates who received their entire education in the Peking school can match the achievements of the eight Kuang fang-yen Kuan graduates named in the preceding paragraph.
[91] Letter Journals, July 5, 1867.   [92] Lou Tseng-tsiang, p. 20.

where in the country. But I have found little information about their distribution and none about their individual roles.[93]

There can be little doubt of the great contribution made by the translation department of the Kiangnan Arsenal to the introduction of Western knowledge into China—particularly of scientific and technical knowledge. The isolation of its influence from that of other agencies engaged in translating and distributing such information during the second half of the nineteenth century is not possible, but it must be counted among the principal contributors along with the Society for the Diffusion of Christian and General Knowledge and John Fryer's Chinese Scientific Book Depot and with such periodicals as Young J. Allen's *Wan-kuo kung-pao* (first called the *Globe* magazine and later the *Review of the Times*) and Fryer's *Ko-chih hui-pien* (*Chinese Scientific and Industrial Magazine*).[94] Hsü Shou, Hua Heng-fang, Fryer, and Allen, who were chiefly responsible for the establishment of the translation department and for the pattern of activity within it, believed that the Chinese language was the only medium by which Western knowledge could penetrate China, and they

[93] The amount of actual shipbuilding by the Kiangnan Arsenal was negligible: six small vessels and two 2800 tonners were completed between 1868 and 1876, after which only one more vessel was built—completed in 1885. Even the ordnance activities of this arsenal were somewhat limited, seldom going beyond the manufacture of small arms and gunpowder (Ch'üan Han-sheng, "Ch'ing-chi ti Kiangnan chih-tsao-chü," *Li-shih yü-yen yen-chiu-so chi-k'an*, no. 23 [1951], pp 145–159). Moreover, in contrast to the Foochow Navy Yard during much of its history, there was always foreign engineering direction in the Kiangnan Arsenal. See the *Chronicle and Directory for China*, year after year.

[94] For a valuable brief survey of the translation of Western books into Chinese, see Tsuen-hsuin Tsien, "Western impact on China through translation," *Far Eastern Quarterly*, 13 (1954), 305–327, which is based on his University of Chicago Ph.D. dissertation of 1952 that bears the same title. On the *Wan-kuo kung-pao*, see Britton, pp. 53–56; on the *Ko-chih hui-pien* see Biggerstaff, "Shanghai Polytechnic Institution," pp. 143–146.

devoted all their energy to the preparation and dissemination of Chinese-language materials. They disagreed with a view expressed by some missionaries and other foreigners that China could absorb what the West had to teach through the graduates of missionary schools and of such schools as the T'ung-wen Kuan and the Kuang fang-yen Kuan who had learned a foreign language.[95]

Any exact measurement of the influence of the translation department is difficult. Between 1871, when the first translation was published, and 1880, over thirty thousand copies of its books, in more than eighty-three thousand Chinese volumes, were sold.[96] Besides regular sales, John Fryer reported widespread pirating of arsenal publications, some of which were copied "by photolithography in small characters and sold at absurdly small prices." [97] In consequence of the Sino-Japanese War there was a great increase in the demand for the arsenal's translations, with the result that it proved "impossible to print some of the more popular of them fast enough." [98] Although, as noted earlier, these translations were not used in the technical teaching departments of the Kiangnan Arsenal, possibly because the foreign teachers there could not read Chinese and therefore were unable to judge their usefulness, they were used in the more advanced missionary schools, in the Peking T'ung-wen Kuan, and, almost certainly, in the Kuang fang-yen Kuan. They were also available to Chinese readers in the Polytechnic Institution and Reading Room in Shanghai and in reading rooms set up for interested Chinese in Amoy and Chefoo.[99]

In 1886 the Shanghai Polytechnic inaugurated a prize-essay contest reserved for members of the official class which was

[95] Fryer, "An account," pp. 14–15.　　[96] *Ibid.*, p. 19.
[97] John Fryer, *Catalogue of Educational Books* (1894), p. 8.
[98] John Fryer, in *Chinese Recorder*, 28 (1897), 382.
[99] Fryer, "An account," pp. 16–17.

conducted regularly over a period of twenty years and which demonstrated that an interest in and knowledge of modern science and technology was much more widespread in China, even among the more conservative section of the population, than most observers had believed.[100] It would be of great interest to know which and how many of the leaders of modern China read and were influenced by publications of the translation department, but such information is scarce and elusive. The kind of comment that is helpful is one which Levenson reports regarding Liang Ch'i-ch'ao, one of China's most influential publicists during the first quarter of the twentieth century. Levenson says that in 1890 "the great world began to speak to him [Liang]." On a visit to Shanghai "he was able to examine, though not rich enough to buy, European books translated into Chinese by the translation department of the Kiangnan Arsenal of Shanghai. In an article written six years later, he revealed what a watershed this year of 1890 had been in his life." [101] Although only one of the influences on Liang in this period, the examination of the translations must have given him significant insights into the larger world.

[100] Biggerstaff, "Shanghai Polytechnic Institution," pp. 141–143.
[101] Joseph R. Levenson, *Liang Ch'i-ch'ao and the Mind of Modern China* (1953), p. 17.

IV

The Foochow Navy Yard School

Establishment

ON June 25, 1866, the governor-general of Fukien and Chekiang, Tso Tsung-t'ang, submitted a memorial to the Throne
in which he commented on two memoranda written by foreigners and proposing, among other things, reforms in China's
defenses; these had been sent by the Court in April to a number of high provincial officials for discussion. One memorandum
had been drawn up the year before by Robert Hart, inspector-
general of the Chinese Imperial Maritime Customs; the other,
drafted by Thomas Wade of the British legation staff, had been
submitted in a note to the Tsungli Yamen in March by Sir
Rutherford Alcock, British minister.[1] In the course of his discussion of these memoranda, Tso advanced a proposal that

[1] IWSM, TC 40: Hart memorandum, pp. 13–22; Alcock note, including
Wade memorandum, pp. 22–36; Imperial edict of April 1, ordering discussion, pp. 12–13.

China should build its own ships and train Chinese to operate them. He had for three years, he said, been considering a project for the training of Chinese in shipbuilding and navigation as a means of strengthening China's defenses, and he welcomed this opportunity to present the scheme to the Imperial court.[2]

In a separate memorial of the same date Tso elaborated his project for a naval dockyard where not only ships would be built but shipbuilding and navigation would be taught as well.[3] In this second memorial Tso stated that he had long recognized the importance of the steamship to China, both for coastal commerce and for naval defense. Several years earlier he himself had had a small steamer built at Hangchow by Chinese workmen, but it had not worked well. He had accordingly consulted with two French naval officers, Paul d'Aiguebelle and Prosper Giquel, the latter an employee of the Chinese Maritime Customs, who had agreed to help him build another steamship following a European design; but the loss of Hangchow to the T'aip'ing rebels had postponed that venture. He continued to believe that China must have steamships to strengthen its defenses, but he felt even more strongly that China must also possess the means for building and operating its own ships.

Tso then went on to propose that a complete navy yard be built at the port of Foochow, a key point in the maritime defenses of China, and that all necessary machinery be purchased for equipping it; furthermore, he urged that European engi-

[2] IWSM, TC 42, p. 48. See the biography of Tso by Tu Lien-che in Hummel, pp. 762–767. As early as 1863, Tso expressed his belief that China must build its own steamships (Gideon Chen, *Tso Tsung T'ang: Pioneer Promoter of the Modern Dockyard and the Woollen Mill in China* [1938], p. 11).

[3] Tso Tsung-t'ang, *Tso Wen-hsiang kung ch'üan-chi* (1890–1897), 18, pp. 1–6. For a translation of most of this important document see Teng and Fairbank, pp. 81–83; translated excerpts from it also appear in Chen, *Tso Tsung T'ang*, pp. 12, 20–21.

neers and skilled craftsmen be employed in the beginning to manage the yard and to teach shipbuilding and navigation to Chinese, in the expectation that after five years the services of foreigners could be dispensed with. The Chinese to be trained as engineers, craftsmen, and ships' officers should be, he thought, recruited from all levels of society and subjected to careful training during which the diligent and capable would be pushed ahead and the stupid and slothful dropped. Tso estimated that it would cost 300,000 taels to launch the enterprise and more than 600,000 taels per year to operate it. The required funds, he suggested, might be secured from the maritime customs duties and the likin taxes collected in Fukien, Chekiang, and Kwangtung provinces—each of which would benefit from the resultant naval protection. At this stage he anticipated that steamships built at Foochow might be used as troop carriers and warships in times of trouble and as cargo ships in times of peace, and thus both China's defenses and its economy would be strengthened.

Tso declared that he was not unmindful of the difficulties inherent in such an undertaking: the selection of a satisfactory location, the purchase of adequate machinery and other equipment, the recruitment of dependable foreign personnel, the raising of sufficient funds, the training of Chinese unaccustomed to building and operating steamships, and the need to cope with the slander and criticism that must be expected from those who were unsympathetic or who sought personal political gain from the shortcomings and possible failure of the enterprise. But he felt strongly that China must build such a shipyard, and he was himself prepared to face the risks involved. He declared that although the Chinese at the time lagged behind foreigners in technical competence they were not stupid and they certainly could learn. He rejected the attitude that was widespread among the tradition-ridden bureaucracy that it would be humiliating for China to imitate Western ship construction, recalling that the Chinese had found it advisable two centuries earlier to adopt Western cannon and pointing out that neighboring Japan had already sent people to England to study shipbuilding. He continued:

When steamships are built, the administration of the tax grain transport will be prosperous, military administration will be improved, the distress of Chinese merchants [who cannot now compete with foreigners] will be relieved, and the customs duties will be greatly increased. The temporary cost will produce profit for generations.

On July 14 an Imperial edict authorized the building of a navy yard at Foochow, as urged by Tso Tsung-t'ang, and the purchase of equipment and employment of foreign technicians to teach shipbuilding and navigation.[4]

In a memorial submitted to the Throne on November 19, Tso reported that he had already conducted detailed discussions with Prosper Giquel and Paul d'Aiguebelle, whom he wanted to serve as foreign directors of the enterprise,[5] and that a contract for the construction and staffing of the navy yard was being prepared. Moreover, he requested permission

[4] Tso Tsung-t'ang, 18, p. 14.
[5] Prosper Giquel, "The Foochow Arsenal and its results" (1874), p. 17. Prosper Marie Giquel (1835–1886) was a French naval officer who served in the Baltic and the Crimea during the Crimean War and in China (as a Lieutenant de Vasseau) from 1857 to 1859, at which time he resigned to join the Chinese Imperial Maritime Customs. He was commissioner of customs at Ningpo in 1861 and was in Hankow at the time of his resignation in 1866. He also commanded troops fighting T'aip'ing rebels and was awarded the honorary rank of brigadier general by the Chinese government. Paul Alexander d'Aiguebelle was also a French naval officer who served in China in the late 1850's and commanded troops engaged with T'aip'ing rebel forces (Henri Cordier, *Histoire des relations de la Chine avec les puissances occidentales*, I [1901], 215–216, 251; Wright, *Hart*, pp. 492–493). Robert Hart's support of the Foochow Navy Yard project, which he regarded as a first step toward the modernization of China, is recorded by Wright, *loc. cit.*

to postpone his departure to assume the post of governor-general of Shensi and Kansu, to which he had been newly assigned, until he should be able to complete arrangements for the navy yard and to see its direction in capable hands.[6] With respect to the last matter, the Emperor had already, two days earlier, authorized a brief postponement of Tso's reassignment in compliance with a request from Ying-kuei and Hsü Tsung-kan, Foochow Tartar general and governor of Fukien respectively.[7] Also on November 19 Shen Pao-chen, recently governor of Kiangsi province, was appointed director-general of the Foochow Navy Yard[8] with authority to memorialize the Throne directly;[9] and on December 3 Shen was ordered by the Emperor to take over the post at once even though on mourning leave. In the same edict Director-general Shen's relations with other provincial officials and with his chief subordinates were defined.[10]

On December 30, 1866, several memorials dealing with the navy yard project were received from Tso Tsung-t'ang, as well as two sets of regulations. In his first memorial Tso stated that a contract had been signed with Giquel and d'Aiguebelle (with a French consular officer signing as guarantor) under which they would purchase necessary machinery and other equipment in France, employ foreign engineers and skilled workmen for the navy yard, and manage the enterprise for a period of five years after completion of the plant. (D'Aiguebelle resigned in 1869, after which Giquel served alone as foreign director until the completion of the period of foreign tutelage in 1874.)

[6] IWSM, TC 45, pp. 19–21.   [7] *Ibid.*, pp. 18–19.

[8] *Ch'uan-cheng ta-ch'en.* The Chinese term for the installation means "ship administration," but I prefer the more meaningful translation, "navy yard." The term "arsenal," used by contemporary Western writers, is misleading. Shen was at home in Fukien on mourning leave for his mother. See his biography by Teng Ssu-yü in Hummel, pp. 642–644.

[9] IWSM, TC 45, p. 21.   [10] *Ibid.*, p. 59.

Agreements had also been made locally with both Chinese and foreign contractors for the construction of docks, ways, an iron foundry, school buildings, dormitories, and other necessary structures on a suitable site at Ma-wei, on the estuary of the Min River below Foochow.[11] Tso again pointed out that the project was an expensive one and might not in the end prove successful, and thus it would become a target for criticism. But he felt that it was necessary for China to undertake long-term defensive measures, and he was willing to assume personal responsibility for this one.[12]

At one point in this same memorial Tso stated that a school was to be opened within the navy yard, to be called the Ch'iu-shih T'ang technical division.[13] Foreigners were to be employed to teach English, French, mathematics, and drafting. Intelligent local boys with some literary knowledge were to be invited to study in this school. In the second memorial Tso elaborated on the teaching role of the navy yard. His purpose was not merely to build ships, he said, but to secure mastery of the techniques of shipbuilding and ship operation. It was not enough for one or two men to acquire such knowledge; China must master these crafts so that it would forever afterward be capable of building and handling its own ships. Hence the necessity to set up the technical school and to attract to it intelligent young men who could learn foreign languages; able to read the foreigners' books and understand their mathematics, they would be able to utilize Western methods in China. Tso, aware that there would not be a rush of students for such unorthodox edu-

[11] Because of its location, Chinese writers frequently refer to this navy yard as the Ma-wei yard.

[12] IWSM, TC 46, pp. 19–22. For quotations from agreements signed by Giquel and d'Aiguebelle see Cordier, I, 250–256.

[13] This name evidently was never actually applied to the school, for it is always referred to in subsequent documents as the Navy Yard School (Ch'uan-cheng Hsüeh-t'ang).

cation, proposed that substantial monthly allowances be offered as an inducement and that the work not be too difficult at first.[14]

The second of a set of ten general regulations for the navy yard attached to the memorials submitted on December 30, 1866, relates to the school and reads as follows:

Special treatment for students in the school is desirable in order to develop men of ability. When the school is established, the students must study English and French, master mathematics, and also be able to draw accurately and to understand clearly the principles of construction. Moreover, with thorough study of the commanding and navigation of ships, this school is the place for the perfecting of men of ability. There must be ample monthly stipends in order strictly to enforce the curriculum and generous promotions in order to attract the ablest students into the service. In the future our naval talent will come from this kind of men, who have completed the study of ship construction and navigation. It is suggested that all who complete the study of ship command and those who learn to build ships in conformity with designs be given military rank. Persons in the civil service who enter the school to study shall still be permitted advancement as civil officials, although used in the navy, in order to encourage effort.[15]

The second set of regulations, eight in number, relates entirely to the school. Important provisions not already covered

[14] IWSM, TC 46, pp. 22–23. The contract signed by Giquel and d'Aiguebelle in December 1866 stipulated: "We will guarantee that five years after the workships of the engines [*sic*] shall have commenced to work, the engineers and workmen whom we shall employ will have taught the Chinese officers and workmen to build a ship according to a given plan, and to make machine-tools with the machines placed in the workshops. We will also open a French school, the pupils of which shall learn that language, and enough of mathematics to construct a ship on a given plan; besides, an English school, the pupils of which shall learn that language, and shall prosecute the studies essential to the commanding of ships" (Giquel, p. 17). Obviously this English translation of the original contract leaves something to be desired.

[15] IWSM, TC 46, p. 24.

in the general regulations were as follows. The term of study was to be five years. Classes would meet every day except for three-day vacations at the time of the spring and autumn festivals and a longer vacation at the New Year. The student and his father or elder brother must sign an affidavit of voluntary entry at the time of admission. No long leaves would be granted, nor would students be allowed to change freely from study to a different occupation. Students must be polite and attentive to their teachers, and outside activities that might interfere with their studies were prohibited. Examinations were to be given quarterly by the foreign teachers. Students ranked at the top would be rewarded with prizes of $10; those ranked in the middle were to be neither rewarded nor punished; and those at the bottom would receive one demerit for laziness. Two demerits would lead to punishment, and three to dismissal; three top awards would give an extra award of material for clothing. All students were to receive free board and room and cost of medicines besides a monthly allowance of four taels. Graduates were to be appointed to appropriate positions building or commanding ships at the salaries prevailing for like positions in foreign countries, with unusual talent rewarded by special promotions. Responsible members of the local gentry were to be appointed to remain constantly in the school to monitor diligence or laziness among both students and teachers.[16]

Another memorial of Tso Tsung-t'ang presented on December 30 recommended the assignment to the navy yard of certain officials of Fukien and Chekiang provinces who were experienced in foreign affairs or naval matters; one of the latter was to recruit a crew in Ningpo to be trained to take over the

---

[16] CCTI, 2, pp. 9–10. The plan to use local gentry to supervise the behavior of teachers and students evidently did not work out because the navy yard was too far away from the city of Foochow to permit members of the gentry to spend much time there (IWSM, TC 50, p. 4).

first ship completed and commissioned by the navy yard.[17] Still another memorial shows that the original intention to have three provinces finance the operation of the yard had been changed. The Fukien maritime customs revenues were expected to provide not only the 400,000 taels appropriated for the construction of the Foochow Navy Yard but also 50,000 taels per month to cover all the costs of its various operations, including the school.[18] A final memorial submitted on the same day requested permission for the continued use of Tso's name, even though he had been assigned to a distant governor-generalship, together with that of the Chinese director-general Shen Pao-chen, in memorials relating to the navy yard, in order to satisfy the European directors of the continued support of the undertaking by a powerful and influential official. Giquel and d'Aiguebelle, Tso said, were fearful that without evidence of his continuing connection with the enterprise the required funds might not be forthcoming and other insurmountable obstacles might be encountered. He had told them that should the monthly customs allocation prove to be insufficient there was a 40,000-tael provincial military fund that might be drawn upon, but they wanted firmer reassurances.[19] An Imperial edict issued on December 30 expressed full confidence in the project and sanctioned all of Tso's recommendations. The Foochow Navy Yard was recognized as his creature, and his views concerning it were to be consulted at all times even though he would be stationed far away in the northwest. The senior provincial officials in Fukien were ordered to give the project their fullest support and to do their best to retain the good will and co-operation of the two French directors.[20]

On August 9, 1867, Director-general Shen reported to the Throne that although the construction of the navy yard was proceeding very slowly "the foundation of the navy yard—the

[17] IWSM, TC 46, pp. 26–27.
[18] *Ibid.*, p. 28.
[19] *Ibid.*, pp. 28–29.
[20] *Ibid.*, pp. 30–31.

school" was already in operation and making steady progress.[21] Later, in a memorial presented on September 27, Shen again mentioned the basic importance of the school and reported having examined the young men studying French and English there, promoting and demoting them according to their achievements. He also reported having given instructions that all students in the school study the *Sacred Edict* of the Emperor K'ang-hsi, the *Classic of Filial Piety*, and essay writing in Chinese, in addition to their more specialized subjects. Although it was proper to acquire foreign skills, he said, there was no excuse for becoming less Chinese.[22] On February 24, 1868, Shen reported to the Throne the opening of two drafting departments in the school, one to teach ship design and the other engine design.[23] These evidently were soon combined, for Shen mentioned only one department of design in a memorial submitted on May 26, 1872, and Giquel also mentioned only one in his final report of November 18, 1873.[24]

Besides training naval architects and engineers, the French engineers and skilled workmen employed by the Foochow Navy Yard were expected to give modern training to ordinary Chinese workmen: carpenters, ironworkers, brassworkers, ship construction workers, and so on. This appears to have worked satisfactorily except that few competent foremen were developed. Most of the workmen were middle-aged and proved to be too set in their ways to learn to do more than follow instructions. Consequently, it was decided during the summer of 1868 that each of the operating divisions of the yard should recruit from ten to forty intelligent boys between the ages of fourteen and seventeen, to be called apprentices (*i-t'u*), who besides working in the navy yard would also study in an apprentice department (I-pu) set up in the school.[25]

[21] IWSM, TC 50, p. 4. [22] *Ibid.*, pp. 22–23.
[23] IWSM, TC 57, p. 6.
[24] IWSM, TC 86, pp. 19–20; Giquel, p. 17.
[25] IWSM, TC 60, pp. 36–37.

Operation under Giquel

On November 18, 1873, Giquel, the foreign director of the Foochow Navy Yard, submitted a report to Director-general Shen "on the results of the instruction, theoretical and practical, given to the Chinese employés [and students] by the European employés" during the preceding seven years. In this report he analyzed the work of the different departments of the Navy Yard School in some detail.[26]

The school consisted of two divisions, referred to by Giquel as the French and English "schools." The French division was made up of three departments: naval construction (Chih-tsao hsüeh-t'ang or Ch'ien hsüeh-t'ang), design (Hui-shih yüan), and apprentices (I-pu). The English division, which constituted what might be called a naval academy, also had three departments: theoretical navigation (Chia-shih hsüeh-t'ang or Hou hsüeh-t'ang), practical navigation (Lien-ch'uan), and engine room (Kuan-lun hsüeh-t'ang).

The oldest French department was that of naval construction, which opened in February 1867 under the temporary direction of A. Borel with twelve students; in April 1868 its direction was taken over by L. Rousset, professor of physics and chemistry, and L. Médard, professor of mathematics. The purpose of this department was to train men to understand "by the help of reasoning and calculation, the function, the dimensions, and the part played by the different parts of an engine, in such a way as to be able to design and reproduce one of its detached members; . . . to calculate, to design, and to trace in the moulding hall, the hull of a wooden ship"; and, finally, to apply this knowledge to the actual work of the navy yard. The basic curriculum consisted of French, arithmetic, algebra, descrip-

[26] Giquel, pp. 17–35. Except when otherwise noted, the material in this section is derived from Giquel, "The Foochow Arsenal and its results," first cited in note 5.

tive and analytic geometry, trigonometry, calculus, physics, and mechanics.[27] On top of this, practical instruction was given in the building of hulls and in the building and operation of machinery. During the last years of training, the students of this department actually worked a part of each day in the various operating divisions of the navy yard, familiarizing themselves with the activities of each and learning how to direct workmen. Also toward the end of the period of study more specialized training was given relating to the particular responsibility the person was to have in the yard after graduation. It was not expected that these engineers would be able to do more than direct construction; competence to design new construction would require more advanced training and experience in Europe.

The curriculum of this department appears to have taken five years to complete. The rate of attrition was very high: of a total of 105 students admitted from the beginning only 39 remained at the end of 1873; 6 had died, and 60 had been dismissed for one reason or another.[28] By the end of 1873 the

[27] J. G. D., an otherwise unidentified visitor to the Foochow Navy Yard early in 1870, reported: "In the French school we saw the pupils of the third class. They demonstrated with quickness and evident understanding, some problems of Euclid. To show that the pupils really comprehended the problems, and did not repeat them parrotlike, the French master insisted, and with success, on demonstrations in converso. The pupils bore this hard task. Adjoining the French school is a study for learning the principles and laws of mechanics. The pupils were young and intelligent, and the examination was satisfactory" (NCH, April 21, 1870). Henry Noel Shore reported that when he visited the "Department of Naval Architecture" (as he designated it) in the early spring of 1876 there were three professors "engaged"—of physics, chemistry, and mathematics (*The Flight of the "Lapwing"* [1881], p. 104).

[28] In discussing the differences in achievement among the students in his own department of theoretical navigation, James Carroll noted that these were "not only attributable to the difference of intellect and ability, which are always to be found among pupils, but in a great measure also to the frequent absences which have occurred to many of them to attend

fourteen surviving members of the first two classes, who had already completed the curriculum, had been assigned to positions in the navy yard according to their abilities. There were at that time two other classes in the department, of four and twenty members respectively, plus one unclassified student. The members of the fourth class were youths with less promise than the others who were being trained for positions requiring less intelligence and ability. Ten of the twenty had entered the school as members of the third class to graduate from the department of design.

The purpose of the department of design, according to Giquel, was "to organize a staff qualified to turn out the plans needed for construction," although his description leaves the impression that it was concerned primarily with engine design. The department was directed during the period of French tutelage by a foreman named A. Louis, assisted by a draftsman named Kerdraon. The basic curriculum consisted of French, arithmetic, plane and descriptive geometry, and a thorough course on the 150-horsepower marine engine; in addition, the students were taught to prepare working drawings and specifications for all kinds of engines, and they also spent some hours daily during an eight-month period in the workshops learning to deal with workmen and familiarizing themselves with the actual details of engines and tools. This curriculum apparently required three years to complete, since the first class, of ten students, which started in 1868, was admitted to the more advanced department of naval construction in 1871.

---

some ceremony connected with family affairs, such absences lasting six weeks and two months at a time, which was so much time lost" (letter to Giquel, NCH, July 14, 1871). Similar prolonged absences unquestionably contributed to the rate of attrition in other departments of the school and in the other modern schools in China. It should be remembered that such absences were forbidden by the regulations; evidently the normal demands of Chinese social usage made it impossible to enforce such a rule.

At the end of 1873 two later classes still remained in the school, each consisting of eleven students.

The apprentice department, established, as noted above, in 1868, provided part-time instruction for young workmen who gave promise of developing as foremen. At first the apprentices were divided in the school according to the divisions of the navy yard in which they worked, but in November 1870 they were regrouped according to the progress they had made. The apprentices at first attended classes only one and one-half hours each evening, after finishing their regular day's work; [29] but from December 1868 they also studied one and one-half hours each morning. The purpose of this department, according to Giquel, was to give to selected young workmen "the ability to read a plan, to design it, to calculate the bulks and weights of the parts of engines, or of hulls, of whatever form, while at the same time causing them to acquire in the workshops the ability requisite for the work of their profession." The curriculum consisted of French, arithmetic, plane and descriptive geometry, algebra, drawing, and a course descriptive of engines. By 1874, nine different Frenchmen had had a hand in the teaching of this department, of whom Messrs. Guerin, Marzin, Latouche, and Piry were singled out for special praise by Giquel. Upon completion of the course, which appears to have required three years or longer, the apprentices could be expected "to make a specification of the designs of an engine, to calculate the masses and weights of each of the parts; they are able, further, to describe the working of it in its most minute details."

Two classes, of twenty-one and nineteen members respectively, had completed this apprentice course by 1874. Giquel reported that the graduates were prepared to assume the responsibilities of foremen except for their youth and need for

[29] "Some of the [foreign] foremen act as teachers in the evening schools, in which arithmetic, the French language, drawing, etc., are taught to young Chinese" (NCH, April 21, 1870).

more experience. The two remaining classes, with nineteen and seventeen apprentices respectively, still were carrying on their studies. Giquel appears to have been particularly well pleased with the achievements of this department. He wrote that some advanced training in Europe would make of these youths not only excellent foremen but even competent superintendents of workshops.

The general aim of the English division of the Foochow Navy Yard School was to train officers to operate the ships built there. Giquel and d'Aiguebelle had promised that within the five-year period of their contract they would teach the students of the navigation departments how to navigate ships within sight of land, but by the end of their training Giquel reported that the students had learned to navigate on the open seas as well. The third department was to train ships' engineers to match the deck officers.

The department of theoretical navigation was directed from the beginning by James Carroll, an Englishman, who was assisted in 1871 by an English-speaking Chinese named Ch'en and in 1873 by another Englishman, a Mr. Skey, and by a member of the first graduating class. Besides the English language, the curriculum included arithmetic, geometry, algebra, plane and spherical trigonometry, nautical astronomy, theoretical navigation, and geography, and it required three and a half years to complete.[30] The first class, which consisted of twenty-

[30] J. G. D. wrote of his visit to this department: "The pupils of [Mr. Carroll's] first class, thirty in number, were submitted to an unpremeditated examination in mathematics, algebra, conic sections, dynamical laws, fluxions, hydrostatics, etc., and answered perfectly well, and with a readiness which was astonishing to us. We were informed that the young Chinese students studied the exact sciences so eagerly that the foreign superintendents had found it necessary to forbid that any student should prolong his studies after 10 or 11 o'clock at night. The young Chinese spoke correct and good English and the jargon of pidgin English is not to be heard" (NCH, April 21, 1870). Shore noted in 1876 that the students of theoretical navigation attended classes six hours each day

three students in the end, graduated in May 1871.[31] The second class, with nine graduates, finished in September 1873. At that time two other classes remained in the department, one having thirteen and the other five students. The graduates of the department of theoretical navigation went immediately into the second department of the English division, the department of practical navigation, unless they were retained as tutors and translators, as in the case of three members of the first class who were not physically strong enough for shipboard life.

The department of practical navigation, which was located at first on the sailing ship *Chien-wei,* did not commence instruction until more than three years after the inauguration of the school. It appears to have been set up by a Lieutenant

---

except Sunday and in addition did a good deal of work out of hours in their own rooms (p. 227).

[31] An editorial in the July 14, 1871, *North-China Herald* discusses the final examination given to this class by a board presided over by a commander of the British navy. Of the twenty-one who took the examination, eight did very well and only three did badly. Geometry and trigonometry were the best subjects, navigation and arithmetic the poorest. In his letter to Giquel, mentioned earlier, published in the same July 14, 1871, issue of the *North-China Herald,* James Carroll reported as follows regarding the studies of the first graduating class: "In *Arithmetic* we have followed Barnard Smith, and I think they will be found to have a perfect knowledge of Fractions, Proportions, Interest, etc. *Algebra.*—Todhunter's Elementary, they thoroughly understand to Quadratic Equations of the second degree, and have a slight knowledge of Ratios, Proportions, Progressions, etc. *Geography.*—Anderson's—General Features of the Globe, and the leading points of each of the continents. *Trigonometry, Plane and Spherical.*—Todhunter's.—all rules relating to the solution of triangles, necessary to understand the problems in Navigation and Nautical Astronomy. *Geometry.*—Todhunter's Euclid.—Three books and part of the sixth book. *Navigation.*—Raper's—Correction of Compasses, the Sailings as usually taught, and the Day's Work. *Nautical Astronomy.*—Finding Latitude by a Meridian Altitude, by an Altitude of the Pole Star, and by Altitudes taken when the object is near the Meridian. Finding Longitude by the Chronometer. Finding the Error of Compass by the Amplitude, by the Azimuth with the Altitude and by the Azimuth without the Altitude. All rules deduced from figures."

Swainson, but the head during most of the remainder of the period of foreign tutelage was Capt. R. E. Tracey, who was assisted by a master gunner and a boatswain—all of the British navy.[32] The students of this department came from two sources: in the beginning ten were recruited by Captain Tracey in Hongkong; the rest were graduates of the department of theoretical navigation. On the training ship the students were taught "the theoretical and practical branches of knowledge requisite in the captain of a ship," including seamanship, gunnery, and command. The most important exercises consisted of extensive training cruises under the command of the outstanding students in the class during which the other students not only had assigned responsibilities but also kept logs on the various maneuvers of the ship. By the autumn of 1873 four students had qualified as captain or mate, four more were then on a cruise from which they would return with like ratings, and six others were expected to qualify the following spring. Twelve additional students had only partially completed their training. It required about two years for graduates of the department of theoretical navigation to complete this practical course.[33]

The third unit of the English division was the engine-room department, designed to train engine-room officers for the ships built at Foochow. W. Allan was the professor from the begin-

[32] The department of practical navigation appears to have been opened ashore as early as the spring of 1870. J. G. D., who visited the school early in 1870, wrote: "We visited the naval school over which Lieut. Swainson R.N. presides. The cadets are numerous. They are taught the arts of navigation and seamanship theoretically and practically. Lieut. Swainson has charge of the gunnery class as well. The pupils go through the heavy gun drill in good form, and they handle the heavy rifled cannon, which is of 5 tons weight, with celerity, and in silence. The boat and field gun, small arms, and cutlass drills were efficiently performed" (NCH, April 21, 1870).

[33] See also the description of the operation of this department in Shen Pao-chen's memorial of Nov. 23, 1873 (IWSM, TC 91, p. 34).

ning; the students were recruited in Hongkong and Shanghai from young men who had had "experience in the working of iron and iron plates" in local foundries and machine shops. The curriculum, besides English, included arithmetic, geometry, drawing, description of engines, rules for operating engines at sea, and the use of the indicator, salinometer, and other gauges. For practical application of the theories taught, the students practiced setting up 80- and 150-horsepower engines ashore and later installed the engines in several of the ships built at the navy yard. By the fall of 1874 fourteen graduates of this department had been appointed engineers aboard the ships already built, and seven other qualified ships' engineers awaited assignment, though one was regarded as still too young for such responsibility.

Shen Pao-chen in a memorial presented to the Throne on May 26, 1872—and later in a joint memorial wih Li Ho-nien and Wang K'ai-t'ai presented March 14, 1873—reported a total of more than three hundred students and apprentices in the various departments of the school.[34]

Instruction at the Foochow Navy Yard was by no means confined to the school. As noted earlier, the principal reason for employing foreign foremen and skilled workmen was to teach Chinese workmen the manifold tasks involved in building and maintaining ships. This instruction was given "on the job" to a selected group of advanced workmen and apprentices in each division of the navy yard, and it included not only the necessary skills required for their particular jobs but also training in the reading and execution of drawings and plans—though none of this group learned a foreign language or received the theoretical training supplied in the school. Searching examinations were given during 1873 to the recipients of this training in each of the various subdivisions, and as a result 244 were judged to be qualified.

[34] IWSM, TC 86, p. 19; TC 89, p. 15.

The original contract had stipulated that the navy yard personnel should be trained to operate all of its various divisions without the aid of foreigners within five years of the completion of the physical plant—that is, by February 16, 1874. Well in advance of that date Giquel and his foreign staff, together with Chinese examiners designated by Director-general Shen, subjected all divisions of the navy yard to thorough tests to ascertain their fitness to carry on.[35] The pattern shop, the engine-fitting shop, the engine setters-up, the metalworking forge, the iron and brass foundries, the boiler shop, the carpentry shop, the borers, the caulkers, the masting and ships' boat shops, the cabinetmakers, the equipment forges, the equipment fitters, the sail loft, the compass and chronometer shops—each was required to carry out a complete exercise under the technicians trained in the school and Chinese foremen without the presence of any foreigner. In each case the results were reported as satisfactory, and Giquel and his associates professed themselves to be satisfied with the ability of the Chinese staff to carry on alone.[36] It should perhaps be noted in passing that in addition to the building of the navy yard facilities and the training of its personnel fifteen ships were launched between June 1869 and February 1874.

The School after 1874

The years from 1874 to 1895 are referred to by Wang Hsin-chung in his monograph on the Foochow Navy Yard as "the period of self-management," a time during which the yard itself was operated entirely by Chinese officials and skilled workmen

[35] See Shen's report on plans for these tests (IWSM, TC 91, p. 18).

[36] See also the description of this testing in Shen Pao-chen's memorial of Dec. 26, 1873 (IWSM, TC 92, p. 17; translation in Giquel, pp. 35–38). Shore reports that de Segonzac informed him in 1876 that the navy yard workmen, "superintended by native foremen educated in the arsenal schools," were "as thoroughly trustworthy and quite as competent as Europeans, though perhaps rather slower" (p. 97).

except for two French technicians brought in late in the 1870's for a year or more to teach the Chinese staff some newly developed metalworking techniques.[37] The yard was unable to maintain its initial high productivity after the period of foreign tutelage came to an end and after the able and dedicated first director-general, Shen Pao-chen, had been promoted to a higher official position elsewhere. Whereas fifteen ships were launched from 1869 to 1874, only nineteen were launched between 1874 and 1897.[38] Although this decline may be attributed in part to the ending of Giquel's energetic and skillful management and of the participation of his competent and experienced team of French engineers and skilled workmen, other factors were the lower caliber of most of the directors-general who followed Shen, the curtailment of operating funds, and a sharp decline in the interest and support of the central government and of provincial officials.

Most of the ten directors-general and acting directors-general during this "period of self-management" served too briefly to be able to familiarize themselves with the operation of the

[37] "Foochow ch'uan-ch'ang chih yen-ke," *Tsing Hua hsüeh-pao*, 8 (Dec. 1932), 27, 30. The two technicians, Heim and Meusburger, are listed in the *North China Desk Hong List, 1879*, p. 42. An article in the *China Mail* declared in 1876 that the Chinese had found it impossible to operate the yard at Foochow without foreign help and so had re-engaged Giquel with authority to employ French technicians as needed (NCH, March 30, 1876). Giquel and his deputy, L. Denoyer de Segonzac, remained on the navy yard staff after all the other Europeans departed in 1874 (CCTI, 9, p. 16). But they appear to have spent most of their time in Europe, buying new equipment for the navy yard and supervising the training of Foochow graduates. Although Shore speaks of de Segonzac as "the engineer" at the navy yard in 1876, he also says that the latest vessel built there was "constructed without any foreign assistance whatever" (pp. 97, 101). Actually French tutelage was not resumed until 1897.

[38] See descriptive lists of these ships facing pages 28 and 48 of Wang's monograph cited in the preceding note. Most of the later ships were larger and of more complicated construction than the small wooden vessels built under French auspices.

yard or to carry through a policy; and none but Ting Jih-ch'ang, who held the post less than a year, had sufficient rank and prestige to be able to press the provincial government for badly needed funds. Moreover, few of them seem to have taken a real interest in the yard, some appear to have been incompetent, and some may even have been corrupt. After 1880 the Fukien Maritime Customs regularly failed to turn over the full 600,000-tael annual allocation to the navy yard; the amount received fell to between 200,000 and 300,000 taels by the 1890's and even below 200,000 taels by 1895.[39]

Shortcomings of the Foochow Navy Yard were called to the attention of the central government from time to time. For example, an Imperial edict issued on July 14, 1880, took note of a recent memorial from the Tsungli Yamen that reported incompetence, sloth, and corruption in the yard. A newly appointed director-general, Li Chao-t'ang, was ordered to investigate and to report for punishment all persons guilty of corruption,[40] but there is no evidence that anything came of it. Following the bombardment of the yard by a French fleet in 1884, during the Sino-French War of that year, a better than average director-general, P'ei Yin-sen, tried during a six-year term to bring about improvements as well as to rebuild what had been destroyed. Among his reforms he revised the salary system, eliminating abuses that had contributed to dissatisfaction and even to corruption. These abuses had arisen because a proper system of paying officials, workmen, and even students various kinds of bonuses, made necessary in order to keep them in the navy yard, had never been regularized, and it was thus almost impossible to check irregularities. P'ei emphasized the need for higher salaries for this kind of employment than were

[39] CCTI, 46, pp. 11, 25.
[40] THHL, KH 35, p. 13. Foreign employees (they must have been Heim and Meusburger) were charged in the Tsungli Yamen memorial with resorting to delaying tactics in order to prolong their own employment.

customary elsewhere in the government, and he succeeded in having a fair and clearly stated scale adopted.[41] The yard appears to have gone into a decline again after P'ei's replacement in 1890, as his successors gradually reduced the number of engineers and skilled workmen employed,[42] but it continued to function in spite of decreasing funds and official neglect. In view of its many difficulties it is surprising that the Foochow Navy Yard managed to carry on at all; yet one ship was launched in each of the years 1891, 1892, and 1895, and routine services were provided for the Fukien naval squadron, as well as for other warships and commercial vessels of the Chinese government.

The Navy Yard School appears to have fared better than the operating divisions during the "period of self-management," although its graduates found it increasingly difficult to secure government positions after the mid-1880's and the school itself seems to have been practically moribund during the early 1890's. A new department of electricity was added on April 8, 1876; it appears to have been attached to the English division because electricity was referred to in the relevant document as an important subject in relation to the command of ships.[43] A telegraph office was added to the navy yard in the mid-1880's, but it appears to have had an operational, not a training, function.[44] In general the school and the operating divisions continued to be organized throughout this period much as planned by Giquel and Shen in the late 1860's;[45] however, it proved

[41] THHL, KH 72, pp. 20–21; KH 74, p. 16; KH 82, p. 2.

[42] CCTI, 46, p. 9.

[43] CCTI, 17, pp. 19–20, 34. Such knowledge would seem to have been no less useful to shipbuilders.

[44] CCTI, 37, p. 11. The office was operated by two graduates of the school, one paid twenty taels per month, the second, sixteen.

[45] CCTI, 47, p. 17. A document sent from the navy yard and acknowledged in an Imperial rescript dated Feb. 5, 1888, divided the school into four departments, French, English, navigation, and ship's engine, with the first two grouped in a front division (Ch'ien hsüeh-t'ang) and the last

impossible to keep up with European technological advances.

In 1885 P'ei Yin-sen complained that the students of navigation had been given too little training at sea during recent
years—only two months each year, which was not enough
experience for officers who were to be entrusted with the command of ships. He accordingly compiled new regulations stipu-
lating that half of each of the three years required to complete
the course in practical navigation be spent at sea.[46] The unavailability of an adequate training ship was a recurring problem in the history of the school. The corvette *Yang-wu*, the larg-
est ship built at Foochow during the period of French tutelage,
served as the school ship in 1875–1876, and the *Wei-yüan*, the
first iron-ribbed warship built at the yard, was in use in 1879.
In 1883 there evidently was no school ship, for it was proposed
that ships regularly attached to the Fukien defense squadron
be used in a dual capacity. After the destruction of most of the
Fukien squadron by the French fleet in 1884, a foreign-built
ship, the *P'ing-yüan*, was purchased and refurbished for use
as a training vessel; and older ships that had survived the
French attack, such as the *Ching-yüan* and the *Yüan-k'ai*, were
converted for such use at later times.[47] While the school buildings sustained only slight damage during the French attack,
books and equipment suffered severely. However, these losses
had been made good by the end of 1886.[48]

---

two in a rear division (Hou hsüeh-t'ang) (CCTI, 37, p. 9). This was
either a temporary change or a mistake in the document, because the
name Ch'ien hsüeh-t'ang (Front School) was applied to the French-
language department of naval construction and the name Hou hsüeh-
t'ang to the English-language department of theoretical navigation (sometimes to both theoretical and practical navigation) both before and after
1888 (CCTI, 24, pp. 12–14; 41, p.8; 48, pp. 30 ff.).

[46] CSWP, 108, pp. 8–9. It should be noted that the curriculum of this
department must have been extended from two to three years after the
Chinese assumed control of the yard.

[47] CCTI, 13, p. 19; 17, p. 34; 21, pp. 23–24; 22, p. 20; 33, p. 25; 48,
pp. 1–3; 50, pp. 17–18.

[48] CCTI, 25, p. 17; 33, pp. 23–25.

Although the operating divisions of the Foochow Navy Yard carried on almost altogether without the help of foreign technicians between 1874 and 1897, it early became clear that the school required some foreign teachers. It is not certain when Te-shang (a Frenchman whose identity I have been unable to ascertain) and L. Médard were appointed professors in the reorganized French division (Médard had previously been professor of mathematics under Giquel), but it must have been fairly soon after the Chinese assumed control.[49] Director-general Ting Jih-ch'ang wrote sometime in late 1875 or early 1876 that experienced Western teachers were needed, implying there were none at that time.[50] James Carroll, who had also taught under Giquel, was reappointed professor of navigation during the summer of 1876, and A. Moreton began teaching in the engine-room department in January 1878.[51] In the summer of 1878 Ting Jih-ch'ang suggested that, in view of the uncertainty as to when graduates might be sent abroad for advanced training, Giquel be asked to find two French specialists in steam, mechanics, and chemistry to teach in the French division.[52] Nothing came of this proposal, possibly because the first group of Foochow graduates was dispatched to Europe the following spring.

By October 1880 Te-shang had resigned because of illness, leaving Médard the only French professor; Carroll had died, and Moreton, upon completion of his initial term of appointment, had departed. Carroll had been replaced in the navigation department by C. H. Brewitt-Taylor in September 1880.

[49] The first mention of Te-shang and Médard I have found after the change is in a document dated June 28, 1878, in which both are listed as professors in the French division (CCTI, 15, p. 32).

[50] CCTI, 13, pp. 19–20.

[51] CCTI, 14, p. 5; 15, p. 32. Carroll was at the school during Shore's visit in 1876. Shore also mentions a Captain Luxmore, R.N., and two other Englishmen who were attached to the training ship *Yang-wu* (p. 233).

[52] CCTI, 14, p. 5.

In November 1883 only Médard and Brewitt-Taylor are mentioned as members of the foreign staff; but the first two graduates of the school to receive full faculty status had been appointed—Cheng Ch'ing-lien, as professor of ship construction in the French division, and Wei Han, who though a graduate of the French division also knew English, as professor in the engine-room department of the English division.[53] Médard resigned and went home at the time of the trouble with France in 1884, and two new English professors arrived on May 1, 1885: G. Le Gros, to teach in the engine-room department, and F. T. Richards, to teach science and mathematics in the French division.[54] Médard was recalled to China and reinstated in the French division in August 1886; in 1888 he, Brewitt-Taylor, and Richards constituted the foreign faculty. By 1889, J. S. Fishbourne had replaced Richards (who went to the Canton Naval and Military Academy), and in 1892 the foreign faculty consisted of Médard, Brewitt-Taylor, Le Gros, and Fishbourne.[55] From the beginning the professors were assisted by Chinese tutors, nearly all of whom appear to have been graduates of the school. In 1884, one of the few years for which figures are available, there were eight tutors in the French division and eleven in the English division.[56]

The salaries of foreign professors were set in 1876 at from 200 to 250 taels per month plus living allowance and cost of travel to and from China; and there had been no change by 1883. I have found no mention of how much Chinese professors

[53] CCTI, 18, p. 10; 22, pp. 31–32. *Chronicle and Directory for China . . . 1882* also lists an E. C. Legh in the "School of Naval Mechanics"— clearly the engine-room department (p. 320).

[54] CCTI, 28, pp. 8–9. I am not sure of the particular positions held by these men. The *Hongkong Directory and Hong List for the Far East for 1886* lists both Le Gros and Richards as professors of mathematics and English (p. 231). This differs from the *Ch'uan-cheng tsou-i hui-pien* account.

[55] CCTI, 37, p. 9; 43, p. 12; 44, p. 22; *Chronicle and Directory for China . . . 1889*, p. 396.

[56] CCTI, 24, p. 12.

were paid. In 1884 the Chinese tutors, according to the department and the experience of the individual, were paid from ten to thirty-six taels per month, besides a living allowance.[57] The regular Chinese officials in charge of each division of the school (there seem to have been four assigned to the English division, for example) were paid salaries of forty taels per month by the navy yard, almost certainly in addition to their regular official salaries and allowances.[58]

The Foochow Navy Yard School, at least until the late 1880's, appears to have had little difficulty recruiting students and to have maintained a steady flow of young men through its various departments. Nearly all students in the French division seem to have come from Fukien province, and most of those in the English division from Kwangtung or Hongkong. In 1878, for example, a new entering class consisted of twenty-one Fukienese and eight Cantonese.[59] The Fukienese probably continued to be drawn from respectable local families, as originally contemplated. Most of the Cantonese apparently were recruited from English-language schools in Hongkong. The two outstanding navigation students of the first graduating class had previously studied English and other modern subjects in Hongkong. In 1876 Director-general Ting Jih-ch'ang sent representatives to Hongkong to recruit forty new students for the English division.[60] This practice must have been fol-

---

[57] CCTI, 14, p. 3; 22, pp. 31–32; 24, p. 12.

[58] The men in those positions during the late 1880's appear to have held the fifth official rank or a lower one. Their responsibilities included disbursement of food allowances, supervision of study, and inspection of all persons entering or leaving the school (THHL, KH 82, p. 2).

[59] CCTI, 15, p. 32. The latter category would include students from Hongkong. Shore reported in 1876 that the students from Foochow and Kwangtung lived separately in the school and had different cooks and that the Cantonese were usually the sharpest. There were about fifty students in the department of theoretical navigation at the time of his visit in February and seventeen on the training ship (pp. 226–227).

[60] CCTI, 13, p. 19. According to Shore, placards advertising the school were placed in conspicuous places throughout Foochow city. The age

lowed subsequently, for Sir John Pope Hennessy, the governor of Hongkong, complained bitterly in a speech delivered at the Hongkong Central School in 1881 that about forty of its best Chinese students, who had been educated with Hongkong government funds for service in that British colony, were enticed away each year by the Foochow Navy Yard and the Chinese Imperial Maritime Customs.[61] Some of the returned students from the Chinese Educational Mission to the United States were assigned to the Foochow school in 1882 but I have been unable to discover exactly how many.[62]

A census of the Foochow student body in May 1884 is given in Table 2 and shows the distribution of students among the various departments. In April 1887 P'ei Yin-sen stated that there were 128 students in the French and English divisions of the school. This would seem to show a sharp decline in enrollment except that P'ei's figure probably does not include apprentices.[63]

In 1896 the Tsungli Yamen declared that Foochow students had become discouraged by the government's failure during recent years to make use of the graduates of that school; and

----

limit of sixteen, he says, was not strictly adhered to, although there was strict examination of all applicants in the classics and in Chinese literature. Carroll, he reports, spoke well of the students, saying that they were more diligent and attentive than English boys, though not taking kindly to manual labor (pp. 228, 234).

[61] NCH, Feb. 15, 1881.

[62] Thomas E. La Fargue says that six of the Chinese vessels attacked by the French at Foochow in 1884 were commanded by students who had returned two years before from the United States. He lists four who lost their lives in the battle and one who escaped (*China's First Hundred*, p. 74). La Fargue is clearly wrong in believing that these youngsters would be commanding ships. The American consul at Foochow reported that there were five returned students from the United States engaged in the battle, all of whom fought gallantly, and that only one lost his life (*Foreign Relations of the United States, 1885*, p. 145).

[63] THHL, KH 82, p. 2.

Director-general Yü-lu reported in the same year that no new students had been recruited for a long time, that the only students at the school when he had assumed his position in July were those who had failed to graduate and had been allowed to continue to study there.[64] Operations in the navy yard had been drastically curtailed because of the decrease in

Table 2. Enrollment in the Foochow Navy Yard School, 1884

Resident graduates *	
Students	4
Apprentices	6
French division	
Naval construction	34
Design	10
Apprentices	62
English division	
Navigation	44
Returned students from the Educational Mission to the United States	4
Engine room	18
Electricity	6
Total	188

* Returned from advanced study in Europe but not yet assigned to posts.
Source: CCTI, 24, pp. 12–14.

funds, with the result that instead of adding recent graduates of the school to the yard staff the total yard staff had been reduced and earlier graduates were thrown out of employment. There appear also to have been more Foochow naval graduates than there were available naval appointments. In 1889 thirty-seven students who had spent three or four years studying in the English division at Foochow were transferred to the Naval and Military Academy at Canton, either because there was already an oversupply of Foochow graduates or be-

[64] CCTI, 46, p. 24; 47, p. 21.

cause there were insufficient funds available at Foochow to enable them to complete their training there.[65]

The monthly payment of four taels to each student, in addition to board, lodging, and medical expenses, as provided in the first regulations, remained the basic stipend through the next three decades. In 1884 eighty-one of the students outside the apprentice department were receiving four taels per month, eighteen were receiving five taels, and fifteen from six to twelve taels. Two students in the electricity department were receiving sixteen taels per month and one twenty—stipends more like those paid tutors than students. The apprentices studying in the apprentice department were paid from one-tenth to one-fifth of a tael per day. Resident graduates—those who had returned to the school after completing advanced training in Europe—were paid from seventy-two to eighty-six taels if students and from twenty to twenty-two taels if apprentices.[66] The new scale of stipends drawn up by P'ei Yin-sen in 1886 provided that new students should receive only a food allowance until examined at the end of three months, after which those permitted to continue would be paid four taels; and apprentices in the school would start with .075 taels per day, only half the amount paid earlier. It was planned that the stipends of both students and apprentices might be increased later as progress was demonstrated.[67]

The most significant educational development at the Foochow Navy Yard after 1874 was the dispatch of graduates of the school to Europe for advanced study. Giquel, in his report of November 18, 1873, to Director-general Shen Pao-chen, had stressed the desirability of sending graduates abroad for further

[65] Chang Chih-tung, 28, p. 3.   [66] CCTI, 24, p. 12.

[67] THHL, KH 74, p. 16. The *Ch'uan-cheng tsou-i hui-pien* includes much scattered material on the various expenses of the Foochow Navy Yard, including those of the school. These figures have been brought together by Wang Hsin-chung in a series of tables published in his *Tsing Hua hsüeh-pao* article already cited (pp. 18–22 and 35–44).

study.[68] In Shen's own memorial presented to the Throne on December 26 of the same year, he had urged that selected graduates of the French division be sent to France to study shipbuilding and to acquaint themselves with the latest technical developments in that field and that picked graduates of the English division be sent to England to study advanced navigation and naval operations. These students should devote from three to five years to such advanced study, he wrote, and upon returning to China they should be replaced by later graduates. Those not strong enough physically to serve in the navy yard or aboard ship might, after completing their foreign studies, be used as teachers of astronomy, mathematics, geography, and so on in the various modern Chinese schools.[69]

Shen's memorial was referred to the Tsungli Yamen for comment, and on January 6, 1874, that body sanctioned the proposal, citing Tseng Kuo-fan's recommendation of the Chinese Educational Mission to the United States as a precedent.[70] It further suggested that the superintendents of trade for the northern and southern ports be instructed to draw up plans. Preoccupation with the Formosan crisis postponed consideration of the matter by the superintendents, but meanwhile, in view of Giquel's departure for Europe to purchase new equipment for the navy yard, five graduates were sent with him to visit European shipyards and industrial plants.[71]

On January 15, 1877, a joint memorial of the two superintendents of trade, Li Hung-chang and Shen Pao-chen (the latter

[68] Giquel, pp. 19, 22, 32.   [69] IWSM, TC 92, pp. 16–17.
[70] See Chap. I, pp. 21–23.
[71] IWSM, TC 92, pp. 23–24; THHL, KH 13, p. 11; CCTI, 12, p. 9. The five students who accompanied Giquel were Wei Han, Ch'en Chao-ao, Ch'en Chi-t'ung, Liu Pu-ch'an, and Lin T'ai-tseng. According to Ch'ih Chung-hu, only three of these students returned to China the following year, Wei Han and Ch'en Chao-ao remaining in France, where they joined the first group of Foochow graduates sent there in 1877 for advanced training (p. 327).

no longer connected with the Foochow Navy Yard), was submitted to the Throne in compliance with the instructions they had received three years earlier. After thorough investigation, the memorialists said, they were convinced that an adequate defense required expertness in shipbuilding and naval operations beyond the level of training that could be given in China and that the graduates of the Foochow school were capable of acquiring the desired expertness if sent abroad for advanced study. Moreover, the rapidity of technological improvement in Europe made it imperative to maintain direct contact with the centers of advancement. France, they said, led in shipbuilding, and England in naval operations. They therefore proposed that thirty promising Foochow graduates be sent to Europe for three years of advanced study, the project to be financed by an appropriation of 200,000 taels, one-half to be supplied from the likin tax of Fukien province, one-fourth from the maritime customs collections in Fukien, and one-fourth from the funds of the Foochow Navy Yard. Some of these students might go beyond shipbuilding and naval operation and take up other important subjects such as chemistry, mining, international law, and diplomacy. Li and Shen recognized that not all students sent abroad for study could be depended upon to measure up to expectations, but they believed that if five out of ten really benefited from advanced training the experiment could be regarded as successful. Finally, they submitted a set of ten regulations to govern the operation.[72]

These regulations provided that the project should be directed by two supervisors, one Chinese and one European, who were to work together and to share responsibility as equals, and that the director-general of the Foochow Navy Yard and the two superintendents of trade were to resolve any differences that might arise between the two supervisors. The supervisors were to make all arrangements for the instruction of the

[72] THHL, KH 13, pp. 11–13; CSWP, 120, pp. 6–7.

students and for their visits of inspection to places of educational value, to watch over their studies, to discipline them when necessary, and to examine them periodically to determine their rate of progress. The salaries and expenses of the students and of Chinese employees were to be paid by the Chinese supervisor, those of non-Chinese employees and teachers by the European supervisor.

Fourteen engineering students and four apprentices from the French division of the school were to be taken to France, and twelve navigation students from the English division to England. Those sent to France were to study first with special tutors, and afterward they would be sent to a shipyard or a marine-engine factory to secure practical experience. During the second and third years, besides their regular studies, they were to devote sixty days each year to inspecting shipyards, naval vessels, industrial plants, mines, and forts in order to broaden their acquaintance with Western technology. The students sent to England were to spend some time during the first year perfecting their English and being tutored in such matters as gunnery and torpedo firing; after this they would be sent to the Portsmouth School at Greenwich [*sic*]. At the end of their first year of study, unless tests showed a need for additional preliminary instruction, they were to be assigned for advanced training to British warships. The naval students also were expected to visit shipyards, factories, mines, and different types of naval vessels to broaden their knowledge. Aboard ship they were to wear British naval officers' uniforms and to conform to British naval regulations.

The three-year advanced training program was to commence with the students' arrival in France and England. Interim examinations were to be given every three months by the supervisors and European teachers, and a final examination was to be administered four months before the end of the three-year period. Those passing the latter would be sent back to

China for employment; what would be done about those demonstrating a need for six months or a year of additional training was to be left to the responsible officials in China for decision. Nothing less than the ability to build the latest model warships and all their components, including engines, without foreign assistance, or competence to command and operate modern warships and to direct fleet tactics and battle formations was to be tolerated. Special study arrangements were to be made by the supervisors for graduates of either the French or English division who preferred to study mining, chemistry, diplomacy, or international law.

All the students were to keep careful diaries of their observations, to be sent back to China at six-month intervals for distribution or other use by the government. Of particular interest would be detailed reports of new technical developments observed in shipyards, factories, or elsewhere, including drawings and specifications. Provision was made for the punishment or dismissal of students who failed to comply with the regulations, for mourning periods in the event of the death of parents of students, for awards to the relatives of students who died while abroad, and for the punishment of the supervisors should they fail to carry out their duties or fail to report each other's shortcomings.

The Emperor approved the project as set forth by Li Hung-chang and Shen Pao-chen, on January 15, 1877.[73] Li Feng-pao, an expectant intendant of the brevet third rank, and Prosper Giquel were appointed the two supervisors, and Li was also assigned supervision over seven army officers who had been sent to Germany for advanced training a year earlier by Li Hung-chang.[74] On March 31, 1877, Giquel departed from Foochow leading a party that consisted of twenty-six students, three apprentices, a diplomatic attaché, a secretary, and an

[73] *Shih-lu,* KH 44, pp. 2–3.   [74] THHL, KH 13, pp. 12, 13.

interpreter. Six additional apprentices joined this group in Europe the following year.[75]

Of the twenty-six students in this first contingent, the twelve graduates of the English division went to England, where six were assigned immediately to British warships for training at sea,[76] five entered the Royal Naval College at Greenwich—four to study the principles and methods of ship operation and one to study surveying and science—before being assigned to sea duty,[77] and the twelfth [78] studied for a while at the Portsmouth School before entering the Royal Naval College. In the course of their sea duty the students visited Spain and the Mediterranean, and some even went as far on the ships to which they had been assigned as the Indian Ocean or across the Atlantic to the United States. After finishing their training at sea they were given additional instruction ashore in electricity, gunnery, and the handling of torpedoes and were sent on tours of inspection to various shipyards and factories. One of them, Yen Tsung-kuang, did not go to sea. Upon completing the scheduled course of study in the naval academy he was sent to France on a tour of inspection, after which he returned to Greenwich to do more advanced work in mathematics, chem-

[75] CCTI, 15, pp. 24–25. For a table listing all the members of this group and the schools, factories, warships, etc., where each received advanced training while abroad, see Wang's *Tsing Hua hsüeh-pao* article, pp. 46–48. There were only twenty-four students in the party leaving Foochow if Ch'ih is right in saying that Wei Han and Ch'en Chao-ao were already in France.

[76] Liu Pu-ch'an, Lin T'ai-tseng, Chiang Ch'ao-ying, Huang Chien-hsün, Lin Ying-ch'i, and Chiang Mou-chih. The first four of these, and Ho Hsin-ch'uan and Yen Tsung-kuang (mentioned in subsequent notes), had been members of the first class to complete the course in theoretical navigation under Carroll and the course in practical navigation under Tracey. See Giquel, pp. 30–31.

[77] Fang Po-ch'ien, Sah Chen-ping, Lin Yung-sheng, Yeh Tsu-kuei, and Ho Hsin-ch'uan.

[78] Yen Tsung-kuang, later better known as Yen Fu.

istry, science, navigation, ordnance manufacturing, and the building of fortifications. In July or August of 1879 Yen was recalled to China to teach in the Foochow Navy Yard School.[79]

Nine of the fourteen graduates of the French division included in this first group sent to Europe studied the construction of ships' hulls and the principles of ships' engines; the remaining five studied mining and metallurgy—all in France. Four of the shipbuilding students spent two years in the Ecole de Construction Navale in Cherbourg, and the other five spent a similar period studying at the Toulon Navy Yard.[80] Upon completing this period of study the eight survivors were sent to inspect French, German, and English shipyards, machine shops, and foundries, and then several of the ablest studied new processes of manufacturing in selected arsenals and ordnance factories. Four of the five students of mining and metallurgy went first to the Le Creusot ironworks, while the fifth entered the Ecole Nationale des Mines in Saint-Etienne.[81] The following year they all entered the Ecole Nationale Supérieure des Mines in Paris. Upon finishing the courses there they were sent to Germany to inspect mines and metal refineries.

The three apprentices who accompanied Giquel studied for a time in a French government school, and subsequent to this they pursued special studies at the Toulon Navy Yard and else-

[79] CCTI, 18, pp. 18–19; 15, pp. 24–25. It is puzzling that not a single one of the ten Cantonese who entered the first class in navigation (only eight appear to have graduated) was sent abroad for advanced study. For a list of the ten, see Pao, p. 223.

[80] Wei Han, Ch'en Chao-ao, Cheng Ch'ing-lien, Ch'en Lin-chang; Wu Te-chang, Yang Lien-ch'en, Lin I-yu, Li Shou-t'ien, and Liang Ping-nien. The last-named died during this period. The first three, plus Wu Te-chang and Liang Ping-nien, had been members of the first two classes to complete the curriculum in naval construction under Giquel and his French associates. See Giquel, p. 19.

[81] Lin Ch'ing-sheng, Ch'ih Chen-ch'üan, Chang Chin-sheng, Lin Jih-chang; Lo Chen-lu. The first, third, and fifth had also been members of the two graduating classes mentioned in the previous note.

where. Of the six apprentices who reached France the following year, three studied in training schools for overseers and foremen, and three spent a year learning iron and steel manufacturing at the Saint-Chamond ironworks, after which they received scientific training at one of the technical schools. The diplomatic attaché, Ma Chien-chung, who later became a personal secretary to Li Hung-chang and a well-known scholar in China, studied Western governments and international law in Paris, either at the Ecole Libre des Sciences Politiques or at the Faculté de Droit of the Université de Paris.[82] The Chinese secretary, Ch'en Chi-t'ung, studied French and also European and international law in Paris, possibly at the same school where Ma was studying; and the interpreter, Lo Feng-lu, studied chemistry in London, at King's College or at the King's College School.[83]

All the students, except one who died in France and two who went home early, returned to China after three years or, in the case of the slower ones, after three years and four months. All had reached Foochow by September 1880. In a final report submitted to the Throne by Li Hung-chang on February 23, 1881, eleven of the returnees were rated as outstanding: Wei Han, Ch'en Chao-ao, Cheng Ch'ing-lien, and Lin I-yu among the marine engineers; Lo Chen-lu and Lin Ch'ing-sheng of the metallurgists; and Liu Pu-ch'an, Lin T'ai-tseng, Chiang Ch'ao-ying, Fang Po-ch'ien, and Sah Chen-ping of the naval cadets. The rest were rated as "useful." [84]

On December 5, 1881, Li Hung-chang memorialized regard-

[82] Teng and Fairbank, p. 88. For Ma's report on his studies at the "Political Institute," see *ibid.*, pp. 95–97.

[83] CCTI, 18, pp. 17–22; THHL, KH 39, pp. 5–6.

[84] THHL, *loc. cit.* Li declared toward the end of 1881 that all the returnees had been assigned to important positions, some commanding small naval craft, some assuming positions in the Foochow Navy Yard, and some assigned to warships being built in Europe for the Chinese navy (THHL, KH 44, p. 12).

ing the sending of a second group of Foochow graduates to Europe. The best of the graduates had been sent in the first group, he said, but fourteen more had been selected for advanced training, eight from the French division and six from the English. In the end, because four of the latter could not be spared, having been called to Tientsin to teach in the new naval academy or on its training ship, only two students of navigation were to be included in the second group, together with seven graduates of the French division. Li Feng-pao, who prior to this time had been appointed Chinese minister to Germany, and Giquel were to continue as joint supervisors.[85] Eight of this group left China probably before the end of 1882; a report of their return after three years of study in Europe, dated May 10, 1886, appears in the *Ch'uan-cheng tsou-i hui-pien*. Five studied in France, two the planning and construction of fortifications and other defenses and one each ordnance, gunpowders and other explosives, and shipbuilding; [86] one made a special study in Germany of the manufacture and repair of naval mines and torpedoes; [87] and two studied navigation and naval command in England.[88] They were accompanied by Wu Te-chang, a member of the first group, who served as interpreter and possibly as assistant to Li Feng-pao. In all probability they studied in the same schools, navy yards, factories, and naval vessels as had their predecessors, and they also made tours of inspection.[89]

A joint memorial was sent to Peking by Li Hung-chang and others on November 16, 1885, urging that a third group of Foochow graduates be dispatched to Europe for advanced

[85] THHL, KH 44, pp. 12–13; Li Hung-chang, 32, p. 24.

[86] Huang T'ing and Wang Hui-lan; Li Fang-jung; Wang Fu-ch'ang; Wei Hsien.

[87] Ch'en Ts'ai-jui.   [88] Ch'en Chao-i and Li Ting-hsin.

[89] CCTI, 32, pp. 11–13. There is no report in the *Ch'uan-cheng tsou-i hui-pien* of the exact distribution of these students in Europe.

training.[90] The need for more trained naval officers to command new ships that were being puchased abroad for the Chinese navy as well as the need for up-to-date marine engineers to operate shore installations was pointed out. Giquel and Chou Mou-ch'i, an expectant intendant who had been serving as proctor at the Foochow Navy Yard, were nominated joint supervisors. It was urged that the period of foreign study for marine engineers be lengthened to six years and that while three years was long enough for naval cadets half of each of those years be spent at sea and this should be so stipulated. Finally, it was proposed that promising graduates of the Tientsin Naval Academy be sent abroad for similar training as rapidly as they were ready.

This proposal having been approved by the Throne, thirty-three students sailed for Europe on April 6, 1886: ten graduates of the English division of the Foochow school and fourteen graduates of the French division, plus nine Tientsin graduates. Giquel had died early in 1886 and was succeeded as foreign supervisor by L. Dunoyer de Segonzac, a former French naval officer who had been subdirector of the Foochow Navy Yard under Giquel in the late 1860's and early 1870's and had served as assistant foreign supervisor of the first two groups sent to Europe.[91]

Thirty members of this third group completed their training abroad, which was reported to have been more thorough than that of their predecessors. Of these, eighteen naval cadets studied in England and returned to China after three years.

[90] Li Hung-chang, 55, pp. 14–15. This document was signed by Li Hung-chang, Superintendent of the Southern Ports Tseng Kuo-ch'üan, Foochow General Ku-ni-yin-pu, and Governor-general Yang Chün-kung of Min-che.

[91] CCTI, 32, pp. 4–5. On Aug. 14, 1886, Giquel was posthumously awarded the brevet first rank, the Yellow Riding Jacket, and the First Class Order of the Double Dragon (CCTI, 33, p. 15).

Three of the eighteen—two from Foochow and one from Tien-tsin—specialized in hydrography as well as in the navigation of ironclad warships.[92] They took a world-wide cruise aboard an English training ship and also pursued special hydrographic studies in England and France. Eight more of the eighteen naval cadets—three from Foochow and five from Tientsin—specialized in naval artillery and small arms, also studying naval tactics, ship command, and the navigation of ironclad warships.[93] Some of them were assigned first to an arms training ship, after which they studied the design, manufacture, and repair of ordnance at the Woolwich Ordnance Factories; the others first studied mathematics, science, hydraulics, and steam at the Royal Naval College in Greenwich, and afterward they trained aboard an arms training ship. One of the eighteen, a Foochow graduate,[94] studied ships' engines at the Royal Naval College and later served as an engine-room officer aboard an English warship; three more specialized in mathematics and science relating to naval vessels, studying at the Royal Naval College two years and at University and King's Colleges of the University of London a third year;[95] and the last three specialized in naval law and the law of piracy and also continued their study of the English language, though it is not stated which school or schools in England they attended.[96]

All twelve graduates of the French division of the Foochow school who completed the six-year advanced training program

[92] Chia Ning-hsi and Chou Hsien-shen; Ch'en En-tao.

[93] Huang Ming-ch'iu, Cheng Wen-ying, and Ch'iu Chih-fan; Liu Kuan-hsiung, Cheng Ju-ch'eng, Ch'en Tu-heng, Wang Hsüeh-lien, and Shen Shou-k'un.

[94] Wang T'ung.

[95] Ch'en Po-han of the Foochow school and Ts'ao Lien-cheng and Wu Kuang-chien of Tientsin.

[96] Chang Ping-kuei and Lo Chung-yao from Foochow; Ch'en Shou-p'eng from Tientsin.

in this third group studied in France. Two of them studied ships' hulls and marine engines at the Ecole de Construction Navale in Cherbourg; [97] two studied mathematics and science relating to ship construction, possibly at the Université de Caen; [98] two studied river control and bridge and railway construction in Paris at the Ecole Nationale des Ponts et Chaussées; [99] and six studied international law and the French language in the Faculté de Droit of the Université de Paris.[100] It should be noted that as in the case of the second group sent to Europe most of the engineering graduates received their advanced training in subjects other than ship construction.[101]

Although the school, like the rest of the Foochow Navy Yard, was considerably less active in the early 1890's than previously because of official neglect and greatly diminished funds, Yü-lu reported later that another group of graduates had been scheduled to go to Europe in 1894 but that the plan had been abandoned after the outbreak of the Sino-Japanese War.[102]

In recommending changes in the operation of the navy yard in 1896, Pien Pao-ch'üan urged that students no longer be sent abroad for advanced training but that instead additional foreign teachers be employed to provide more thorough instruc-

[97] Ch'en Ch'ang-ling and Lu Shou-meng. The Chinese text says: advanced engineering school of the Ministry of Navy.

[98] Cheng Shou-chen and Lin Chen-feng. The Chinese text says: the *no-man* advanced school of the Ministry of Education. This I take to mean Norman or Normandy. It has been suggested that the text should read *no-ma* rather than *no-man,* probably referring to the Ecole Normale Supérieure in Paris, but I believe "mathematics and science relating to ship construction" would less likely be taught in the latter school than in one in Normandy.

[99] Ch'en Ch'ing-p'ing and Li Ta-shou. In Chinese: advanced engineering school of the Ministry of Public Works.

[100] Lin Fan, Yu Hsiao-k'ai, Kao Erh-lien, Wang Shou-ch'ang, K'e Hung-nien, and Hsü Shou-jen. In Chinese: advanced school of law of the Ministry of Education.

[101] CCTI, 41, pp. 8–11.   [102] CCTI, 47, p. 18.

tion in astronomy, mathematics, engineering, and navigation at Foochow.[103] However, the Tsungli Yamen, to which Pien's recommendations were referred by the Emperor for comment, though approving the addition of foreign teachers to the staff of the school, insisted that the best graduates continue to be sent abroad to secure the knowledge and experience that could not be supplied by teachers in Foochow but only in European schools, forts, and ships. Only by this means could China keep up with the latest developments in shipbuilding, said the Tsungli Yamen. Moreover, it urged that Foochow graduates who had previously studied in Europe but whose knowledge had become rusty through disuse or who were out of touch with the latest technological advances be sent abroad once more for additional training and observation.[104] An Imperial edict ordered the Pien proposals, as amended by the Tsungli Yamen, carried out.[105]

Yü-lu, who assumed charge of the navy yard in July 1896, sent a memorial to the Emperor a couple of months thereafter calling attention to a continuing need to train competent personnel and to improve equipment and techniques so that the most up-to-date warships might be built by China. The outstanding graduates of the Foochow school had been sent to France and England for further study in the past, he wrote, and many of them were now supervisory engineers in the yard or teaching in various modern schools in both south and north China, justifying the procedure that had been followed. At present, he went on, there were a number of students in the Foochow school who had completed their studies, and he therefore asked permission to select the best of them to be sent abroad for more advanced training. The precedent of the

[103] CCTI, 46, pp. 10–11. Pien had been ordered by the Emperor in December 1895 to investigate the navy yard thoroughly following charges of extravagance and waste made by a censor. This was one of the recommendations Pien presented to the Throne following his investigation.

[104] CCTI, 46, pp. 24–25.　　　[105] *Ibid.*, pp. 28–29.

third group should be followed, allowing the naval cadets three years in which to complete this training and the students studying ship construction six years. The funds to finance the project were to be drawn, as previously, one-half from Fukien likin taxes and one-fourth each from maritime customs collections in Fukien and from the funds of the navy yard, all to be paid in yearly installments in order to spread the burden. The Emperor approved this proposal on January 25, 1897.[106]

On June 2, 1897, the Emperor acknowledged receipt of another memorial from Yü-lu announcing the impending departure of the fourth group of Foochow graduates to pursue advanced studies in Europe. Ten had been selected, six from the French division and four from the English, but the Chinese minister to England had telegraphed that the Royal Naval College at Greenwich was full at the moment and that the Chinese students could not be admitted for the time being. Therefore only the six graduates of the French division were being sent—all of them to France, where they were expected to learn the latest methods of ship construction in the appropriate institutions of higher learning.[107] They were to spend six years abroad and to be supervised by Wu Te-chang, an expectant prefect of Kiangsu who had been one of the students sent to Europe in the first group in 1877 and was the interpreter attached to the second group sent in 1883.[108] This fourth group did not complete its studies, for it was recalled in 1900, after only three years, by Shan-lien, currently in charge of the navy yard, on the grounds that insufficient funds were available for its continued support.[109]

In the same memorial of the early autumn of 1896 in which he had urged the dispatch of this fourth group of students to

[106] CCTI, 47, pp. 17–19; 49, p. 1.
[107] Shih En-fu, Ting P'ing-lan, Lu Hsüeh-meng, Cheng Shou-ch'in, Huang Te-ch'in, Lin Fu-chen.
[108] CCTI, 49, pp. 1–2.   [109] CCTI, 53, pp. 3–4.

Europe, Yü-lu had recommended that before hiring skilled foreign technicians to step up the operation of the navy yard or more foreign teachers for the school, as had been urged by Pien Pao-ch'üan,[110] the numerous graduates who had previously completed training abroad but who had not been able to secure appointments in the yard be recalled from idleness or from positions they had found it necessary to take elsewhere. Finally, pointing out that no new students or apprentices had been admitted to the school for years, he proposed that a new entering class of youths between thirteen and seventeen years of age be recruited. These proposals were also approved by the Emperor.[111]

In a memorial acknowledged by the Emperor on May 11, 1897, Yü-lu reported on about April 1 that out of a very large number of applicants eighty new students had been admitted to the department of naval construction and sixty to the apprentice department. Revised curricula had been worked out for both these departments with the assistance of the new foreign supervisor of the navy yard, Ch. Doyère, the former requiring six years to complete, the latter three years. Both curricula began with subjects from the French elementary school curriculum: the marine engineering students studied arithmetic, introductory geometry, and simple physics (also, unquestionably, French, though Yü-lu does not mention it), the apprentices French and also arithmetic and introductory geometry, though presented more simply. After this start the engineering students were to move into a curriculum said to be based on that of the French naval academy, which was mainly mathematical but also included drafting and introductory courses in natural science and chemistry, followed in the fifth and sixth years by advanced mathematics courses through applied mechanics and integral and differential calculus and more chemistry. They were also to study Chinese every day. The

[110] CCTI, 46, pp. 10, 11.   [111] CCTI, 47, pp. 19–21; 49, p. 1.

apprentices were to combine theoretical studies with drafting, the mastery of hulls and engines, and the securing of practical experience in the various divisions of the navy yard. A training class for foremen was attached to the apprentice department to advance workmen showing marked intelligence and ability.[112]

For some unexplained reason new students were not being recruited at this time for the naval division of the Foochow school, which in 1900 was reported virtually to have been discontinued. In that year Médard was given in the *Chronicle and Directory for China* as director of the "French school," and a few of the French engineers listed as attached to the navy yard probably served as teachers in the French division.[113] Another source states that the Frenchmen attached to the Foochow Navy Yard made strenuous efforts to reopen the naval division under French instructors, evidently without success.[114]

In contrast to the situation in 1900, the naval division appears to have been in full operation by 1905 under a faculty of three Chinese professors. At that time there were forty-one students enrolled in the department of navigation, taking a five-year course that included English, mathematics, the sciences, and navigation; and there were nineteen students in the engine-room department.[115] At the same time the French division seems to have disappeared, although it is possible that only its French teachers had departed and that it was, like the naval division, taught by its own Chinese graduates.[116] Pao

---

[112] CCTI, 48, pp. 30–31.   [113] P. 258.

[114] *The Engineer* (London), June 8, 1900, p. 600.

[115] Nathaniel Gist Gee, *The Educational Directory for China* (1905), pp. 133, xix.

[116] The French division is not mentioned in the 1905 Gee *Directory*. The *Directory and Chronicle for China* . . . *1908* (p. 783) still listed Médard as director of the "French school"; but Chen, *Tso Tsung T'ang* (p. 42 n.), says that the French staff worked in the navy yard only from 1897 to 1902. See also Pao, p. 224.

Tsun-p'eng says that no new students were recruited for any department of the Foochow school from 1907 to 1913. However, in October 1913—that is, after the fall of the Ch'ing dynasty—the school was separated from the navy yard by the Ministry of Navy and reorganized to form three separate schools: the department of naval construction became the Chih-tsao Hsüeh-hsiao under the presidency of Ch'en Lin-chang, the naval division became the Hai-chün Hsüeh-hsiao under the presidency of Wang T'ung (both graduates of the old school), and the apprentice department became the I-shu Hsüeh-hsiao.[117]

Shortcomings and Modest Success

The Foochow Navy Yard was the leading naval shipbuilding establishment in China, at least until the end of the Ch'ing dynasty.[118] Between the withdrawal in 1874 of the French engineers and master workmen who had built it and the arrival of five new French technicians in 1897,[119] the yard was operated entirely by graduates of the French division of the school, many of whom had received additional training in France.[120] As noted earlier, the rate of ship production fell off after 1874, but construction continued fairly steadily, even if more slowly; and the Fukien defense squadron appears to have been adequately serviced by the yard throughout the period.

Six members of the first group of graduates to study in France were mentioned in 1887 as being in charge of construction in the Foochow yard, and in 1890 the same six were commended

[117] Pao, p. 224; Ch'ih, pp. 357–358.

[118] This was the view of H. S. Brunnert and V. V. Hagelstrom of the Russian legation in China in 1910. Ships were also said to be built at the Kiangnan Arsenal at that time; and ship repairing was done at the navy yard at Whampoa and the Kiangnan Arsenal as well as at the Foochow Navy Yard (*Present Day Political Organization of China*, pp. 345–346).

[119] CCTI, 46, p. 12.   [120] CCTI, 47, pp. 17 ff.

for the high quality of their work there.[121] Two members of the second group sent to France were appointed teachers in the French division of the school after their return, but one of these and a third member of the group were used in the end as mere translators.[122] Other graduates of the French division were employed as teachers in modern schools at Shanghai and elsewhere along the coast.[123] But there simply were not enough positions to absorb the 178 marine engineers produced by the Foochow school, and many of them, even including a number who had completed advanced training in Europe, were compelled to accept employment wherever it could be found. Some secured engineering positions with foreign companies, but others had to take posts as interpreters with foreign firms and even with foreign consulates.[124]

It was noted earlier that most of the graduates of the French division sent abroad in 1882 and 1886 studied subjects other than shipbuilding—in part, no doubt, because it was recognized that there were not enough shipbuilding positions for all of them when they returned—and that half of the 1886 group studied law, a subject completely unrelated to the purpose for which the Foochow Navy Yard School had been established. It should not be forgotten, however, that the Li-Shen memorial of January 15, 1877, which originally recommended the sending of Foochow graduates to Europe, stipulated that some of them might study "other important subjects such as chemistry,

[121] THHL, KH 84, p. 15; CCTI, 40, p. 15; 42, p. 7. The six were Wei Han, Ch'en Chao-ao, Cheng Ch'ing-lien, Wu Te-chang, Yang Lien-ch'en, and Li Shou-t'ien.

[122] THHL, KH 82, p. 5. Huang T'ing taught French.

[123] CCTI, 47, p. 17–18; KFYK p. 55. It has already been mentioned that two Foochow graduates taught French at the Kuang fang-yen Kuan at different times.

[124] CCTI, 46, pp. 22–24. Pao states that eight classes graduated from the department of naval construction, with a total of 178 members (p. 225).

mining, international law, and diplomacy." I have no idea what became of those who studied law or road and bridge construction; clearly there was no place for them in a shipyard or arsenal. Perhaps they became teachers of French or mathematics in other schools. Although I have found no evidence that they were able to use the special knowledge they had acquired abroad for the benefit of their country, as Li and Shen must have hoped in 1877, it is possible that they did so without becoming prominent enough to be listed in the biographical collections consulted.

There was difference of opinion regarding the quality of the training secured by the students of the French division, both in the school and abroad, as demonstrated by the quality of work done in the Foochow Navy Yard. An Imperial edict dated July 14, 1880, cited complaints that the ships being built at Foochow were out of date.[125] In 1886 P'ei Yin-sen tried to counter continuing criticism of the yard by declaring that the engineers in charge were fully capable of building modern warships, large marine engines, and torpedoes and by pointing out that one iron-ribbed ship and two speedy dispatch boats had been completed during the preceding year.[126] However, warships were also being built in Europe for the Chinese navy, and this indicated that Chinese shipyards were unable to supply the need.

In 1896 Director Pien Pao-ch'üan frankly conceded that ships recently built at Foochow were outmoded and incapable of defending China, hence not worth the money that had been put into them. The engineers, even those who had studied abroad, he believed, were not adequately trained for the re-

[125] THHL, KH 35, p. 13. This was, of course, before the return of the first group of graduates sent abroad for advanced training.

[126] CSWP, 108, p. 9. The Foochow report in the Maritime Custom's *Decennial Reports, 1882–1891* said that "although foreign aid and advice are now entirely dispensed with, some powerful ironclads either have been completed or are in course of construction" (p. 427).

sponsibilities laid upon them. They could only piece ships together in accordance with blueprints, he said, and had no real mastery of shipbuilding.[127] In commenting on this statement the Tsungli Yamen blamed the shortcomings of the yard on the inadequacy of funds available for shipbuilding rather than on the training of the engineers, but it went on to suggest that insufficiently trained engineers be sent abroad again for additional study.[128] Taking cognizance of the criticism, the Emperor on July 28, 1896, ordered the Foochow Navy Yard to employ foreign technicians once more and to buy modern equipment so that China might be capable of building large, modern warships.[129]

Yü-lu declared in 1897 that the navy yard's shortcomings were not to be blamed on a lack of desire on the part of the engineering staff for improved methods but rather on the fact that their training had become obsolete during the subsequent years of rapid technological progress in the West. He pointed out that for a decade the yard had been completely out of touch with the engineering advances taking place in the West. He urged that those European-trained graduates who were now scattered be recalled to the navy yard so that their knowledge, as well as that of the resident engineers, might be brought up to date by the recently hired foreign technicians.[130] Wang Hsin-chung, in his *Tsing Hua hsüeh-pao* article, expresses the judgment that the costs of the Foochow Navy Yard, including its school, were too high for the results achieved. Moreover, he regards it as a shame that foreign technicians had to be called in once more after the Sino-Japanese War.[131] By 1900 the number of French engineers and skilled workmen, plus their medical and religious advisers, totaled twenty-three, and there appears to have been little change for several years thereafter. However, they evidently had all gone home by 1907 for

[127] CCTI, 46, p. 10.   [128] *Ibid.*, pp. 22, 25.   [129] *Ibid.*, p. 28.
[130] CCTI, 47, p. 20.   [131] P. 56.

Pao mentions that the Foochow Navy Yard ceased to operate for a while in that year.[132]

The English division of the Foochow Navy Yard School, of which the navigation departments graduated a total of 241 in nineteen classes and the engine-room department 210 in fourteen classes,[133] supplied both deck and engine-room officers for the entire Chinese navy until the late 1880's; after this the newer naval academies at Tientsin, Whampoa, and Nanking began to provide junior officers for the Peiyang, Kwangtung, and Nanyang squadrons respectively. As early as 1882 Li Hung-chang stated that Foochow naval graduates had attained the second and third military rank, and in 1885 he reported that all the small ships making up his Peiyang squadron were at that time commanded by Foochow graduates who had studied abroad.[134] In 1892 it was remarked that most engine-room appointments in the Peiyang squadron still went to Foochow graduates, and it was therefore difficult to place graduates of the Tientsin Naval Academy.[135] Rawlinson says that nine of the twelve captains of the ships of the Peiyang squadron that fought against the Japanese fleet off the mouth of the Yalu River on September 17, 1894, were Foochow graduates, including Commodore Liu Pu-ch'an, second in command to Admiral Ting Ju-ch'ang. Ting was an old-fashioned army officer who was particularly dependent upon Commodore Liu because of his own lack of modern naval training.[136]

Opinion regarding the quality of Foochow-trained naval of-

[132] *Chronicle and Directory for China . . . 1900*, p. 258; *Directory and Chronicle for China . . . 1903*, p. 304; *1906*, p. 806; Pao, p. 224. The 1908 *Directory and Chronicle* still listed French employees, but its information probably was not up to date.

[133] Pao, pp. 225–226.

[134] NCH, Nov. 29, 1882; Li Hung-chang, 55, p. 14.

[135] NCH, May 13, 1892.

[136] "The Chinese Navy, 1839–1912" (Harvard Ph.D. dissertation, 1959), p. 741. See also W. F. Tyler, *Pulling Strings in China* (1929), pp. 41–42; Cordier, III, 248–251.

ficers differs. As early as the summer of 1874 the *North-China Herald* reported the visit to Shanghai of a Foochow-built ship under the command of graduates and advanced students of the school. The article praised the ship's efficiency and discipline and expressed the opinion that "the Foochow cadets will be able to render a creditable account of their doings if brought into active service." [137] In the fall of 1881 the *North-China Herald* commended the Chinese navy highly at a time when all its officers still came from the Foochow school. [138] On the other hand, an Imperial edict of July 14, 1881, reported Chinese criticism that naval students who had studied for years on high salaries still did not know how to navigate a ship. [139] And P'ei Yin-sen declared in 1885 that Foochow naval graduates who had completed advanced study abroad had lost their heads and made a poor showing during the French attack on the Fukien squadron near Foochow on August 23, 1884, demonstrating the inadequacy of their training. [140] Actually, although some officers deserted their ships at the first French broadside in that uneven battle, others fought gallantly and as skillfully as their inferior ships would allow. [141]

In the Battle of the Yalu in 1894, mentioned above, Captains Lin Yung-sheng of the *Ching-yüan* and Teng Shih-ch'ang of the *Chih-yüan* were said to have commanded their ships with vigor and skill, but Commodore Liu Pu-ch'an and the other ship commanders have been criticized for showing little aggressiveness, and one, Fang Po-ch'ien, fled with his ship in the midst of the battle and was later executed for desertion. [142]

---

[137] Aug. 15, 1874. [138] Sept. 27, 1881.

[139] THHL, KH 35, p. 13. [140] CCTI, 27, p. 11.

[141] James F. Roche and L. L. Cowen, *The French at Foochow* (1884), pp. 16–18. For a full and thoughtful discussion of the naval aspects of the Sino-French War of 1884–1885 and the role played by graduates of the Foochow school, see Rawlinson, "The Chinese Navy," chap. xi.

[142] Fan Wen-lan, *Chung-kuo chin-tai shih* (1949), 1, pp. 265–266. All four of these were early Foochow graduates; the three other than Teng

W. E. Tyler, a British naval officer who served as an adviser on the flagship *Ting-yüan* both during the Yalu battle and later at Weihaiwei when the remainder of the squadron was destroyed, declares that the three chief villains were Commodore Liu and two captains, Lin and Fang.[143] He also speaks disparagingly of Captain Yeh Tsu-kuei but reports that Sah Chenping, who did not participate in the Yalu battle, acquitted himself well at Weihaiwei; and he speaks favorably of the character and behavior of Commander Li Ting-hsin, who also served on the flagship.[144] The extent to which Foochow-trained officers shared in the corruption and laxity said to have prevailed in the Peiyang squadron at the time of the Sino-Japanese War is not clear. J. O. P. Bland declares that the three officers mentioned above, Liu, Lin, and Fang, worked the fleet "as a commercial undertaking for their own benefit." [145]

Some Foochow naval graduates served as teachers in other modern schools. It was noted earlier that four who had been ready to go to England for advanced study in 1881 were sent instead to Tientsin to teach in Li Hung-chang's new naval academy.[146] And the naval academy at Whampoa, which was a copy of the one at Foochow except for minor adjustments to local conditions, used Foochow graduates as teachers of English.[147]

---

had been members of the first group sent to England for advanced training.

[143] Liu and Fang have already been identified; the Captain Lin may have been Lin T'ai-tseng, who was a member of the first group sent to England in 1877.

[144] *Pulling Strings in China*, pp. 41–42, 193–194. Yeh and Sah were in the first group sent to England; Li was in the second group. Rawlinson, who has carefully examined the naval aspects of the Sino-Japanese War and the parts played by Foochow and Tientsin graduates, feels that the contradictory evidence regarding the behavior of Chinese naval officers requires that condemnation be restrained. See his "The Chinese Navy," chap. xv.

[145] *Li Hung-chang* (1917), pp. 228–229.

[146] THHL, KH 44, pp. 12–13.   [147] KFYK, pp. 54–55.

Probably the most famous graduate of the English division of the Foochow school was Yen Fu, known in his younger years as Yen Tsung-kuang. It will be recalled that he received broader training than his fellows while studying abroad and was called back to China before the others, to teach at his old school. In the early 1880's he was appointed professor of navigation and mathematics in the Tientsin Naval Academy, where he was a teacher and administrator for nearly twenty years. In 1902 he was appointed chief editor of a new Translation Bureau established by the government in Peking; in the closing years of the dynasty he served as a political and naval adviser; and after the 1911 Revolution he held important posts under Yüan Shih-k'ai and, for a period, the chancellorship of the Peking National University. His greatest fame came from his translations of major Western political, economic, and philosophical writings.[148] Admiral Sah Chen-ping was perhaps the second most prominent Foochow graduate. He, too, taught in the Tientsin Naval Academy for a time, after which he commanded a succession of ships in the Peiyang squadron and then became commander of that squadron in 1903, commander in chief of the Chinese navy in 1909, and minister of navy in 1919.[149] Admiral K. K. Lang (Lan Chien-shu), another early graduate, succeeded Admiral Sah as commander in chief of the Chinese navy in 1918.[150]

[148] See biography by Chow Tse-tsung in Howard L. Boorman, ed., *Men and Politics in Modern China* (1960), pp. 161–166. Among his most influential translations were Thomas Huxley's *Evolution and Ethics,* John Stuart Mill's *On Liberty,* Adam Smith's *Wealth of Nations,* and Montesquieu's *The Spirit of the Laws.*

[149] 1925 *Who's Who in China,* pp. 640–641. According to Brunnert and Hagelstrom, the Chinese navy still consisted principally of four squadrons in 1911: the Peiyang, Nanyang, Fukien, and Kwangtung squadrons (p. 344).

[150] 1931 *Who's Who in China,* p. 224. His name does not appear on the incomplete list of Foochow graduates I have been able to compile from official sources. Another prominent admiral, Liu Kuan-hsiung, who served as minister of navy in various cabinets between 1911 and 1919 and was active in national and provincial politics during that period, has

Lo Feng-lu, who graduated in the first Foochow class and served as interpreter with the first group of graduates sent to Europe for advanced training, was Chinese minister to Great Britain, Spain, and Belgium concurrently from 1896 to 1901.[151] And Wu Te-chang, a member of the first group to study in Europe and the Chinese supervisor of the group sent in 1897, was Chinese minister to Austria-Hungary in 1902 and 1903.[152]

The political and cultural obstacles that confronted the graduates of the Foochow Navy Yard School—and, in fact, the graduates of all the new schools established between 1861 and 1894—were formidable and discouraging. In spite of the difficulties they faced, however, the Foochow graduates contributed to the development of a modern navy and to the general modernization of their country; and a few of them rose to positions of leadership in the early years of the twentieth century.

the Foochow school listed as his alma mater in the 1925 *Who's Who in China* (p. 543); but the document in the *Ch'uan-cheng tsou-i hui-pien* that names the students sent to England for advanced study in 1886 says he was a graduate of the Tientsin Naval Academy (32, p. 4).

[151] *Ch'ing-shih Kao*, 212, pp. 12–14.   [152] *Ibid.*, pp. 15–16.

Glossary

NOT included here are names, book titles, or terms which appear with characters in the following Bibliography, in Arthur W. Hummel, ed., *Eminent Chinese of the Ch'ing Period* (Washington, 1943, 1944), in *Who's Who in China* (3d ed.; Shanghai, 1925), or in H. S. Brunnert and V. V. Hagelstrom, *Present Day Political Organization of China* (Shanghai, 1912). Omitted also are the names of students who are never mentioned except as such.

Chang An-hsing　章安行
Chang Sheng-tsao　張盛藻
Chang Shu-sheng　張樹聲
Ch'en Chao-ao　陳兆翱
Ch'en Ch'i-chang　陳其璋
Ch'en Chi-t'ung　陳季同
Ch'en Hsiu-ying　陳秀瑩
Cheng Ch'ing-lien　鄭清濂
Ch'eng-lin　成林
ch'i-jen　旗人

Chia-shih hsüeh-t'ang　駕駛學堂

Ch'iang-p'ao Hsüeh-t'ang　鎗砲學堂

Ch'ien hsüeh-t'ang　前學堂

Chih-tsao hsüeh-t'ang　製造學堂

Ch'ing-ch'ang　慶常

Ching-shih Ta-hsüeh-t'ang　京師大學堂

chiu-chang suan-fa　九章算法

Ch'iu-shih T'ang　求是堂

Chou Mou-ch'i　周懋琦

Chou Tzu-ch'i　周自齊

Ch'uan-cheng Hsüeh-t'ang　船政學堂

Ch'uan-cheng ta-ch'en　船政大臣

Chung-hsi Hsüeh-t'ang　中西學堂

Chung-hsüeh wei t'i, hsi-hsüeh wei yung　中學爲體　西學爲用

E-lo-ssu-wen Kuan　俄羅斯文館

Fang Po-ch'ien　方伯謙

Fang-yen Hsüeh-t'ang　方言學堂

Feng-i　鳳儀

Foochow Navy Yard　船政

fu-k'e　附課

Hai-chün Hsüeh-hsiao　海軍學校

Hou hsüeh-t'ang　後學堂

Hsi-hsüeh Kuan　西學館

Hsi Kan　席淦

Hsi-kuo chin-shih hui-pien　西國近事彙編

Hsia Chia-hao　夏家鎬

hsüeh ssu-yüan chieh　學四元解

Hu Wei-te　胡惟德

Hua-t'u fang　畫圖房

Huang T'ing　黃庭

Hui-shih yüan　繪事院

I-hsüeh Kuan　譯學館

I-pu　藝圃

I-shu Hsüeh-hsiao　藝術學校

i-t'u　藝徒

I-yao Kuan　醫藥館

Jui-lin　瑞麟

Kiangnan Arsenal　江南製造局
ko-chih　格致
Ku Wen-tsao　顧文藻
Kuan-lun hsüeh-t'ang　管輪學堂
Kuang fang-yen Kuan　廣方言館
Kuei Wen-ts'an　桂文燦
K'un-ming Lake Naval Academy　昆明湖水師學堂
K'un-yü t'u-shuo　坤輿圖說
Kung-i Hsüeh-t'ang　工藝學堂
Kung-yeh Hsüeh-t'ang　工業學堂
Kuo-shih-ch'un　國世春
Li Chao-t'ang　黎兆棠
Li Shou-t'ien　李壽田
Lien-ch'uan　練船
Lin Chih-tao　林志道
Lin Lien-hui　林聯輝
Lin T'ai-tseng　林泰曾
Lin Yung-sheng　林永升
Liu I-ch'eng　劉蟲珵
Liu Pu-ch'an　劉步蟾
Lo Feng-lu　羅豐祿
Lu Tseng-hsiang　陸增祥
Ma-wei　馬尾
Nan-yang Kung-hsüeh　南洋公學
Nanyang shui-shih Hsüeh-t'ang　南洋水師學堂
P'ao Hsüeh-t'ang　砲學堂
p'ao hsüeh-t'u　砲學徒
P'ao-tui ying　砲隊營
Pei-yang I-hsüeh Kuan　北洋醫學館
P'ei Yin-sen　裴蔭森
Pin-ch'un　斌椿
Ping-kung Chung-hsüeh-t'ang　兵工中學堂
Ping-kung shih-men Hsüeh-t'ang　兵工事門學堂
Po-hsüeh Kuan　博學館
Sa-yin-t'u　薩蔭圖
Shan-lien　善聯
Shen To　沈鐸

sheng chien 生監

Shu Kao-ti 舒高地

Shui-lu-shih Hsüeh-t'ang 水陸師學堂

Shui-shih Hsüeh-t'ang 水師學堂

suan-hsüeh 算學

ta-k'ao 大考

Tai Ch'en-lin 戴陳霖

Te-ming 德明

Te-shang 德尙

Teng Shih-ch'ang 鄧世昌

Tien-pao Hsüeh-t'ang 電報學堂

t'ien-wen 天文

Tsou Po-ch'i 鄒伯奇

Tsung-kuan . . . ta-ch'en 總管大臣

T'ung-wen Kuan 同文館

Tzu-ch'iang Hsüeh-t'ang 自強學堂

Wan-kuo kung-pao 萬國公報

Wang Chi-t'ung 王季同

Wang Feng-tsao 汪鳳藻

Wang T'ung 王桐

Wei Han 魏瀚

Wu Chung-hsiang 吳仲翔

Wu-pei Hsüeh-t'ang 武備學堂

Wu Te-chang 吳德章

Wu Tsung-lien 吳宗濂

Yang Chao-yün 楊兆鋆

Yang Ch'en 楊晨

Yang Lien-ch'en 楊廉臣

Yang Pao-ch'en 楊寶臣

Yang Shu 楊樞

Yang T'ing-hsi 楊廷熙

Yeh Ch'eng-hsien 葉承先

Yeh Tsu-kuei 葉祖珪

Yin-ch'ang 廕昌

Ying-kuei 英桂

Yu Hsiao-k'ai 游學楷

Bibliography

Western-Language Works

Allen, Young J. Diary. Material from this manuscript diary was supplied by Allen's grandson, George R. Loehr.

Biggerstaff, Knight. "The Ch'ung Hou mission to France, 1870–1871," *Nankai Social and Economic Quarterly*, 8 (1935), 633–647.

——. "The establishment of permanent Chinese diplomatic missions abroad," *Chinese Social and Political Science Review*, 20 (1936), 1–41.

——. "The first Chinese mission of investigation sent to Europe," *Pacific Historical Review*, 6 (1937), 307–320.

——. "The official Chinese attitude toward the Burlingame mission," *American Historical Review*, 41 (1936), 682–702.

——. "The secret correspondence of 1867–1868: Views of leading Chinese statesmen regarding the further opening of China to Western influence," *Journal of Modern History*, 22 (1950), 122–136.

——. "Shanghai Polytechnic Institution and Reading Room: An attempt to introduce Western science and technology to the Chinese," *Pacific Historical Review*, 25 (1956), 127–149.

——. "The T'ung Wen Kuan," *Chinese Social and Political Science Review*, 18 (1934), 307–340.

Bland, J. O. P. *Li Hung-chang*. London, 1917.

Boorman, Howard L., ed. *Men and Politics in Modern China*. (First preliminary volume.) New York, 1960.

Britton, Roswell S. *The Chinese Periodical Press, 1800–1912*. Shanghai, 1933.

Brunnert, H. S., and V. V. Hagelstrom. *Present Day Political Organization of China*. Shanghai, 1912.

Calendar of the Tungwen College. See *T'ung-wen Kuan t'i-ming lu* under "Chinese-Language Works."

Cameron, Meribeth E. *The Reform Movement in China, 1898–1912*. Stanford, 1931.

Candler, Warren A. *Young J. Allen*. Nashville, 1931.

Chang, Chung-li. *The Chinese Gentry: Studies on Their Role in Nineteenth-Century Chinese Society*. Seattle, 1955.

—— and Stanley Spector, eds. *Guide to the Memorials of Seven Leading Officials of Nineteenth-Century China*. Seattle, 1955.

Chen, Gideon. *Lin Tse-hsü: Pioneer Promoter of the Adoption of Western Means of Maritime Defense in China*. Peiping, 1934.

——. *Tseng Kuo-fan: Pioneer Promoter of the Steamship in China*. Peiping, 1935.

——. *Tso Tsung T'ang: Pioneer Promoter of the Modern Dockyard and the Woollen Mill in China*. Peiping, 1938.

China Year Book, The, 1914 and *1919–1920*. London and Tientsin.

Chinese Recorder, The. A Protestant missionary journal from 1868 to 1941, published briefly in Foochow and thereafter in Shanghai.

Chronicle and Directory for China, Japan, and the Philippines for the Year 1868 and subsequent years. Hongkong. Called *Directory and Chronicle* . . . from 1903.

Cordier, Henri. *Histoire des relations de la Chine avec les puissances occidentales*. 3 vols. Paris, 1901–1902.

Couling, Samuel. *The Encyclopaedia Sinica*. Shanghai, 1917.

Devéria, G. "Histoire du collège des interprètes de Péking," in *Mélanges Charles de Harlez*. Leiden, 1896.

Dudgeon, J. "Sketch of Russian ecclesiastical intercourse with, and the Greek Church in, China," *Chinese Recorder,* 4 (1871), 35–40, 68–74, 96–99, 186–192, 206–214.

Duus, Peter. "Science and salvation in China: The life and work of W. A. P. Martin," *Papers on China* (Harvard University), 10 (1956), 97–127.

Fairbank, John King. *Trade and Diplomacy on the China Coast: The Opening of the Treaty Ports, 1842–1854.* 2 vols. Cambridge, 1953.

Feuerwerker, Albert. *China's Early Industrialization: Sheng Hsuan-huai (1844–1916) and Mandarin Enterprise.* Cambridge, 1958.

Foreign Relations of the United States for 1880, 1883, 1887, and *1889.* Washington.

Franke, Wolfgang. *The Reform and Abolition of the Traditional Chinese Examination System.* Cambridge, 1960.

Fryer, John. "An account of the department for the translation of foreign books at the Kiangnan Arsenal, Shanghai." Reprinted from the Jan. 29, 1880 *North-China Herald.* Shanghai, 1880.

———. *Catalogue of Educational Books.* Shanghai, 1894.

———. *Educational Directory for China.* Shanghai, 1895.

———. Letter Journals, February 1867 to March 1871. Fryer Papers, University of California (Berkeley) Library.

Gee, Nathaniel Gist. *The Educational Directory for China.* [Shanghai], 1905.

Giquel, Prosper. "The Foochow Arsenal and its results." Translated from the French; reprinted from the *Shanghai Evening Courier.* 1874.

Gumpach, Johannes von. *The Burlingame Mission.* Shanghai, 1872.

Gundry, R. S. *China Present and Past.* London, 1895.

Holcombe, Chester. *The Real Chinese Question.* New York, 1909.

Hongkong Directory and Hong List for the Far East for 1886. Hongkong.

Hsü, Immanuel C. Y. *China's Entrance into the Family of Nations: The Diplomatic Phase, 1858–1880.* Cambridge, 1960.

Hummel, Arthur W., ed. *Eminent Chinese of the Ch'ing Period.* 2 vols. Washington, 1943, 1944.

Imperial Maritime Customs. *Decennial Reports, 1882–1891, 1892–1901,* and *1902–1911.* Shanghai, 1893, 1904, 1913.

——. *Reports on Trade at the Ports in China Open by Treaty to Foreign Trade for the Year 1866*. Shanghai, 1867.

Irwin, Richard G. "John Fryer's Legacy of Chinese Writings." Unpublished manuscript, Berkeley, 1950.

King, Harry Edwin. *The Educational System of China as Recently Reconstructed*. Washington, 1911.

Kuo, Ping Wen. *The Chinese System of Public Education*. New York, 1915.

La Fargue, Thomas E. *China's First Hundred*. Pullman, Wash., 1942.

——. "Chinese Educational Commission to the United States," *Far Eastern Quarterly*, 1 (1941), 59–70.

Levenson, Joseph R. *Confucian China and Its Modern Fate*. Berkeley, 1958.

——. *Liang Ch'i-Ch'ao and the Mind of Modern China*. Cambridge, 1953.

Loehr, George R. "Young J. Allen and mandarins," *Emory University Quarterly*, 4 (1948), 102–109.

Lou Tseng-tsiang. *Souvenirs et pensées*. Bruges, 1945.

Lund, Renville Clifton. "The Imperial University of Peking." University of Washington Ph.D. dissertation, 1956.

Lutz, Jessie Gregory. "The Role of the Christian Colleges in Modern China before 1928." Cornell Ph.D. dissertation, 1955.

Martin, W. A. P. *A Cycle of Cathay*. Edinburgh and London, 1896.

——. "The Tungwen College" (1907), in H. B. Morse, *The International Relations of the Chinese Empire*, III (1918), 471–478.

Mathews, R. H. *Chinese-English Dictionary*. Cambridge, 1943.

Mayers, W. F. *Treaties between the Empire of China and Foreign Powers*. Shanghai, 1906.

Meng, Ssu-ming. "The Organization and Functions of the Tsungli Yamen." Harvard Ph.D. dissertation, 1949.

Michie, Alexander. *The Englishman in China during the Victorian Era*. 2 vols. Edinburgh and London, 1900.

Minerva: Handbuch der gelehrten Welt. Strassburg, 1911.

Morse, Hosea Ballou. *The International Relations of the Chinese Empire*. 3 vols. Shanghai, 1910, 1918.

——. *The Trade and Administration of China*. Shanghai, 1908.

Needham, Joseph, with Wang Ling. *Science and Civilization in China*. 3 vols. Cambridge, Eng., 1954, 1956, 1959.

North-China Desk Hong List, 1879. Shanghai.

North-China Herald and Supreme Court and Consular Gazette. A British-owned weekly newspaper published in Shanghai from the middle of the nineteenth to the middle of the twentieth century.

Papers Relating to Foreign Affairs, 1867–1868. Washington, 1868.

Parker, A. P. "The government colleges of Suchow," *Chinese Recorder*, 24 (1893), 534–540, 579–584.

Peake, Cyrus H. *Nationalism and Education in Modern China*. New York, 1932.

——. "Some aspects of the introduction of modern science into China," *Isis*, 22 (Dec. 1934), 173–219.

Pelliot, Paul. Review of O. Franke and B. Laufer, *Epigraphische Denkmäler aus China* in *Journal asiatique*, 11th ser., 4 (1914), 179–185.

Pilcher, L. W. "The new education in China," *Chinese Recorder*, 20 (1889), 305–310, 343–348, 403–410.

Powell, Ralph L. *The Rise of Chinese Military Power, 1895–1912*. Princeton, 1955.

Rawlinson, John L. "The Chinese Navy, 1839–1895." Harvard Ph.D. dissertation, 1959.

——. "The Lay-Osborn flotilla: Its development and significance," *Papers on China* (Harvard University), 4 (1950), 58–93.

Roche, James F., and L. L. Cowen. *The French at Foochow*. Shanghai, 1884.

Shore, Henry Noel. *The Flight of the "Lapwing."* London, 1881.

Stoecker, Helmuth. *Deutschland und China im 19. Jahrhundert*. Berlin, 1958.

Teng, Ssu-yü, and Knight Biggerstaff. *An Annotated Bibliography of Selected Chinese Reference Works*. Cambridge, 1950.

Teng, Ssu-yü, and John K. Fairbank. *China's Response to the West: A Documentary Survey, 1839–1923*. Cambridge, 1954.

Timkowski, George. *Travels of the Russian Mission through Mongolia to China*. 2 vols. London, 1827.

Tsien, Tsuen-hsuin. "Western impact on China through translation," *Far Eastern Quarterly*, 13 (1954), 305–327.

Tyler, W. F. *Pulling Strings in China*. London, 1929.

Wen Ching. *The Chinese Crisis from Within*. London, 1901.

Whitaker, Joseph. *Almanack, 1890*. London, 1890.

Who's Who in China. 3d ed., Shanghai, 1925; 4th ed., Shanghai, 1931.

Wilhelm, Hellmut. "The problem of within and without: A Confucian attempt in syncretism," *Journal of the History of Ideas*, 12 (1951), 48–60.

Wisner, O. F. "Western education in south China," *East of Asia Magazine*, special educational number, June 1904, pp. 73–89.

Wong, K. C., and Wu Lien-teh. *History of Chinese Medicine*. 2d ed. Shanghai, 1936.

Wright, Mary Clabaugh. *The Last Stand of Chinese Conservatism: The T'ung-Chih Restoration, 1862–1874*. Stanford, 1957.

Wright, Stanley F. *Hart and the Chinese Customs*. Belfast, 1950.

Wylie, A. *Notes on Chinese Literature*. Shanghai, 1922.

Yung Wing. *My Life in China and America*. New York, 1909.

Zi, Etienne. *Pratique des examens littéraires en Chine*. Shanghai, 1894.

Chinese-Language Works

Chang Chih-tung. *Chang Wen-hsiang kung ch'üan-chi*. 229 chüan. Peiping, 1928.

張之洞　張文襄公全集

Chang Ching-lu, comp. *Chung-kuo chin-tai ch'u-pan shih-liao*. 2 vols. Shanghai, 1953, 1954.

張靜廬　中國近代出版史料

Chang Po-ch'u. "Shanghai ping kung-ch'ang chih shih-mo," *Jen-wen yüeh-k'an*, vol. 5 (June 15, 1934).

張伯初　上海兵工廠之始末　人文月刊

Ch'en K'ang-ch'i. *Lang-ch'ien chi-wen*. Preface dated 1880. 21 chüan. 1910.

陳康祺　郎潛紀聞

Cheng Ho-sheng. *Chin-shih chung-hsi shih-jih tui-chao-piao.* Shanghai, 1936.

鄭鶴聲　近世中西史日對照表

"Ch'i Ju-shan tzu-chuan," *Chung-kuo i-chou,* nos. 233–291 (Oct. 1954–Nov. 1955). Taipei.

齊如山自傳　中國一周

Ch'ih Chung-hu. "Hai-chün ta-shih chi," in Tso Shun-sheng, *Chung-kuo chin-pai-nien shih tzu-liao hsü-pien,* pp. 323–363. Shanghai, 1933.

池仲祜　海軍大事記　左舜生　中國近百年史資料續編

Ch'ing-ch'ao hsü wen-hsien t'ung-k'ao. 4 vols. Shanghai, 1935.

清朝續文獻通考

Ch'ing-shih kao. 529 chüan. 1927–1928.

清史稿

Ch'ou-pan i-wu shih-mo. 260 chüan. Peiping, 1930.

籌辦夷務始末

Ch'uan-cheng tsou-i hui-pien. 54 chüan. Latest document dated April 10, 1902.

船政奏議彙編

Ch'üan Han-sheng. "Ch'ing-chi ti Kiangnan chih-tsao-chü," *Li-shih yü-yen yen-chiu-so chi-k'an,* 23, pt. 1 (1951), 145–159.

全漢昇　清季的江南製造局　歷史語言研究所集刊

Fan Wen-lan. *Chung-kuo chin-tai shih.* Shanghai, 1949.

范文瀾　中國近代史

Feng Kuei-fen. *Chiao-pin-lu k'ang-i.* Preface dated 1861. 2 ts'e. 1892.

馮桂芬　校邠廬抗議

Fryer, John (?). "Nan-yang shui-shih hsüeh-t'ang k'ao-shih chi-lüeh," in *Ko-chih hui-pien,* 7, no. 4 (Winter 1892), 47–48.

南洋水師學堂考試紀略

Hai-fang tang. 5 pts. in 9 vols. Taipei, 1957.

海防檔

Hsü T'ung-hsin. *Chang Wen-hsiang kung nien-p'u.* Shanghai, 1946.

許同莘　張文襄公年譜

Hu Huai-shen. "Shanghai hsüeh-i kai-yao," *Shanghai-shih t'ung-chih-kuan ch'i-k'an,* no. 2 (1933).

胡懷琛　上海學藝概要　上海市通志館期刊

Huang-ch'ao cheng-tien lei-tsuan. 500 chüan. Shanghai, 1903.

皇朝政典類纂

Huang-ch'ao ching-shih-wen hsü-pien, comp. by Ko Shih-chün. 120 chüan. 1888.

皇朝經世文續編　葛士濬

Kan Tso-lin. "Kiangnan chih-tsao-chü chih chien-shih," *Tung-fang tsa-chih,* 11 (1914), no. 5 (Nov.), 46–48, no. 6 (Dec.), 21–25.

甘作霖　江南製造局之簡史　東方雜誌

Kiangnan chih-tsao-chü chi. 10 chüan. Shanghai, 1905.

江南製造局記

Ko-chih hui-pien. A scientific journal published irregularly between 1876 and 1892 in Shanghai by John Fryer.

格致彙編

Kuang fang-yen Kuan ch'üan-an. No place or date indicated; last dated document May 27, 1894. My copy was transcribed from a block-print volume belonging to the Institute of Chinese Cultural Studies of the University of Nanking.

廣方言館全案

Li Hung-chang. *Li Wen-chung kung ch'üan-chi.* 165 chüan. Nanking, 1905–1908.

李鴻章　李文忠公全集

Pao Tsun-p'eng. *Chung-kuo hai-chün shih.* Taipei, 1951.

包遵彭　中國海軍史

Shanghai chih-tsao-chü i-yin t'u-shu mu-lu. Shanghai, 1910?. My copy was transcribed from a block-print edition in the Kiangsu Provincial Sinological Library at Nanking.

上海製造局譯印圖書目錄

Shu Hsin-ch'eng. *Chin-tai Chung-kuo chiao-yü shih-liao.* 4 vols. Shanghai, 1928.

舒新城　近代中國教育史料

——. *Chin-tai Chung-kuo liu-hsüeh shih.* Shanghai, 1927.

近代中國留學史

Ta-Ch'ing hui-tien. 1818 and 1899 eds.

大清會典

Ta-Ch'ing li-ch'ao shih-lu. 1938.

大清歷朝實錄

Ting Chih-p'in. *Chung-kuo chin ch'i-shih nien lai chiao-yü chi-shih.* Shanghai, 1935.

丁致聘　中國近七十年來教育記事

Tso Tsung-t'ang. *Tso Wen-hsiang kung ch'üan-chi.* 128 ts'e. 1890–1897.

左宗棠　左文襄公全集

Tung-hua hsü-lu. Kuang-hsü period. 220 chüan. Shanghai, 1909.

東華續錄

T'ung-wen Kuan t'i-ming lu or *Calendar of the Tungwen College.* Peking, 1879, 1888, 1893, 1898. First two in English and Chinese; last two in Chinese only.

同文館題名錄

Wang Hsin-chung. "Foochow ch'uan-ch'ang chih yen-ke," *Tsing Hua hsüeh-pao,* vol. 8 (Dec. 1932).

王信忠　福州船廠之沿革　清華學報

Wang Wen-chieh. "Shih-chiu shih-chi Chung-kuo chih tzu-ch'iang yün-tung," *Fukien Culture,* 3 (Dec. 1947), 1–38.

王文杰　十九世紀中國之自強運動　福建文化

Wei Yüan. *Hai-kuo t'u-chih.* Preface dated 1842. 60 chüan. Yang-chow, 1849.

魏源　海國圖志

Wen-hsien ts'ung-pien. Published in Peiping by the Palace Museum from 1930 to 1937.

文獻叢編

Yang Mo. *Hsi chin ssu-che shih-shih hui-ts'un.* 1910.

楊模　錫金四哲事實彙存

Index